COMMUNICATION SKILLS

SECOND EDITION

LEENA SEN, Ph.D.
Professor, Communications Area, and
Head, Centre for Communications Studies
NMIMS University
Mumbai

PHI Learning Private Limited
New Delhi-110001
2011

Rs. 225.00

COMMUNICATION SKILLS, 2nd ed.
Leena Sen

© 2007 by PHI Learning Private Limited, New Delhi. All rights reserved. No part of this book may be reproduced in any form, by mimeograph or any other means, without permission in writing from the publisher.

ISBN-978-81-203-3301-7

The export rights of this book are vested solely with the publisher.

Thirteenth Printing (Second Edition) ... ... **August, 2011**

Published by Asoke K. Ghosh, PHI Learning Private Limited, M-97, Connaught Circus, New Delhi-110001 and Printed by Meenakshi Art Printers, Delhi-110006.

Contents

Part 2
VERBAL COMMUNICATION AND
PRESENTATION SKILLS

Foreword

I am delighted to write about the work of my colleague Dr. Leena Sen on *Communication Skills.*

Communication essentially involves establishing communion of minds, which entails oneness or identity of understanding. Such a union of minds is fundamental to human existence in society and in organizations. In fact, it can justly be called the lifeblood of Management as any blockage in its flow can cause serious problems and disruptions. Recognizing this, all management training development and educational programmes generally include inputs on development of communication skills, which include skills of listening, reading, speaking, and writing.

In her work aimed at business school students and young managers, Dr. Sen has dealt with the whole gamut of areas in organizational and managerial communication including corporate communication, multicultural communication, verbal and non-verbal communication, listening skills, communication skill sets for managers, presentation skills, written communication skills and public relation skills.

In the present-day world, when organizational operations are bedevilled by lack of communication across the levels, and the language skills are in short supply, the contribution of Dr. Leena Sen is indeed most welcome. I have no doubt that practising managers and students will welcome the book and will use it to their advantage. I take this opportunity to congratulate her in bringing out this timely book.

Y.K. BHUSHAN
Senior Advisor
ICFAI Business School
Mumbai

Preface

This edition has been revised and updated on the basis of suggestions and observations received from management students, the academic community, and practising managers.

Each chapter has an exercise at the end. This has been done to provide a chance to the reader to check understanding of the concepts and application of the skills. Some of the tips have been formatted for a structured approach to the tips offered.

Among new concepts introduced are Fog Index/Readability Index, Business terms/Acronyms/Abbreviations, Email etiquette, Virtual team skills, and Social skills.

The chapters in this edition have been grouped in five parts.

PART 1: Managerial Communication

Chapter 1 acquaints the reader with the power of the 3 V's of communication—the Verbal, the Visual, and the Vocal. It offers the conceptual models of ISEP and ISEC that are complementary to successful communication. It also examines formal and informal communication networks, highlighting the role of the grapevine in organizations. "A good manager should be a good listener" goes the saying. Through everyday examples from business organizations, it has been explained in Chapter 2 why listening is difficult and how and why executives need to pay attention to this delicate skill to understand the other person. Chapter 3 highlights the basic skill-sets that a manager needs to possess to be able to deal with various business situations. Besides the theoretical inputs, illustrations from the business world have been provided so that it is possible to see how to maintain a strong interpersonal relationship at workplace. It is one of the many important managerial skills expected at work.

PART 2: Verbal Communication and Presentation Skills

The nuances of verbal communication have been discussed in Chapter 4 with several examples to illustrate the impact of the powerful C's of communication. Chapter 5 examines in detail the factors that are crucial for preparing a presentation-from the pre-presentation stage of jitters to achieving success for a winning presentation.

PART 3: Non-Verbal Communication

Chapter 6 presents a comprehensive view of Non-verbal communication. The acronym KOPPACT explains different kinds of body movements and the total synchronization of body gestures to understand what gesture cluster is. The concept of neuro-linguistic programming (NLP) explains, with examples, how it can be used for effective interpersonal communication.

PART 4: Written Communication

The status of written communication in business has been discussed in Chapter 7, elaborating why the business school students and managers need to learn the functional importance of effective business writing. It explains the formats of business letters, memos, and report writing. Most importantly, it explains the greatest hurdle that comes in the way of writing a good letter or a memo—that of flawed thinking process.

PART 5: Communicating in a Multicultural World: The New Manager's Role

Chapter 8 enumerates the communication dimensions of a multicultural business environment, the impact of globalization on organizational and interpersonal communication styles, and cross-cultural problems that get thrown up in day-to-day interactions. It offers a model for cultural integration. In Chapter 9, the practice of good corporate communication has been emphasized. The function of public relations, wrongly perceived as 'cosmetic communication' associated with propaganda and lobbying, is being redefined. Today's managers need to have some ideas about this function of handling corporate communication which goes a long way in enhancing the reputation of an organization in the eyes of the outside world. Writing a press release and speaking to the media are the added responsibilities of a manager.

The Second Edition of this text offers exercises and additional inputs that the readers would find useful. Any suggestions for further improvement of the book would be warmly appreciated.

LEENA SEN

Preface to the First Edition

Management is a complex practice of communicating with other people. In an age when a lot is being experienced in organizations in terms of career uncertainties, rightsizing, the pressure of working in a multicultural environment, and the pressure of reaching out to the stakeholders through corporate communication channels, the need for good communication skills is being increasingly felt by managers at all levels. The ability to communicate effectively in various business situations has to be developed. From speaking well to writing well, the whole gamut of communication skills is simply astonishing. Today's managers have to be well equipped to handle these situations through the most important management tool of all—that of communication skills.

What this book offers to the management students is a practical approach to communication problems, supported by examples from real-world business organizations. Organized into nine chapters, the book discusses in detail how to acquire the right skills and behaviours to manage efficiently and achieve a high performance level, especially in today's competitive business scenario.

Chapter 1 acquaints the reader with the power of the three Vs of communication—the Verbal, the Visual, and the Vocal. It offers two unique conceptual models of ISEP and ISEC that are complementary to successful communication. It also examines the formal and informal communication networks, highlighting the role of the grapevine in organizations. The nuances of verbal communication have been discussed in Chapter 2 with several examples to illustrate the impact of the powerful Cs of communication. Chapter 3 presents a comprehensive view of non-verbal communication. The acronym, KOPPACT, explains the different kinds of body movements and the total synchronization of body gestures to show what gesture cluster is. An interesting feature of the chapter is the section on neuro-linguistic programming (NLP).

'A good manager should be a good listener', goes the saying. Through everyday examples from business organizations, it has been explained in Chapter 4 why listening is a difficult task and how and why executives need to pay attention to this delicate skill to understand the other person. Chapter 5 highlights the basic skill-sets that a manager needs to possess to be able to deal with various business situations. Besides the theoretical inputs, illustrations from the business world have been provided so that it is possible to see how to maintain a strong interpersonal relationship at workplace. Chapter 6 examines in detail the factors that are crucial for preparing a presentation—from the pre-presentation stage of jitters to achieving success in presentation.

The status of written communication in business has been discussed in Chapter 7, elaborating why the business school students need to learn the functional importance of effective business writing. It explains the correct formats of business letters, memos, and report writing. Most importantly, it explains the greatest hurdle that comes in the way of writing a good letter or a memo—that of flawed thinking process. Chapter 8 enumerates the communication dimensions of a multicultural business environment, impact of globalization on organizational and interpersonal communication styles, and cross-cultural problems that get thrown up in day-to-day interactions. It offers a model for cultural integration.

In Chapter 9, the practice of good corporate communication has been emphasized. The function of public relations, wrongly perceived as 'cosmetic communication' associated with propaganda and lobbying, is being redefined. Today's managers need to have some idea about this function of handling corporate communication to manage the organization's reputation with the outside world. Writing a press release and speaking to the media are the added responsibilities of a manager.

This book is aimed at business school students at the post-graduate level and the aspiring managers who would have to face the challenges of intense competition in business—where communication skills play as much an important role as knowledge does. It will also be a useful reference for young executives and management professionals who need to communicate the business ideas that would lead to successful business actions.

LEENA SEN

Acknowledgments

I have put into print all that I have learned and taught about communication skills. Years of researching from various sources, interviews of executives, and my own experiences of working with corporate people helped me put my thoughts in an ordered fashion. I am indebted to a number of people. First, I would like to thank my publishers, Prentice-Hall of India, for motivating me to write this book and for the meticulous processing of the manuscript.

I express my deep gratitude to Professor Y.K. Bhushan, Senior Advisor, ICFAI Business School, Mumbai, immediate past Director General, NMIMS, and President Emeritus, ISTD, for agreeing to write the Foreword for this book.

I would also like to thank Mr. K. Gopalan, Chairman (Top Performer's Leadership Center, Singapore), Bernhard-Merswolke, Chariman (Merswolke & Veer Group, Germany), Ingo Lampen-schulten, Executive (Buying-Lincron, Germany), Hiroaki Sugawara, Managing Director (Lic Corporation, Japan), Manish Banerjee, Ex-Senior General Manager, (Philips India Ltd.), and Jim Chidwick, Business Development Manager (Spice Islands Apparels Ltd. India), and my academic friends and students for their ready support and appreciation of the work I have done.

Finally, I would like to thank my husband, Bilin Sen, ex-CEO Stanrose (Mafatlal), Business Advisor (Textiles & Garments, Tatas) and Director (Spice Islands Apparels Ltd. India), for motivating me with his valuable inputs.

I dedicate this book to him—the quiet encourager!

LEENA SEN

Part 1

Managerial Communication

CHAPTER 1

Communication: The Most Important Management Tool

Communication is a skill that you can learn.
It's like riding a bicycle or typing. If you're willing
to work at it, you can rapidly improve the quality
of every part of your life.

— BRIAN TRACY

When we speak of communication as the most important management tool, we must understand the elements that make it vital for our daily functioning at workplace. The word 'communication' has been derived from the Latin word *communis*, meaning "common". A person with whom we wish to exchange or share an idea will understand what we speak and write only when we try to communicate it in a way that will be understood by the other person.

An idea by itself cannot be understood. It has to be encoded either in words or in signs and symbols. An idea is always abstract or intangible, and has to be brought to life through our ability to express it in a concrete way. This is not always an easy task. There are many variables involved in the act of communication. Here is what can occur at any workplace between a senior and his/her subordinate:

Ms. Amla Cherry was busy as usual with her daily work pressure of following up with her clients and preparing the schedule for their flights abroad. The business had begun to show signs of prosperity with a burgeoning list of clients. The volume of work put her under the pressure of commitments to all her clients. She felt the need for a helping hand so that she could be relieved of the pressure of work and fulfill commitments to her clients.

Ms. Charu Daniel was recommended because she had good oral and written communication skills. This made Amla happy as it would take away some of her burden of making regular telephone calls and writing of letters and sending press releases. One day Amla was engrossed in her work when Charu abruptly entered Amla's room and placed some papers on the table saying, "This is what you had asked me to write and I have done it. Is there anything else that you want me to do? I have to leave early because I have an appointment to keep."

Amla looked at her in astonishment and kept wondering what kind of a person her organization had employed.

What is it that strikes us at once about this incident? What does it tell us about the nature of communication, the absence of certain factors that make our communication unpleasant, and factors that should be present so that our communication is effective? Did Charu go wrong somewhere? Why did Amla look at Charu that way?

NATURE OF COMMUNICATION

Communication is the art of being understood

— PETER USTINOV

Many writers have identified the advantages of good communication skills. In different ways they have suggested that good communication:

- Leads one to personal effectiveness
- Helps one to network with other people
- Helps one to collaborate with all the others at the workplace
- Influences motivation for enhanced performance
- Builds better understanding between the boss and the subordinates
- Creates better interpersonal relations
- Increases listening ability
- Enables employees to appreciate the need for change
- Creates better environment for knowing why there is resistance to change

And a number of other benefits of effective communication!

All these benefits cannot be automatically achieved. One can understand the nature of communication by examining the factors that make communication a dynamic process. Only by consciously being a part of the process can we realize how the intricate and interactive nature of the process of communication can pose a challenge to us. To experience the challenge and overcome it, we have to train ourselves to be good communicators. *The ability to communicate effectively, therefore, is a learned behaviour.* When we communicate by applying the techniques and the skills, we do build better understanding with people in our environment despite differences amongst us. Organizational differences are a part and parcel of working but there are ways to deal with them, and the best way is to create a climate of understanding through communication skills.

DEFINITIONS OF COMMUNICATION

Communication can be defined as a

- ◆ transactional process that involves an exchange of ideas, information, feelings, attitudes, or beliefs and impressions;
- ◆ multi-level process in an organization because it involves the organizational hierarchy, from the top to the bottom, and across the horizontal levels;
- ◆ cultural interaction with people in groups for conversing and sharing ideas in social gatherings and not talking shop;
- ◆ disseminating process that involves passing on information to masses through the media;
- ◆ transformational process that motivates and fosters growth and mutual understanding;
- ◆ dynamic process that challenges 'what you say' and 'how you say' at that particular moment;
- ◆ mental/psychological process of talking to oneself in mind, and
- ◆ (an) interaction process with the corporate.

Simply put, communication is the expression of an idea, that may be **verbal**, **visual** (nonverbal) or **vocal** that is read, perceived and heard by another person. The **three 'Vs'** of a communication act **must act in tandem**.

In order that we succeed in our efforts to communicate our thoughts effectively, we need to understand that communication does not take place only by using words. If we want our messages to be understood and accepted, we must take into account the existence of the nonverbal accompaniments of communication. **Gestures, voice, pitch,** and **facial contact** are powerful nonverbal signals, which form an integral part of oral communication. The '**what**' (substance) of communication must complement the '**how**' **(style.)** Only then can we measure the success rate of our communication. It is because of the presence of the non verbal factors that oral communication has been defined as an everoccurring art. This is what Peter Ustinov means when he says *"Communication is the art of being understood"*. We cannot simply spell out or write our ideas any way we like. When that happens, the failure rate of communication increases, leading to misunderstanding and communication breakdown. The success or failure of our communication with people in organizations also depends on our relationship with the person at the point of time when communication takes place. Hence, part of mastering the art of communication depends on mastering the art of being aware of your relations with the receiver of your message.

It is important that the speaker pays attention to the invisible presence of the non-verbal factors in the act of communication. At no cost should they be bypassed. When we talk, these factors come into play and add force to our words and expressions. When we are angry, we use angry words such as **hate, disgust, good for nothing, useless, incompetent,** and so forth. And a high pitch, raised voice, knitted eyebrows and tense facial muscles generally accompany these words. When we are in a happy mood and want to exchange ideas with others, we get into a sharing frame of mind and we use congenial words/phrases like "let's discuss this point; can we spend some time and discuss this important issue"? and such other terms characterized by self-control and mental balance. What happens to the accompanying non-verbal factors? The pitch is under control, the voice is not raised, the facial muscles are not tense, and there is a smile on our face.

The presence of these non-verbal factors in written communication is equally important. Long paragraphs, cluttered text, poor use of white space in the page, poor layouts of business letters, memos, reports and other business documents, are serious nonverbal errors. They affect the level of interest in the readers. Readability suffers in the process. Skilled communicators pay great attention to these factors. A letter of inquiry may get rejected simply because it has not been carefully designed and written.

If we want our communication to be positive and forceful, we need to be aware of the power of the non-verbal factors in our oral and written communication besides choosing the right words to match our thoughts and feelings.

THE INTENT AND THE CONTENT OF COMMUNICATION

The relationship between thoughts and expressions is the relationship between intent and content of a message. Any communication is bound to be positive and pleasant only when our thought process is under control and we are in a positive frame of mind to communicate and also receive communication. Positive communication, which is minus negative thoughts and words, is closely connected with the communicator's existing frame of mind and the core competencies. In fact, a person whose inner qualities/core competencies are positive is likely to be a better communicator than a person whose perceptions, values, outlook and attitude are not positive. However, given the nature of communication, which is highly intricate and interactive, it is not possible to have a complete control on ourselves. The concepts of ISEP and ISEC illustrated below explain the tacit relationship between our thought process (intent) and the words we use to communicate (content of a message).

At a workshop on communication, conducted by K. Gopalan, Chairman, Top Performers Leadership Centre, Singapore, some years ago, the interesting concept of ISEP was put forth, which touched my heart. The journey through exercises, focussed on self-realization, made me see clearly the close connection between our thinking patterns and our communicating patterns. Thus, I framed the concept of ISEC (inner side of effective communicators). The two put together form the coin of effective communication. The perfect blend of ISEP and ISEC can bring success to a communicator. But, this is not always very easy to achieve.

The concepts of ISEP and ISEC (see Model 1.1) are at the basis of all effective communication. An effective communicator not only has to have mastery over the functional skills of communication but also on the personal qualities. The concept of ISEP illustrates some of the core competencies of an effective communicator.

Similarly, the concept of ISEC illustrates the power of the 'C's of communication.

The concepts of ISEP and ISEC emphasize that communication is not only about learning a few functional skills in isolation but also about knowing the 'why' and 'how' of communication.

The value of correct use of words is keenly felt these days when we read about corporate scams. Wick Simmons, Chairman

MODEL 1.1 Concepts of ISEP and ISEC

Inner side of effective people (ISEP)		*Inner side of effective communicators (ISEC)*	
Effective communication is at the base of all relationship building			

To be a learner *To take responsibility*

- Unlearning
- Learning
- Re-learning

- Be committed

To have total involvement

- Be open
- Avoid focussing on unimportant details
- Listening with an open mind

To have a purpose

- Achieve a new level of attention by disciplining oneself to reserve one's opinions, evaluations and judgements

Conciseness *Consideration*

Courtesy

- Avoiding all discriminatory thoughts and words

- Your attitude
- Need for adaptation

Completeness

Concreteness

- Avoiding Abstract Language

Clarity *Correctness*

- Avoiding all ambiguity

- Being ethical

and CEO, The Nasdaq Stock Market, Inc., in his Foreword to the book *Building Public Trust—the future of corporate reporting,* writes:

> Today's capital markets are at the leading edge of complex information technology. But some things are simple and always will be simple. The effectiveness of the world's capital markets depends on public trust, and trust depends on the timely availability of complete, relevant, and reliable information—in a word, it depends on appropriate levels of transparency. (p.vi)

The following extracts illustrate how organizational conflicts and poor management decisions influence the manner in which communication takes place, thereby propounding the theory that the **intent influences the content.**

1. "The message spread throughout the Corporation. The company is in doldrums, not likely to survive. All executives are being advised to look for next jobs. No projects on hand." But the officers also asked soul-searching questions, "what is our fault in this? The management is blaming us for its own blunders. They are asking us to quit. Where do we get these kinds of facilities like hospitals, residential houses, schools etc? Why

should we leave; rather we shall stay here but may not give our best." Their willingness to work started drying up after hearing such unkind and reckless words from the Management. (*The Power Brokers*, p. 186).

2. A young entrepreneur came to deliver a lecture to the budding young executives of an Indian firm about the services that his company was capable of providing. Having done his doctorate in nuclear technology in America and now practising as a consultant in India, he was inspired by the spirit of nationalism to render service to his mother land.

   As he spoke about his company, the words began to fly past the audience. With a sparkle in his eyes and a tone of conviction about why his company would survive the difficult conditions of doing business in India, he seemed well in control of his idea and the manner in which he delivered his message. He was at peace with himself and tuned to the audience that listened to him with rapt attention.

What do these two examples tell us about the psychology of the communicators? What emphasis do they shed on the intent and the content of messages?

The values of ISEP and ISEC are not only meant for interpersonal communication, but are also integral to all types of communication. You as an aspiring, good communicator need to know about the various types of communication and how you can integrate the qualities for effective communication.

TYPES OF COMMUNICATION

1. Personal or intra-personal communication
2. Interpersonal communication
3. Organizational communication
4. Mass communication
5. Social communication
6. Transformational communication
7. Corporate communication
8. Group communication

In **Intrapersonal communication**, the individual communicates in his/her mind through the process of thinking and feeling. By doing so, he/she is able to process the information and seek time to establish an understanding with others. Carl Rogers has observed that if an individual does not practise intrapersonal communication, he/she is likely to lose touch with himself or herself and thus suffer mental agony. Intrapersonal communication enables an individual to shape self-concept and develop one's convictions. It helps one to think, plan, analyze and interpret ideas and messages. It also gives the opportunity to think of new ideas and be creative about new decisions, approaches and solutions to organizational problems. This type of communication has great value to an individual and to an organization.

Interpersonal communication involves interaction between two persons, or a small group, on a one-to-one basis. The advantage of interacting with fewer people makes it possible for people to open up and discuss matters to one another's convenience. The possibility of exchange of views and opinions on the spot makes this type of communication very valuable to an organization. Staff meetings, briefings about work to be carried out, feedback and customer relations are examples of this type of communication.

Organizational communication is at the very root of a successfully governed, well-understood and networked organization. Without a positive communication climate, no organization can either function or survive the complexities that besiege it everyday. Communication takes place constantly in an organization. It is inseparable from any function in an organization. From the board room decision to team briefings to shop floor instructions and departmental meetings, communication takes place because information has to be passed on, discussions have to take place, and work has to go on.

Mass communication is for disseminating news about the organization to the stakeholders and to the public. Through staff newsletters, press releases, annual reports, interviews to the media, the organization passes on information about changes in policies, new projects, mergers and acquisitions, and any information that should interest the mass about the organization.

Social communication occurs when people interact with one another in groups outside the organization, converse and share ideas in social gatherings and generally exchange pleasantries without talking shop. While it is different to communicate within an organization, social communication demands that people know the social skills of greeting one another, making oneself known to the host/hostess/the organizers, and mingle with the crowd without getting too rigid and socially gawky. Very often businesses happen in such social parties than in the formal environment of an organization. One should be equipped with the relevant skills.

Transformational communication goes beyond transactional or interpersonal communication. It originates from the main source, the sender. The sender conscientiously builds a larger frame of reference for a healthy understanding to develop. Also known as supportive communication, counsellors, teachers, human resource managers practise transformational communication by listening to the grievances of the employees and seek solutions to the problems. Non-governmental organizations and voluntary social organizations also use this type of communication to provide succour to the disadvantaged and the needy.

The four elements of transformational communication are thinking, sensing, intuiting and feeling (Carl Jung's psychological functions).

Corporate communication is the way in which a company builds and keeps contact with employees, dealers, business houses and all stakeholders. It is a work that is carried out not only by the board and the CEO or the MD of the company but also by also by all responsible employees. All specialists from various departments such as advertising, public relations, sales and marketing, finance, business promotion, production, and human resource and planning have to play a key role to achieve the organization's planned objectives. Although it is the corporate communication person who monitors the flow of information across the organization and outside it and keeps contact with those who affect its life and growth, each employee has to play a key role in enhancing the organizational culture.

Group communication occurs when meetings are held for face-to-face discussions on issues that affect the working lives of employees. The group works towards common goals and follows the norms that govern its functioning. Verbal and non-verbal communication skill sets are vital to a purposeful interaction between group members. A successful group meeting allows each member to interact in a climate of open exchange of thoughts without anyone disrupting the discussion or suggestions made. The spirit of a good group lies in its respect for shared values and beliefs. The communication pattern is interdependent.

PROCESS OF COMMUNICATION

In this era of globalization, knowledge management, and corporate governance, the prime factor that concerns the workforce from the top hierarchy to the levels below is the ability to communicate effectively. The more organized and clear the communication pattern is, the greater will be the impact of the message on the receiver. A number of corporate scams in recent times are examples of communication that have gone awry.

How does the sender ensure that the message has been well transmitted and understood by the person on the other side? Is there any way by which the message can be modified and corrected if needed?

Since communication is the transmission of information from the sender to the receiver, it is necessary to understand the relationship between the two when communication takes place. The word 'process' indicates that it is an activity that is connected with a series of steps which are deliberately undertaken to reach a specific goal. The process demands that both the sender and the receiver pay attention to the finer aspects or elements of successful communication.

A communication process comprises the following elements and activities:

◆ The sender
◆ The sender has an idea
◆ The sender encodes the idea into a message
◆ The message travels through the channel
◆ Noise in the transmission process
◆ The receiver gets the message
◆ The receiver decodes the message
◆ The receiver provides the feedback
◆ The frame of reference of the sender and the receiver
◆ The context of the receiver

Figures 1.1–1.3 illustrate the challenges that are integral to the process of communication. These challenges need to be competently handled for successful communication to take place.

Communication is the process by which ...

1. Information, Ideas, Opinions, Views, Attitudes, Feelings, Beliefs, Message

are

2. Conveyed, Passed on, Exchanged, Shared

by/to

3. Transmitter (Tx)/Sender
   Receiver (Rx)/Listener
   Is Effective Only When It

4. Reflects in the Mind of Rx as a True Image Of the Thoughts Conveyed by the Tx

for the

5. Receiving and Understanding of the Message

FIGURE 1.1   Process of communication.

1. **The sender.** The sender of a message can be any individual, from the watchman and peon in an organization to managers, vice-presidents and company CEOs and managing directors.

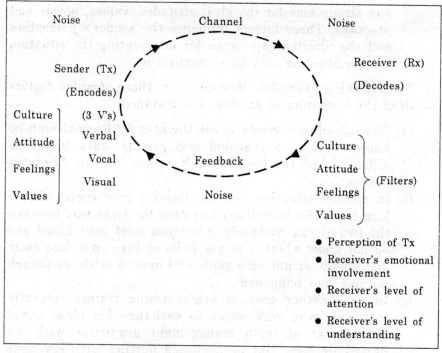

FIGURE 1.2 Process of communication.

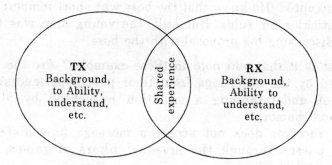

FIGURE 1.3 Frame of reference.

2. **The sender has an idea.** The process of communication begins when the sender is struck by an idea. An idea is a stimulus that sets the sender thinking about it. There may be many stimuli crowding the sender's mind all at the same time. The stimulus that interests and possesses the sender's attention becomes an idea. The sender may then wish to share/convey/exchange the idea with another person. However, many complex factors influence the formation of the idea. For example, the sender may be influenced by the existing mood, his/her cultural habits,

and strong bias for the idea, attitudes, values, norms and practices. These factors influence the sender's perception and the filtering experience for interpreting the situation and forming the idea for transmission.

The following examples illustrate how these complex factors can affect the formation of an idea. For instance:

(a) The subordinate wants to ask the boss for leave though he knows that it is year-end and getting leave might be difficult. And the boss is likely to say 'no'. He hesitates asking.

(b) In another situation, you are meeting your friend after a long time. Not everything has gone the right way between the two of you. Suddenly, when you meet your friend you do not know whether to say hello or turn your face away and ignore, or put on a smile and greet warmly as though nothing had happened.

(c) In yet another case, a bright young trainee, recently recruited, was very eager to exchange his ideas about recruitment of fresh management graduates with his immediate boss. But he hesitated putting forth his ideas because he was not sure whether the idea would be accepted. He knew that the boss was short tempered and a stickler for rules. But still, the young man was bent on discussing his proposal with the boss.

What is it that you note in these examples? Are the senders influenced by the situations from their past experiences? Is the process of understanding a situation influenced by attitudes, values, and memory?

The receiver does not accept a message immediately. The message passes through the personal filters of values, beliefs, attitudes, and opinions.

All senders think that their ideas will be accepted because they assume that the receiver will be receptive to these ideas. Most of us think that way. However, ideas do not get accepted that easily. There is always some difference or opposition to an idea. The success of effective communication depends on the sender's ability to accurately predict how the idea will impact the receiver and what kind of skills would be necessary to create a positive impact.

3. **The sender encodes the idea into a message.** Encoding is the process by which the sender converts the idea into a message by using verbal or non-verbal

mediums of communication. These can be words, signs, signals, gestures, symbols, or body movements. The conversion of the idea into a message connects the sender to the receiver. In order to ensure that the message is well understood, the sender uses words and non-verbal signals that the receiver is familiar with. If not, the message gets rejected. For example, if the receiver rejects a letter or a job resume because they are full of clichés and jargon, it means that the sender has not been careful with the necessary skills required for making the messages effective. This is how the use of ambiguous or carelessly chosen words often leads to the bypass of the actual message resulting in confusion and misunderstanding. Hence, skilled communicators pay attention to every detail of message composition.

4. **The message travels through the channel.** Channel is the vehicle that carries the message to the receiver. The various channels include postman, computer, fax, letter, telephone, memorandum, report, picture, film, radio, TV, and books that are used to deliver messages. It is important for the sender to know the suitable channel for the kind of message that has to be transmitted. The choice of the channel depends on the purpose of communication, the sender's needs, and the profile of the receiver.

5. **Noise in the channel/the transmission process.** Anything that disrupts or interferes with the transmission process is called *noise* or *barrier* to communication. Channel noises can cause disturbances in telephone, computer, television, radio, the fax machine, or errors in typography in e-mail messages, unclear pronunciation in oral com-munication (voice as a channel of communication), poor facial expressions (face as a channel of communication) or poor gestures (body as a channel of communication). Poor selection of the channel for transmission of the message can also be a noise to the receiver.

6. **The receiver of the message.** The receiver is any individual to whom the message has been transmitted. Like the sender, the receiver also has a set of personal filters—attitudes, values, ideas, opinions, beliefs, feelings and culture. The element of perception plays a major role in the receiver's acceptance or rejection of the message. The sender might think that the message has been very effectively composed and transmitted and hence will be

received. The receiver, however, might have a different perception about the message. The success or failure of communication depends on how the receiver receives the message. Perception plays a major role in influencing communication. It is the way by which people seek meaning in their environment. Hence, it is aptly said that communication is message perceived, and not message sent.

7. **The receiver decodes the message.** Decoding is the process of translating words, signs, symbols into meanings. The receiver has to move through the entire filtering process before successfully decoding and accepting the message. Successful decoding is correct understanding of the intent of the message as transmitted by the sender. Like skilled senders who aim at creating mirror image while encoding and transmitting the message, skilled receivers of communication also aim at decoding and understanding the message as the sender would have liked it to be received. This is not again an easy task. No communication can be completely successful or completely understood because no two persons are the same. They have different life experiences. Also, too many noises disrupt the entire process of communication. Both the sender and the receiver have to manage the noises well if they want their communication to be successful.

8. **Feedback sent by the receiver.** Feedback is the receiver's response to the sender's message. The responses can be both verbal and nonverbal. It is an important factor in the communication process because it helps the sender to know whether the message has been understood or not. Very often, senders deliberately seek feedback by asking such questions as, "does this example seem relevant in this context? What do you think?" or "how about looking at this problem in a slightly different way?" or "am I making myself clear?" Feedback demands great attention from the receiver of the message. Good listening skills, ability to read between the lines, and ability to interpret a meta-message or a hidden message, are expected of a competent receiver of communication. Successful communication, therefore, is a two-way process. Both the sender and the receiver have an equal share of responsibility in the cycle of communication.

9. **Frame of reference of the sender and the receiver.** Successful communication takes place when the sender's

frame of reference matches the receiver's and vice-versa. Frame of reference is a combination of ideas, beliefs, opinions, attitudes, values, knowledge, culture, past experiences and many other elements. It is the same thing as the filters that people wear. The biggest challenge that the sender faces is in drawing the receiver into his or her own frame of reference. This is not again easy. Too many noises occur at this stage and these need to be overcome for successful communication to take place. But when the two frames meet, as has been illustrated in the diagram, communication is said to be a mirror reflection of the intended message.

10. **The context of communication.** Every communication takes place within a context. Context is formed by the combination of circumstances that influence the piece of communication at a certain point of time. The factors that influence a context are physical surrounding, emotions and reactions of people to whom the communication is transmitted, their attitudes, and opinions. These factors differ from situation to situation. Therefore, no two transmissions can be replica of each other because the situations are different. The context influences both the encoding and the decoding stages. A piece of communication in annual general meeting may have a different impact and meaning than when delivered to the employees within an organization.

An organization can function efficiently only if it creates a system of communication networks that will specify who will communicate with whom. Only a proper communication system can lead the organization to function as a cohesive body that is well networked for the daily work to go on smoothly. Imagine a company where no such networks exist and where everybody sends conflicting, confusing and overlapping memos and reports to everyone else. Such a company can only be described as unregulated, disorganized and chaotic, where people are responsible neither for sending information nor for receiving it. An organization cannot function that way.

COMMUNICATION NETWORKS IN AN ORGANIZATION

Communication networks refer to regular patterns of interaction among people and a systematic flow of information. The two kinds of networks that exist are:

◆ Formal network of communication
◆ Informal network of communication

Formal Network

The management lays down the formal communication networks. The network is reflected in the organizational chart that shows the hierarchy of command. The formal network is also labelled as the 'chain-of-command' model. All organizational policies and decisions originate from the top hierarchy and they flow down through the managers and supervisors to the lower-level employees. Modern day managements, however, encourage a lot of open communication with employees so that a free communication climate is generated for exchange of information. Such a working climate helps organizations to know their employees better, who in turn can understand the organizational goals and objectives. It also helps the top brass to remain in tune with the changing trends in the market, increase efficiency and productivity and, most importantly, build employee morale.

Today, many organizations lay down clear communication policies that have to be followed by employees across the levels. Regular interactions help the human resource department to keep assessing the areas of improvement.

The organizational chart of a company will show that information mainly flows in three directions:

◆ Downward
◆ Upward
◆ Horizontal

(i) **Downward communication.** This occurs when superiors send down messages to their subordinates. Decision makers like the CEO and the managers pass down information about job plans, job rationale, relevant instructions, policies and procedures so that the organizational culture and nature of work are clearly understood by the employees. It is a sort of an indoctrination process that takes place. It is aimed at impressing the organization's mission and vision upon the subordinates and how they can play a dynamic role in fulfilling them. The superiors also discuss the feedback for correction of errors so that the subordinates can work better with a clearer sense of responsibility and commitment.

The biggest barrier to downward communication, however, is the long line of communication from the top level to the lower levels. The longer the line of downward communication, the greater is the chance for the distortion of the message. Since it is one-way communication, there is no opportunity for immediate feedback. Most of the time, it is in written form.

Other barriers that plague downward communication are superiors' perception of the subordinates and vice versa, element of mistrust (employees who mistrust a superior may block the relay of downward messages), lack of contact with the superior, superiors perceived as biased source of information than the organization's grapevine.

However, modern managements do realize the importance of downward communication and have therefore shortened the line by encouraging team-work and interacting directly with the team leaders. A study at General Electric (GE) revealed that clear communication between the boss and the workers was the most important factor in job satisfaction. GE launched a programme to encourage managers to communicate directly with employees, including informal meetings to encourage interactions.

Managements also have begun to pay considerable attention to the powerful impact that newsletters, company intranets, house organs, and videos can play in speeding up the entire process of information flow. Open downward communication has great motivational value.

(ii) **Upward communication.** Messages that are sent by subordinates to superiors are labelled as *upward communication.* When employees are expected to perform and show results, it is natural that they might experience some difficulties in carrying out the specified tasks. In upward communication, employees discuss their problems with superiors and also seek suggestions for improvement, sort out unsolved work problems, seek solutions to recurring conflicts, discuss steps for quicker completion of projects, and such other related matters. Such regular meetings with subordinates also give the superiors oppor-tunities to find out what the subordinates are doing and, most importantly, what they feel about each other, the assigned work, and about organizational working climate.

The channels used for communication are face-to-face talks, memos, reports, e-mails and phone messages.

There are barriers, however, to upward communication. There may exist a perceptual gap between the superiors and the subordinates. People at lower hierarchical levels may distort information when communicating to persons of higher ranks either for pleasing the boss or impressing the boss for a promotion. The stronger the subordinate's interest in advancement and promotion, the greater is the chance for distortion.

Today's managements have begun to see the positive results of open upward communication, and so the modern management practice is to encourage the 'open door' policy. When managers encourage meetings with the subordinates, they get a chance to interact with the subordinates and know their minds. A personal and human touch with subordinates goes a long way in building trust-relationship with the subordinates and it also helps in sustaining their morale. We all know about Jack Welch's "walking the talk" *mantra*.

Open upward communication has many advantages. Positive approaches from the superiors can convert distrustful, intriguing and scheming employees into productive individuals. An open and healthy communication climate acts as a touchstone for quality. The present workplace environment of mergers and acquisitions, cost cutting measures, rightsizing and recruitment of temporary workers is creating a great deal of uncertainty among subordinates. In fact, almost everybody is a victim of today's swift developments at workplace. Such fast changing situations need an empathetic understanding, and hence today's managers need to be prepared to deal with emotionally surcharged situations. At no cost should the top management overlook the employees' sense of trust, pride, esteem and respect in such changing situations.

(iii) **Horizontal communication.** Also known as lateral communication, messages, here, are passed on between employees working at the same organizational levels. For example, communication is transacted between the heads of the accounts/production/maintenance/creative/marketing and communication divisions. Similarly, workers in the office and the workers on the site are laterally connected.

The advantages are many. Employees enjoy a congenial environment for discussing their work where the conventional hierarchies do not exist. Task coordination, brainstorming ideas for projects, sharing and managing information and knowledge, a constant endeavour to build rapport are some of the benefits of lateral communication network.

However, the bitter side to such interactions also exists. Not always do these exchanges go off smoothly. The most common drawback is the prevalence of professional rivalry among members. The achievers might think about themselves as superiors to others and hence expect preferences from the top management. Others may not like to share information and knowledge with the achievers. Very often, specialization also makes people rigid about their points of view, and this influences them to reject another perspective to the problem. The drawbacks of lateral network are, therefore, ego, prejudice, turf wars, territoriality, jealousy, rivalry, and a superior attitude.

Informal Communication Network: Grapevine

As formal communication networks have inherent problems of command and control, the idea of informal communication network emerged with employees playing the lead role. The informal communication network is also labelled as *grapevine*. Shared personal experiences, career interests, interpersonal attraction, curiosity about people, things happening within the organization, and social interaction are the reasons behind its existence. Grapevine is mainly the network of 'who talks to whom' which does not figure on the organizational chart. Such talks and interactions take place in the corridor, near the water cooler, in the wash room, the lunch room, near the notice boards where people cluster around to express their feelings without any inhibitions. They feel that such talks allow them to breathe fresh air and enjoy their interactions.

Research indicates that grapevine has been conventionally linked with gossip or rumourmongers. It is generally believed that people who are less serious minded and indulge in loose talks are the ones who keep the grapevine alive and strong in an organization. This may not be always a correct way of interpreting the informal network of communication. Grapevine exists because the formal network does not always provide adequate information about organizational life. So employees seek information from grapevine to satisfy their curiosity. It may be about a superior's bias towards a certain employee, the possibility of number of public holidays being reduced, shift hours being changed, or somebody preferred by the top management is assigned a new project, and so on. Employees take interest in such talks because they are 'juicy', 'interesting', and have 'freshness' about the stories.

Grapevine also exists in organizations because information is **powerful**. Whoever possesses information and is prepared to barter it will find themselves in positions of strength. Gary Kreps calls such people **informal leaders** and makes an interesting observation about them:

> People who seek organizational power and influence, especially those who do not have powerful formal hierarchical positions within the organization, often attempt to gain power by gathering key information about the organization and its members and

disseminating it through the grapevine. Kreps calls them the "Machiavellian personality types".

However, contrary to the popular belief, the grapevine can be a powerful network of communication in an organization. The management often uses the service of the informal leaders to disseminate information about organizational developments. This way the management can control the spread of untrue rumors and unfounded fears. Kreps observes,

> Rarely do informal leaders like to be caught in a lie. They want and need accurate information to maintain their informal power over other organization members. Vicious, untrue rumours are just as dangerous for the informal leaders as for their victim because untruths can undermine the informal leader's position and power.

Modern managements have realized the power of the grapevine. They have moved away from the rigid management structure in which only a few of them shared vital information. With the flattened hierarchical organizational structure, now followed in many organizations, increased team work and collaborative style of functioning have brought employees in close proximity. This gives them a chance to interact well and know the latest buzz in the corridors. Employees feel important because they get a chance to keep themselves informed about various things happening and they need not be dependent on the informal leaders, who sometimes can become the power brokers.

The change in modern organizational structure has reduced the power of the grapevine and almost made it a source of loose and unhealthy talks. The more work-centred the workforce is, the better will be the interactive environment of the organization.

However, it is important to note that when formal communication network is weak and ineffective, there is bound to be a great deal of irresponsible talk creeping into the organization, and the grapevine then becomes more abuzz. Grapevine flourishes during periods of uncertainty and due to lack of clearly spelt out formal communication networks. Employees must know who is to report to whom. Role definitions and role responsibilities for employees are important for the success of an organization.

SUMMARY

The chapter has briefly acquainted you with the dynamic nature of communication. The definitions of communication tell you that in communication you deal with ideas. But these ideas cannot be communicated unless you code them appropriately in words, or in signs, or in symbols. The three 'V's play a significant role in making your communication effective to your recipient. Communication is verbal, visual, and vocal.

Successful communication transmits values, attitudes, and feelings through properly chosen words. The models of ISEP and ISEC illustrate why and how communication is a responsible task.

You, as a part of an organization, will have to conduct yourself responsibly, not only in face-to-face situations with bosses and subordinates but also with people from different backgrounds and organizations. The process of communication tells you that there are several elements that play an integral part to make it interactive. Unless these elements are effectively dealt with, the impact of communication may be lessened. It is important for a skilled communicator to understand that the frame of reference must be established for any communication to be successful.

At workplace, you will have to know how to go about with your work. An organization has both formal and informal communication networks. You need to understand how the formal network functions. Downward, upward, horizontal/lateral communication are different in many ways. While downward communication is command and control type, upward communication suffers because subordinates may or may not be very open in their interactions with their superiors. The perceptual gap often creates this lack of interaction between the superiors and the subordinates. The lateral level of interaction demands a good deal of polished interpersonal skills from the managers. The informal network of communication, popularly called the *grapevine*, unlike the formal network, is people oriented. When the formal network fails to keep the employees informed about the happenings in the organization, the informal network functions with greater speed.

Although these networks have inherent problems, modern managements, through team-work, meetings and open-door policy, have reduced the influence of the grapevine. Of course, grapevine can also be put to good use. The models and the few examples from day-to-day experiences offer you glimpses into the complex nature of communication. Many more industry and organizational examples will be given as you journey through the chapters.

TEST YOURSELF: ONLY ONE OPTION IS CORRECT. TICK IT. DO IT YOURSELF.

1. When I think of communicating with someone, I generally focus on the

   (a) correctness of speech

(b) content

(c) 'how' and the 'what' of the presentation

2. **The ability to communicate effectively is**

   (a) a learned behaviour

   (b) an acquired behaviour

   (c) a casual behaviour

3. **Gestures, voice, pitch, facial contact, are**

   (a) powerful verbal signals

   (b) not important to oral communication

   (c) natural accompaniments of oral communication

4. **The common frame of reference between the sender and the receiver of a message means**

   (a) the sender and the receiver are still caught up in their "message noises"

   (b) both the sender and the receiver have common understanding of the message

   (c) the mirror reflection of the message has not been established

5. **Grapevine is active in an organization when**

   (a) formal network of communication is weak

   (b) too many people meet at the same time to talk

   (c) there is some problem at workplace

6. **The biggest barrier to downward communication is when**

   (a) the organization is small

   (b) there is a long line of communication from the top level to the lower levels

   (c) upward communication is considered more important than downward communication

7. **The other name for horizontal communication is:**

   (a) Lateral communication

   (b) Collateral communication

   (c) Collaborative communication

8. **Jack Welch's 'walk the talk' *mantra* illustrates:**

   (a) Open door policy

   (b) Check on employees' policy

   (c) Encourage grapevine policy

9. **By and large today's organizational communication climate is**

   (a) more formal and less informal

   (b) more informal and less formal

   (c) more professional and less casual

10. **Transformational communication is at the very basis of**
    (a) corporate social responsibility
    (b) corporate stakeholders responsibility
    (c) corporate financial responsibility

FURTHER READING

Adler, R.B. and J.M. Elmhorst, *Communicating at Work*, McGraw-Hill, Toronto, 1996.

Bell, Arthur H. and M. Smith Dayle, *Management Communication*, John Wiley & Sons, Inc., Toronto, 1999.

Booher, Dianna, *Speak with Confidence: Powerful Presentations That Inform, Inspire, and Persuade*, McGraw-Hill, Toronto, 2003.

Fisher, Dalmar, *Communication in Organizations*, 2nd ed., Jaico Publishing House, Chennai, 1999.

Guffey, Mary Ellen, *Business Communication: Process and Product*, South Western College Publishing, Toronto, 2000.

Hamilton, Cheryl, *Communicating for Results—A Guide for Business and the Professions*, 5th ed., Wadsworth Publishing Co., Washington, 1997.

Kreps, Gary L., *Organizational Communication: Theory and Practice*, 2nd ed., Longman, London, 1990.

Lesikar, Pettit and Flatley, *Lesikar's Basic Business Communication*, 8th ed., Irwin McGraw-Hill, Toronto, 1999.

Locker, O. Kitty, *Business and Administrative Communication*, Irwin McGraw-Hill, Toronto, 2000.

Miculka, Jean, *Speaking for Success*, South-Western Educational Publishing, Washington, 1999.

Murphy, H.A., H.W. Hildebrandt, and J.P. Thomas, *Effective Business Communication*, 7th ed., McGraw-Hill, Missouri, 2000.

Thill, John V. and Bovee Courtland L., *Excellence in Business Communications*, 4th ed., Prentice-Hall Inc., Englewood Cliffs, New Jersey, 1999.

CHAPTER **2**

The Importance of Listening

You not only listen with your ears, you also listen with your eyes!

In *Seven Habits of Highly Effective People*, Stephen Covey identifies listening as an important skill. Tom Peters, author of *In Search of Excellence* and *A Passion for Excellence* emphasizes that one of the keys to business success is effective listening. In a revealing observation, he states, "My correspondence occupies many a file cabinet after years of dealing with managers in turbulent times. The most moving letters, by far, are the hundreds about "simple listening". ... I suspect that 50 per cent of its contents would deal with just one narrow topic ... listening to customers." (Tom Peters, "Learning to Listen")

According to researchers, listening is the most neglected of all the skills of communication. Most people confuse listening with hearing. The objective of this chapter is to study the nuances of the skill of listening and become a better listener. Superficial listening is poor listening and it can cause losses to a company. Negotiations demand that you listen to the opposite party carefully. Decisions can go wrong otherwise.

Considerable amount of research has already been carried out on this valuable aspect of communication. According to researchers, listening comes at the top of the list in the four forms of communication:

1. Listening
2. Speaking
3. Writing
4. Reading

Top executives spend almost 65 to 90 per cent of the working day listening to people.

WHAT IS LISTENING?

Listening requires more intelligence than speaking.

— TURKISH PROVERB

The intricate process of listening has been very succinctly explained by S.I. Hayakawa.

> Living in a *competitive culture*, most of us are most of the time chiefly concerned with getting our own views across, and we tend to find other people's speeches a tedious interruption of the flow of our own ideas. Hence, it is necessary to emphasize that *listening does not mean simply maintaining a polite silence* while you are rehearsing in your mind the speech you are going to make the next time you can grab a conversational opening. *Nor does listening mean waiting alertly for the flaws in the other fellow's arguments so that later you can mow him down. Listening means trying to see the problem the way the speaker sees it*, which means not sympathy, which is feeling for him, but means *empathy*, which is experiencing with him. Listening requires entering actively and imaginatively into the other fellow's situation and trying to understand a frame of reference different from your own. This is not always an easy task.

At workplace, often people are heard saying, "My boss just doesn't listen to what I have to say," or "she/he is such a poor listener," or "only if she/he had listened to me, this would not have happened."

This is what happened to a senior manager in a private firm (the name of the person has been changed upon request):

Ratna, a senior executive with ABC firm, was at her table that morning, in a pensive mood, ruminating over the recent development in her organization. A task that was assigned to her by her immediate boss, for the last two years, suddenly seemed to have been snatched away from her. She wanted to know the reason.

That morning, she decided to meet the GM and have an open talk about the swift change that had taken place. In fact, that morning as she arrived at her workplace, she met the new person who was now assigned the task and who wanted to have tips from her about the successful manner in which she had handled the project. His phony and pretentious behaviour and artificial manner of talking not only seemed jarring but also political. Almost spontaneously Ratna said, "I do not have to tell you anything about the manner in which I handled the work. You will get all the details from the departmental staff. Nothing was kept secret from them. Every paper, every document is filed."

That afternoon as she busied herself over telephone calls from the press, the corporate people and a visitor in her room, she received a call from her boss. Not the GM, her boss! He wanted to know why the information that the new person wanted was not given to him. As he rambled, Ratna tried to tell him that it was not the right time to discuss as she had a visitor in her room and requested him to discuss the matter later in the day.

No matter how many times she tried telling him that, the message just didn't seem to penetrate his mind. He just didn't listen and went on and on. When Ratna intervened, as a last resort, all he did was to slam the telephone receiver and bring the conversation to an abrupt end! The suddenness with which the incident took place made Ratna feel a little embarrassed. It was visible from her body language. She knew the visitor had noticed it. And that was the time when Ratna decided to quit the firm. It was impossible to work in an organization where bosses did not know how to listen. How could they run an organization, she reflected!

Some people just don't know how to listen, is what Ratna said to herself, with a wary smile! Some bosses perhaps just do not want to listen!

We can communicate an idea around the world in seventy seconds, but it sometimes takes years for an idea to get through 1/4 inch of human skull.

— CHARLES KETTERING
Inventor and General Motors Executive

What makes the process of listening such an arduous task? What are the possible reasons that come in the way of a person who would like to listen intently? Is it possible to be an active listener by eliminating the non-essential messages without offending/alienating the speaker?

There is so much to learn from Ratna's story. Listening is hard work and most people are not even aware of the fact that poor listening can result in disasters in terms of poor decisions, poor negotiations, poor employee relations, poor corporate governance, and most importantly, in terms of one's image as a fair human being.

In a survey of management students and executive

participants, listening was ranked first together with verbal and non-verbal communication skills. Students with no work experience seem to consider oral skill to be most important. Those who have work experience understand the importance of listening skills. At workplaces, when deadlines and targets have to be met, it is suicidal not to pay attention to the flow of information, whether from the boss or from the market or the clients.

MISCONCEPTIONS/MYTHS ABOUT LISTENING

Like misconceptions about communication, there are some wrong notions about listening too, perhaps because listening is not given the kind of attention that it deserves either at school/college levels or at management education level. One can make out from the number of training workshops/classes that are conducted for professional competencies. There are workshops held for training on assertive skills, NLP, written communication, public speaking and so forth. Listening takes a back seat perhaps because it is interpreted as an abstract, invisible, and subjective experience. The truth/reality is poor listening results into corporate disasters.

♦ **Listening is the same thing as hearing**

"I have heard you, enough. Don't say that to me again," said the irritated husband.

"But you haven't even listened to me!" exclaimed the wife.

Listening *is not* an automatic process. We may hear but we may not listen. Listening is different from hearing. In *hearing*, the sound waves strike the eardrum, causing vibrations. These are then transmitted to the brain. Listening occurs only when the brain swings into action by reconstructing these 'electrochemical' impulses by giving meaning to the sounds. Hearing cannot be stopped; it is a passive activity. Listening is not. Ratna's boss merely heard the sounds; he did not listen! True listening is a dynamic process. It involves more than the passive act of hearing. Hearing is with ears, but listening is with mind.

♦ **Listening is the same thing as breathing: What is so special about listening?** Breathing is a continuous process; listening is not. Listening is like deep breathing. When the yoga teacher instructs that deep breathing is good for health only then we take it up as a healthy exercise. Or, when making presentations, you might experience that deep breathing helps you to get over the fear factor. Listening therefore is a conscious activity like deep breathing and, therefore, is not a passive one.

The physical act of hearing, unfortunately, is so often taken as listening that it results into poor communication, which further results into misunderstanding or communication breakdown. You may ask yourself how often others have misunderstood you or you have failed to understand others because you were not receiving the thoughts correctly.

◆ **All listeners receive the same message** If this were so, then some listeners in the seminar or conference would not go off to sleep or not enjoy the speech/presentation/ lecture! All listeners do not receive the message in a uniform manner. Listening is a very demanding activity. It demands not only full attention but also a *proactive interest in* what the speaker is talking about. This may not be always easy for all listeners.

Read the following episode:

The farewell party was on! The seniors were being given a farewell party by the juniors! A great tradition in management education! Camaraderie, reflections, sharing of thoughts and memories! One of the premier management institutes in the country was holding the event.

The director of the institute was requested to deliver a short speech keeping the mood and the spirit of the event.

The director was an eloquent speaker. He delivered a motivational speech, interspersed with touches of gentle humour, about management education, finding the real path of making it big in life while not forgetting the values, the focus, and the two years of rigorous training and learning.

All eyes were fixed on him. Most students were serious, tense, and cold. Some were clearly indifferent. Few proactive listeners, however, enjoyed every bit of the speech as was visible from their body language. Their smiling faces, twinkling eyes, and occasional head nods, in agreement with what the speaker said, indicated their level of enjoyment. Obviously they had tuned themselves with what the director was saying!

Sensing that perhaps the speech was becoming a little stretched for most of the graduating students, the director cut short and wished the group a prospective future ahead!

What has happened here? Did everybody receive the message the same way? No, they didn't. That is why there are *discrepancies* in what we hear.

LISTENING BARRIERS

Despite the fact that listening is taken for granted, researchers have estimated that a manager listens only at a 25 per cent efficiency level. Immediately after presentations, according to a research, only 25 per cent of what the listener has listened to can be recalled. This only shows how listening suffers because of inherent problems.

There are quite a few of them, from psychological/mental to physical, emotional, linguistic, and socio-cultural barriers.

Psychological Barriers

1. **Prejudgment/ hasty evaluation**

Shallow listening prevents the listener from looking critically into the finer aspects of what the speaker says. In the process, the listener, passes a hasty/unfounded remark about the speaker.

2. **Superficial frame of reference**

It is failure to understand the mental framework of the speaker. Every person brings with him or her own background of likes and dislikes and knowledge. Very often this background can be contrary to the listener's background. This creates a barrier in understanding.

3. **Closed-mindedness**

Lack of interest in various topics brings about the inability to take interest in the speaker's topic.

4. **Inability to pay attention**

A wandering mind and day dreaming habit prevent the listener from concentrating on what the speaker says.

5. **Prejudice/envy/ jealousy/dislike/ hatred**

Personal limitations can bar a listener from keeping an open mind to receive thoughts and opinions. A prejudiced listener looks for a chance to derail a talk/conversation.

6. **Ego involvement/ egocentrism**

Difference of opinion, or a feeling of hurt limits the listener from concentrating on the speaker's words and thoughts. The listener might think that his/her ideas are more important than what the others think. An egoistic attitude alienates the listener from others. *Being right* is their motto because they cannot be *wrong*. Such self-centred listeners are poorly rated than those who are open to ideas.

7. The urge to debate or advise	This refers to an irrepressible urge to contradict the speaker and make a point. Your whole attention is to design your rebuttal by allowing your mind to race at a mile a minute. There are people who are the **know alls**. They look for chances to intervene and make their point noted before the speaker has finished.

Environmental Distractions

1. Physical distractions	Noisy surroundings, loud music, noise of machines, noisy office equipment, noise of horns of vehicles from road traffic, etc. affect listening.
2. Loud talking	Cultural habits of people at workplace, and conversations at the top of their voices can disturb others at work.
3. Visual barriers	Posters on wall may catch your attention while you are engaged in a conversation with your boss, or distracted by a person's clothes, heavy jewelry, eye shadow, etc.

Emotional/Personal Barriers

1. Beliefs and attitudes	Your strong opinions on issues of religion, sex, politics, business policies, may prevent you from agreeing with the speaker.
2. Sad memories	Loss of a dear one in a tragedy or if any reference is made to incidents of a similar kind may prevent you from listening.
3. Fear	You may not like to oppose your boss for fear of losing an opportunity to prove yourself for a post, or being misunderstood.
4. Anxiety	The state of health of someone dear to you may keep you disturbed at workplace and hence not able to pay attention.
5. Anger	You perhaps expected a promotion and when not given, you may feel sore about it.

Linguistic/Semantic Barriers

1. Speaker's style of speaking and mannerisms	Some speakers have affected manners or a rhetorical manner of speaking. The hollowness of speech may irritate you and block your mind from listening. Very often

jingoistic fervour in a politician's speech creates this block affecting the listening span of sections in the audience.

2. **Difficult words and use of jargon**	Jargon means high phrases and words (gobbledygook) that are peculiar to a trade or profession. It also means meaningless writing. They may irritate the receiver of the message.
3. **Lag time**	The time taken by the speaker between words and sentences can either irritate or bore you and hence prevent you from listening.
4. **Different frame of reference**	The speaker's mental framework may be different from yours. For instance, the meaning of a certain word, say **capitalism** or **socialism** may act as trigger words and create resistance in you and consequently reduce your listening level.
5. **Mispronounced words or words with double meanings**	All these can create problems with understanding and hence listening may get hampered.

Socio-cultural Barriers

1. **Different cultural background.**	Different accents and pronunciation of words by people from different cultures can be a major problem in international communication.
2. **Personal space and public space.**	Lack of this can also cause discomfort to people from different cultural background, for example, Asians are different from their Western counterparts. An Asian participant in a workshop may feel uncomfortable if the speaker, a westerner, comes too close to explain a point.
3. **Sense of time.**	This is also a major problem. Research indicates that while a Western businessperson likes to get down to business immediately, the Asian counterpart may like to indulge in small talk or have tea before settling down to discuss business.

Physiological Barriers

1. **Hearing impairment**	It is a physical disability and requires medical attention.
2. **Hunger**	Pangs of hunger can obstruct or reduce listening span.
3. **Tiredness**	Overwork and exhaustion can prevent a listener from paying attention.
4. **Pain**	Physical or emotional pain can block listening altogether.

How Good a Listener Are You?

If you have the following habits, then certainly you are not a good listener:

1. *Declare that the subject is uninteresting.* Poor listeners justify their inattention by declaring that the topic is uninteresting. Such listeners have a limited interest range and hence are incapable of deriving joy in a speaker's speech. At workplace, topics may sometimes be quite functional and routine but one has to pay attention to understand the technical aspects for doing a particular work efficiently.

2. *Criticize the content of the speech.* Sometimes listeners look for only facts and not elaboration or explanation of the facts. Isolated facts can often be disjointed and fail to create a context for the ideas to be understood. Infact, facts become more meaningful when they are placed against a particular background and are backed by feelings.

3. *Criticize the speaker's manner of talking.* Poor listeners are typically attracted to the speaker's dress, clothes, walking style, mannerisms, voice, grammar, etc. Instead of concentrating on the text, the poor listener focuses only on the peripheral aspects of listening.

4. *Pretend to be attentive.* A poor listener fakes attention by periodic head nods, fixing a plastered smile, and staring at the speaker, while thinking of something else. Such listening habits, if a manager adopts, can seriously affect a decision-making process and result into communication breakdown.

5. *Take down excessive notes.* Selective note taking is different from detailed note taking. Instead of making a

tree or a map of the points, or writing down phrases or key words, a poor listener engages in the act of taking every word that the speaker speaks. Detailed note-taking prevents the listener from grasping the essence of the speech.

6. *The urge to spar.* This listening block seizes the listener with the strong desire to argue, disagree and deny. The main focus is on finding points on which the argument can take place.

7. *Jump to conclusion.* When listening is superficial, the listener is bound to be hasty with passing judgments about the speaker's substance. A superficial listener never pays attention to complex or difficult material, and hence bases judgment on superficial understanding of matter.

TYPES OF LISTENING

Marginal Listening

A poor listener is a marginal listener. Marginal listening refers to a listener's poor listening habits. Distractions, inattention, day-dreaming, wandering attention and avoiding understanding of complex points by finding escape routes, characterize marginal listening.

Evaluative Listening

Evaluative listening traps a listener into the temptation of passing hasty judgments or unfounded evaluations about the speaker. Such a listener fails to get into the speaker's frame of reference and understand an idea from the speaker's point of view.

Active/Empathic Listening

A good listener is always an empathic listener as Hayakawa had said. Such a listener pays close attention to what the speaker says, intervenes very little, uses encouraging head nods and words of appreciation, and is willing to listen completely. This, of course, does not mean that the listener agrees with what the speaker says. Difference of opinion can always be there but the listener is prepared to listen completely for a critical understanding of the matter. Analytical or active listeners separate fact from emotion in an effort to critically understand the speaker's statements. Such a listener practises a *lot of mental paraphrasing. All managers must aim to be active listeners.*

Different Stages in Listening

In order to be a good listener, it is necessary to understand the different stages in listening. These are now described (see also Figure 2.1)

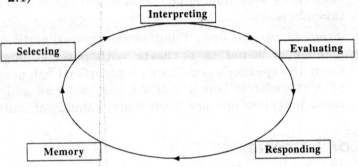

FIGURE 2.1 Different stages of listening process.

1. *Sensing/selecting stage.* The listener selects, from among *multitude of stimuli,* only the one that seems important at that point in time and converts it into a message.

2. *Interpreting stage.* The listener is engaged in the act of decoding the message. It is at this stage that the listener is faced with multiple barriers—semantic, linguistic, psychological, emotional, or environmental.

3. *Evaluating stage.* A great deal of critical listening takes place at this stage. The listener assigns meaning to the message, draws inferences, takes an overview of the message, and seeks accuracy of information and evidence. Often, the listener is disturbed by previous experiences, beliefs, and emotions, and these often come in the way of the evaluation process.

4. *Responding stage.* This is the stage when the listener is ready to respond. This is the feedback stage that is important to a speaker. The listener's non-verbal signals tell the speaker whether she/he has been understood or not. The speaker also has to be able to understand whether the listener is faking attention.

5. *Memory stage.* This is the final stage of listening. Effective listening helps listeners to retain chunks of what they have listened. *'Memorability' is an important*

index for listeners to test how much matter has been stored into the memory bank. Unfortunately, no matter how brilliant a speaker is, most listeners can retain only 10–25 per cent of a speech/presentation/the next day. That is why good speakers always make it a point to organize their matter sequentially, supported by good visuals for a presentation so that listeners are able to recall what they have listened to.

OVERCOMING LISTENING BARRIERS

Since listening is an arduous task and also extremely important at workplace, it is essential that we have a clear idea about how we can improve our listening ability. Effective listening leads to excellence in work!

1. Be a willing listener by controlling all barriers, and build a proactive interest to think or act congenially for better understanding.
2. Ensure that all environmental distractions/noises do not occur.
3. A long lecture/seminar/conference might demand that you are not hungry or tired to listen to the talks. So ensure that you have taken proper rest and food for the task on hand.
4. It is important that you discipline yourself as a listener by controlling all psychological barriers. Neither day-dreaming, nor dislike for the speaker is going to help you. Hence, it is important to control all disruptive psychological barriers to enable yourself to be a proactive listener.
5. Carrying a notebook/a writing pad to take down brief notes/ key points is a good habit to force effective listening on oneself. Application of mind to matter is an enjoyable work.
6. Practising good body language, sitting correctly, establishing eye contact with the speaker are effective enablers for good listening to take place.

HOW TO INCREASE LISTENING EFFICIENCY

Here is a formula that has worked wonders at training programmes for managers. A decade ago, two communication researchers, Tony Alessandra and Phil Hyunsaker, in their book, *Communicating at Work* had recommended a well-researched formula about how listening can be improved. They called it the formula of **CARESS**. The acronym brings together the six basic skills that *guarantee success* rate in listening:

C: **Concentrate**	Focus attention on what the speaker is saying
A: **Acknowledge**	Demonstrate appreciative body language without faking attention
R: **Research**	Practise self-talk to understand what the speaker is saying
E: **Exercise control**	Exercise emotional control by restraining impatience
S: **Sense the non-verbal message**	Observe the body language of the speaker. Is the intended message supported by body language?
S: **Structure**	Put the message in an order

The **CARESS** formula helped the managers to steer themselves through the challenging process of

- ◆ Concentration
- ◆ Control of mental distractions
- ◆ Taking down of points
- ◆ Withholding of hasty evaluations
- ◆ Withholding of judgments or arguments till the end of the speech
- ◆ Mental paraphrasing

Here is an exercise that you may try out. Imagine the following extract is a speech that was delivered by an expert in the field. Your job is to paraphrase as you read it:

> The values of equities have constantly eroded over the recent past. Nevertheless, the long-term economic prospects appear positive. We therefore suggest that long-term investors retain their positions in sound equities. Those who have additional funds to commit and those who have refrained from a commitment should buy on weakness. These investors should search out sound equities that combine secure current yield with the likelihood of future price appreciation.

BENEFITS OF EFFECTIVE LISTENING

When you prove yourself to be a good listener, you gain several advantages, whether in your professional life or in your personal and social life. The payoffs are numerous.

1. *Helps in creating happy work environment.* Proactive listeners always make it a point to understand the real meanings of messages that are transmitted incessantly. This they do by discovering the speaker's beliefs, values, and sense of commitment, expectations, and goals. When we listen sincerely and with empathy, we understand our colleagues better, thus adding to a happy work environment. Good listening is conducive to efficient work.

2. *Reduces tensions and hostilities.* Positive listening establishes a wider and flexible frame of reference so that people are willing partners in the act of listening. This paves the way for a healthy exchange of views and opinions, thus reducing the possibilities of psychological tensions and bad blood. A healthy attitude to listening plugs the negative fall out of grapevine. Mistakes and misunderstandings are sorted out mutually.

3. *Saves time.* Good listeners are always time conscious and concerned about how the material can be used for the benefit of the organization. They actively seek application of information to policies and procedures.

4. *Improves management-employee relations.* Open door policy reconfirms employees' faith and trust in the management. When employees know that they are being listened to and that they enjoy the freedom to express their grievances, a feeling of positive attitude develops. In making decisions, good managers take into account the feelings of their employees.

5. *Leads to early problem solving.* A good amount of valuable time of the organization is saved when managers/employees collaborate in understanding a problem jointly and find solution to the problem. The shop floor supervisor and the production manager of an organization would view the problem of the workers more realistically when they both sit down to discuss the production needs and the market conditions together.

6. *Increases sales and profits.* Needless to say that when an organization listens to its employees' suggestions, the level of satisfaction, commitment, and the values and goals of the organization find the top priority in the employees' list. An environment of trust and mutual consideration produces a climate of togetherness and healthy interaction.

THE BODY LANGUAGE OF AN ACTIVE LISTENER

In the chapter on non-verbal communication, you will study about various aspects of body language. Here are a few tips that might help you to be a good listener in a classroom, or in a conference/ interview or presentation.

FIGURE 2.2 'His explanation seems convincing! Let me think it over! An example of active listening posture.

Tips on the body language of an active listener

1. An attentive face (we listen with our ears, face and mind).
2. A closed-mouth smile (pleasant) and direct eye contact.
3. A comfortable sitting position on the chair (not looking clumsy or sitting on the edge of the chair).
4. No distracting body gestures like tapping of foot, drumming of fingers, covering of mouth, and talking to the person sitting by the side.
5. Hands can be lightly clasped or fingers can be placed under the chin/across the cheek, suggesting interest in the speaker's talk.
6. Occasional head nods in appreciation of what is being said encourages the speaker as this is a positive body language.
7. Applauding whenever the speaker values strong points.

All Leaders have to be good Listeners: "Listening Leaders Apply SIER"

Listening has become my career. I am the daughter of a mother and father who each had their own brand of listening skills. My mom taught me to listen for the unspoken emotion. My dad taught me to watch while I listen since body language speaks so loudly. I believe being a good listener has made me a better marketer because whenever I am faced with a new product, ad, or service, 'I hear' through the ears of others before 'I hear' for myself.

MARY LOU QUINLAN
("Oprah of Madison Avenue")
Hailed by the *Wall Street Journal*

In their book *Listening Leaders*, Steil and Bommelje recommend the application of the SIER model:

S: Sensing (receiving the message)

I: Interpreting (understanding the message)

E: Evaluating (judging the message)

R: Responding (reacting to the message)

The authors emphatically state that at the base of effective leadership are the effective listening skills. They are "inseparable". Further, they state that "Effective listening is imperative for anyone who desires to lead cohesive, productive, and significant teams and organizations." (p. 1)

SUMMARY

In this chapter, we have shown that effective listening is an active process and not a passive one. It takes considerable amount of effort to concentrate on messages for understanding to take place. Because it is an arduous process, it challenges the listener's mental faculties. Therefore, it is said that listening is not hearing and that a listener not only hears through the ears, but listens also through the eyes. Good listening is a prerequisite for success in professional careers. It is a significant area of effective communication skills, and when we listen critically, we succeed in establishing a rapport with people. Hayakawa's advice on listening explains how a person can become a good listener by actively and imaginatively entering the frame of reference of the other person. As he says, this is not always an easy task.

TEST YOURSELF: ONLY ONE OPTION IS CORRECT. TICK IT. DO IT YOURSELF.

1. **Listening to me is**

    (a) not as important as speaking to explain ideas because I am better at it

    (b) not as important as writing to get response because I believe in accurate information

    (c) equally important as all other communication skills

2. **Listening is not the same thing as hearing because it is**

    (a) a psychological process and is there-fore far more demanding

    (b) a physiological activity where the ears play an important role

    (c) the same thing as hearing the words and responding to them

3. **Listening as a process involves**

    (a) only two main stages—sensing and memory stages.

    (b) five stages—sensing, interpreting, evaluating, respond-ing, and memorizing stages.

    (c) catching the strong stimulus and converting it into a message is the only important stage.

4. **There are many barriers to listening. Tick the one which you think is the most applicable to you.**

    (a) Close mindedness

    (b) Hasty evaluation

    (c) Egocentrism

    (d) Anger/Jealousy

    (e) Different cultural backgrounds

    (f) Wandering mind

    (g) Hearing impairment

5. **Which type of a listener are you? Tick one of the following that applies to you.**

    (a) I am able to separate my negative emotions from facts when I listen to people and hence I am an **active listener**.

    (b) Long speeches and poor speaking skills force me to skip listening for the real matter and hence I am an **evaluative listener**.

    (c) I have a wandering mind and cannot stop day dreaming when listening to people and hence I am a **marginal listener**.

6. **Which of the following bad listening habits do you suffer from? Tick the one that applies to you.**
   (a) Uninteresting subject
   (b) Poor content of the speech
   (c) Poor speaking style
   (d) The urge to spar

7. **Write down the full meaning of the acronym CARESS.**

8. **The body language of an active listener is reflected in**
   (a) shifting body posture
   (b) attentive facial expressions
   (c) covering of mouth and talking to the person sitting by the side

9. **Active listening is**
   (a) nodding head as an attempt to appreciate the point
   (b) trying to see the point as the speaker sees it
   (c) ignoring the speaker's point and framing one's own

10. **There are many misconceptions about listening. Tick the one that you agree with the most.**
    (a) Listening is the same thing as breathing.
    (b) All listeners receive the same message.
    (c) Listening is the same thing as hearing.

FURTHER READING

Adler, R.B. and J.M. Elmhorst, *Communicating at Work*, 5th ed., McGraw-Hill, Toronto, 1996.

Adler, R.B., Rosenfeld and N. Towne, *Interplay: The Process of Interpersonal Communication*, Holt, Rinehart and Winston, Inc., Tokyo, 1989.

Alessandra, Tony and Phil Hunsaker, *Communicating at Work*, A Fireside Book, Singapore, 1993.

Hamilton, Cheryl with Parker, Cordell, *Communicating for Results: A Guide for Business and the Professionals*, 5th ed., Wadsworth, Washington, 1997.

Harvard Business Review on Effective Communication, Harvard Business School Press, 1999.

Lesikar, Pettit, Flatley, *Lesikar's Basic Business Communication*, 8th ed., Irwin McGraw-Hill, Toronto, 1993.

Steil, Lyman K. and Bommelje, Richard, K., *Listeners Leaders*, UBS Publishers' Distributors, Delhi, 2004, reprinted in India 2006.

CHAPTER 3

Basic Skill-Sets of a Manager

Man lives by affirmation even more than he lives by bread

— VICTOR HUGO

Just as people become good speakers through practice and hard work, similarly people become good managers through knowledge, business experiences and realities of workplace.

This chapter tells you briefly about various business situations that managers have to deal with as efficiently as they can. And for all this, they are dependant on the most important managerial tool—that of communication. You will now study how a manager has to weave the skills to build good interpersonal relations at workplace, overcome differences through constructive criticisms, communicate in a team, manage conflicts, negotiate successfully, learn to be a good interviewer, and speak well on telephone. Management is about people coming together to fulfill the objectives of an organization and help a system to function efficiently. Communication is central to all of these functions of a manager. When managers fail, systems follow suit. Organizations need managers and managers need to learn effective communication skills to make a system work.

Interpersonal Skills

'People skills' are an essential ingredient for success in any career. These skills help create a positive communication climate in which people feel valued. Any good organization will make it a point to ensure that the working climate is not <u>vitiated</u> by any internal or external conflicting factors. The key to building a positive climate is to ensure that strong interpersonal relationships are maintained. People must respect the other person, even during a conflict or disagreements. The story of communication is the story of its barriers. For success at work, these barriers need to be overcome. And for this, we need to be aware of people's expectations, their beliefs and opinions on varied subjects, and reciprocate their feelings and thoughts. Relationships and understanding do not take place automatically. We succeed in establishing under-standing and relationship with people when we use our communi-cation style that suits the other person. In the chapter on Non-Verbal Communication, chapter 6, we will know about the power of neuro-linguistic programming. When we program ourselves to suit the person on the other side, we enter a clearer frame of reference. This helps us establish better understanding. However, it is not easy to do so. Since communication pattern is dependant on people's style of behaviour, it is vital to know about these styles. The different kinds of behaviour that managers, customers, and workers demonstrate, are:

1. The closed style
2. The blind style
3. The hidden style
4. The open style

The factors that are common to these styles are:

◆ *Feedback*, i.e. response from others in terms of infor-mation, facts, opinions
◆ *Disclosure* which means voluntarily sharing information, opinions and feelings.

Note that most people have mixed styles of operation. No one has a fixed style of functioning or a style that is good or bad. Each style has its strengths and weaknesses.

The Closed Style

Managers with this kind of style have poor interpersonal skills. They neither actively seek feedback nor do they find it comfortable to disclose information to others. This kind of style not only makes managers feel uncomfortable but such managers also make others around them feel uncomfortable with their closed communication style. They are also less successful in dealing with employees and such other problems. Their communication style is somewhat like the following:

- 'Don't ask me, I do not know anything about it'.
- 'If I were in your place I would not have written the report like this'.
- 'Where is the need to send the report to the boss? He will come to know about it anyway.'
- 'Why do you waste time working so hard? Nobody is going to be bothered.'
- 'I don't care what you people think about the problem. The rule says that employees cannot get these benefits.'

Such closed styles make collaborative work absolutely impossible. Managers who adopt such styles cannot take decisions, guide employees, or make friends at workplace. They are the loners, preferring to work alone and prove to be productive as long as they do not have to interact with others. Interpersonal skills are at the low end feedback as well as of disclosure.

Strengths

◆ They are at their best only when they are left to themselves, free of interpersonal demands.

Weakness

◆ Uncommunicative, unsocial, unresponsive to others' needs.

The Blind Style

Managers with this kind of style are low on feedback but high on disclosure. They are critical of employees and demand perfection from them. Errors or failures are seldom tolerated. It is because of this reason that such managers are labelled as authoritarians. "I know best", describes such managers aptly. They are opinionated and hence do not think that it is necessary to gather feedback from others. For a fire-fighting situation, however, such a style is useful. The person commands authority and troubleshoots a problem. However, like the closed managers, the blind managers too are uncomfortable with interpersonal relationships. Since they are rigid in their views, they are impatient with others. Their communication pattern will be something of the following nature:

- 'Look here! I know what the employees are looking for. If you pamper them too much, they will begin to demand more.'
- 'I know the rules of telephone communication! You don't have to teach me!'
- 'If you people continue to come to work late, you all will be thrown out of your job.'
- 'I won't tolerate this kind of mistake anymore!'
- 'If you think you can do the job better, then please do it yourself!'
- 'Do not lecture me please! I know what I am doing.'

Managers with blind style, as Hamilton says, "overuse disclosure, they underutilize feedback. There are several reasons why blind managers don't seem to want much feedback from employees. First, because they think they know more than their employees, they see no more reason to ask for employee ideas or opinions. Second, blind managers often believe that employees must be treated firmly and impersonally. Asking for employee opinions might encourage employees to interact on a more personal level to take advantage of the situation."

Strengths

◆ Organized, firm in opinion, risk taker, trouble shooter, loyal.

Weakness

◆ Poor delegation, demanding and impatient, opinionated, 'I know it all' attitude, poor listener, personalize opinion, poor sense of objectivity.

The Hidden Style

Managers with this style are low on disclosures and high on feedback. Such people are generally sociable but avoid giving their opinions. They are different from closed communicators. Managers with hidden style are not afraid of meeting people as the close communicators are. The hidden style prevents the managers from expressing their opinions and feelings although these are the people who keep their eyes and ears open to collect feedback. Their communicating pattern is something like this:

- 'How was your work today? Very tiring?' (Trying to gather feedback)
- 'When do you think you can meet us?'

- 'Hello, Sam! Are all of you comfortable with the new office timings? Hope you have no problems.' (Hoping that Sam would say 'yes' and the manager would be able to gather the latest feedback)
- 'I have nothing to add to the discussion. Everything has been said.' (The manager prefers to keep quiet especially when he thinks that his opinions may not be regarded)
- 'Well, I do not think the full report needs to be sent to the boss. The important points may be summarized and sent.' (The report is edited because the top management may not like all the observations made in the report)

In a nutshell, hidden managers may seem sociable, as illustrated under 'Hidden Style' but may not really be so. Since they are low on disclosures, they shield themselves while expecting to be accepted by others. One of the reasons that make them quite popular with people is that they are high on listening skills and on feedback. Employees may think that such managers are empathetic and hence can be trusted. However, this may not be so. Research indicates that managers with hidden style camouflage their functioning style in order to find out what the employees are really saying about whom! Such managers keep fuelling the grapevine all the time. The need for social acceptance within the organization and also charting the popularity scale drives them to use feedback as a way to find out organizational details.

However, they also have their good points. These are the managers who can iron out differences and contribute in creating a harmonious communicating climate.

Strengths

- Generally liked.
- High speed interactions with people make them popular.
- They are good at organizing events.
- They are sweet talkers (since gathering feedback is their main concern).

Weaknesses

- Low disclosure makes them suspicious of others.
- Since they flit around, they do not really contribute to productivity.
- Suspicion makes them disloyal.
- Tendency to be on the right side of <u>officialdom</u> makes them perceived as manipulators or double-faced.

The Open Style

These are the managers who are blessed with *people skills*. They are high on both feedback and disclosures, but they use them carefully and sensibly. Enriched by a true concern for people's welfare, such managers <u>exude</u> a warm personality, empathy for others, motivate employees and transform them for their own good. In a way, they are the 'Samaritans' who bring a lot of cheer to the place and kindle the souls of the stressed out employees, think about the prospects of an organization, and play a significant role in developing employees for maximum productivity.

They have an open style of functioning. That is, their collaborative style helps employees to come together to discuss organizational problems and find solutions. Their proactive nature makes them open, transparent, warm hearted, a good listener with an open mind, and makes them appreciate people's contribution genuinely. These managers use communication as an effective tool of management. They are very careful in using words because they have the ability to take a critical and careful view of the overall situation. Their positive role is reflected in their choice of words and thoughts. Their communication pattern will be somewhat similar to the following:

- "I really appreciate the way you are working hard on this project. Keep it up. I am sure it will be approved by the top management." (Note the positive words and the tone)
- "I think the boss may not like the way the report has been written. Why not structure it more logically so that the ideas are clearer?" (The use of 'I' instead of the <u>ubiquitous</u> 'You' that a boss always uses for a junior, particularly in Indian organizations)
- "Perhaps you have your own reasons to make those recommendations about price rise. Let me listen to your reasoning."
- "Nisha, you managed the office really well when I was away on my educational tour!"

Strengths

- Their caring nature is genuinely liked by the employees.
- They have a flexible communication style.
- They are trustworthy, dependable, honest, and sincere.
- They, being natural leaders, build their organizations.

Weaknesses

- Since they are high on feedback and disclosures, often blind superiors do not trust them.

- ◆ The element of spontaneity often makes them open up at inappropriate times and this sends a wrong message to people.
- ◆ They are the fast thinkers and concerned about organizational transformations, hence, may feel frustrated with bureaucracy and long lines of communication.

Of the four interpersonal styles, obviously the open style is best suited for interactions with people in an organization. Of course, it must be borne in mind that a mix of all the four styles is sometimes needed and it is wise to operate in such a manner. This is because, not all organizations have an open communication climate.

All managers have to develop skills in their interactions with people both at work and in their social meetings. The emphasis on 'soft skills' is making many organizations promote their staff because of their 'people skills' rather than on technical skills alone. Managers who succeed in being flexible with people in their day-to-day operations achieve a lot of interpersonal effectiveness. Their face-to-face communication, open body language, listening skills, ability to deal with barriers and overcome them, and a genuine sense of consideration make them interpersonally very rich. Their rapport building skill is amazing as is their ability to treat people with respect and a sense of dignity.

DEALING WITH CRITICISMS

All managers have to deal with the unpleasant task of giving feedback that may not always be pleasant to the ears. And yet, the work has to be done! Criticism is a fact and part of life. In the chapter on written communication, you will study how a big idea can be delivered a little later (BILL). A manager with good interpersonal skills is bound to handle the situation more sensitively than one who is poor at it. Communication research in this area indicates the following ways in which managers can deal with criticism:

1. Make an attempt to know more about the work done. Do not criticize immediately.
2. Limit the criticism to only one point at a time. This will help the employee to understand better.
3. If too many default areas are pointed out all at one time, they will put the employee on the defensive.
4. As a manager, it is necessary to point out limitations of people in an accurate manner. The employee may like to

know the details. Support the criticisms with factual explanations. Such explanations have greater validity.

5. It is important to keep the 'you view point' in mind while dealing with criticism. This way the manager will be able to enter the frame of reference and create a better understanding with the employee. This will also help the manager to keep the tone under control. A raised voice affects the facial muscles, which in turn will distort the message delivery.

6. A contextual understanding of the situation in which a certain act took place will help the manager to understand the problem in a wider perspective. A manager with high interpersonal skills will care for the employee's self-esteem and his/her own dignity. Criticism should not diminish any one's self-respect. A good manager perhaps will say something like this:

"I wish you had brought the matter to my notice. Together we could have examined the problem and found a solution."

This way the manager can earn the goodwill of the employee.

7. One of the grave errors that managers commit is to be judgmental while dealing with criticism. All kinds of discriminatory and emotive words must be avoided in such interactions. Poor listening skills and hasty evaluations can mar a manager's handling of a situation.

8. If necessary, the manager should volunteer to ask for more information or clarification.

In short, an interpersonally sensitive manager does not encode negatively and hence does not use negative words and negative tone.

MANAGING CONFLICT

Just as it is said wherever there are human beings, there is a grapevine, similarly it is also said wherever people are there conflicts are bound to occur. Conflict is a part of life and more so at workplaces. Every manager has to deal with such situations. But there are ways of dealing with conflicts. Like the different types of interpersonal styles, conflict-resolving styles are also of different types.

There are generally six ways of dealing with conflicts:

1. Avoiding
2. Accommodating
3. Competing
4. Collaborating
5. Compromising
6. Asserting

If a manager says, "Leave behind the papers I'll look into them later" there is every possibility that the manager does not wish to get into the details of a complex problem. What the manager has chosen to do is to avoid facing conflict. Day in and day out, managers may be subjected to unsatisfactory work from juniors, or pressures from the boss for immediate results. The manager may prefer tolerating such situations because confrontation may not lead to any kind of result.

If a manager says, "Alright! I guess I understand why you want us to do the work this way. Perhaps this style makes a better sense." Giving up your point to accommodate the other person's suggestion can sometimes bring better result. It could also lead to better negotiation.

If a manager says, "I don't care what the workers say about this proposal of coming at eight in the morning. If they don't, they will be fired from their jobs." This kind of a power-based or competing approach can lead to disasters.

A better way is to say, "OK! I understand your problems. Try out the new timing for a few weeks. If it does not work, we'll change the timing."

The compromising or collaborating approach makes a better sense. Both parties must make an attempt to understand a common problem and be a part of it. Both have to make an effort to resolve the conflict.

If a manager says, "Nisha, the three reports that you typed last week contained errors in spellings. Please correct the errors and next time check the matter before you submit." (Specific description). The manager wants to be specific about the nature of error and minces no words about Nisha's slipshod work. The manager asserts.

The manager could have said, "Nisha, your careless work will not be tolerated any more! Why are there so many mistakes in the reports? Looks like, you take your work lightly!" (This is an accusation. Consider the tone)

The correct way to handle conflicts is to address an issue directly—whether you collaborate, compromise or compete. You need to be assertive in your skill of handling conflicts.

COMMUNICATING ASSERTIVELY

Managers with assertive style are direct, honest, and empathetic while dealing with others at workplace. They are good listeners, positive in their approach to finding a solution to a conflict, and works toward a 'win-win' situation. They negotiate carefully and are willing to cooperate. Hence this kind of behaviour leads to success. It encourages an open understanding and relationship. The language that an assertive person speaks is something like this:

- "I think I must finish this report before I decide to go home. Boss needs˙it tomorrow." (Being honest with oneself about one's responsibility toward work.)
- "Joydeep, I know you are tired right now. I'll discuss your work tomorrow. I have gone through the report you submitted today. There are a couple of things that have not been explained correctly. See me in the morning." (a considerate boss chooses the right time and frame of mind for talk. It enhances better understanding because listening will be at its best)
- "At tomorrow's meeting, I do need to clarify the points about the distribution of work and roles of the new recruits in my department." (Good encoding leads to better transmission of thoughts and generates clearer understanding)
- Joydeep, the report needs to be more focussed on the kinds of channels that we are looking for. A vague reference is not going to help us to promote our product." (specific mention is made to the subject that has to be discussed.)
- "I feel very hurt when you criticize my work in front of others in my absence. I wish you would be discreet with me so far my work is concerned." (Pointing out in clear terms like this always makes a good deal of sense because the person does notice the controlled tone and the expression of your feelings.)
- "Of late, I have noticed that you are avoiding me. Have I done you anything wrong? Please tell me! I also feel disturbed about it." (The genuineness of the communication/request makes the other person look up to you.)

A direct, and sincere effort to solve conflicts always leads to gains. The broader frame of reference and willingness to be a participant in finding solution to a problem enable a manager to successfully deal with the situation. Of course, in a hierarchical environment or where indirect style of communication is to be followed, directness or assertiveness may not always work. Directness works in low-context cultural countries where the word is the supreme. In high-context cultural countries like India, it is the non-verbal communication pattern that rules like it does in Japan, Korea, and several other high-context cultural countries. This is a major point of concern to all managers working in a multicultural work environment. The best thing to do is to assess the situation and find out how much of assertiveness/direct style will work. A mix of styles to suit the working environment is a better solution. The tips on neuro-linguistic programming tell you how to match, mirror and pace the other person's communication style for creating better understanding.

Negotiating Skills

Business is eternally plagued with problems which often can be solved through negotiations. Finding solutions is not easy, but efforts have to be made. Simply delivering sweet talks in the discussions may not yield any result. It is important that one understands the basic issues involved so that through discussions, one finds a way out. Negotiation occurs when parties involved in discussions over business proposals/business conflicts/business terms and conditions, attempt to find out a mutually agreeable solution. The solution that emerges from the negotiation cements goodwill and understanding between the parties involved in the negotiating process, and in turn, a favourable business relationship.

Negotiations take place at every stage. Therefore, it is a mistake to think that negotiations take place only in conference rooms or in a formal environment. Do we not negotiate our ways for small matters like the bus conductor refusing to listen to you for an emergency stop or explaining to the boss why it would be in the interest of the organization to have the professional service of IT experts?

But negotiation cannot be struck at one shot. It is a tedious process and one needs to be educated about the subtleties of the whole process. It is intended here to give you an idea about the process and the communication skills that are involved.

The ability to communicate effectively is rarely an inherited gift. We have to develop the ability through a lot of hard work. The preceding chapters provide all the necessary information for developing the communication skill sets. These skills are put to a real test in negotiations. The power to convince the opponent is what is needed most in any negotiation process.

Negotiation has been defined as "the art of exchanging ideas with the intention of changing relationships favourably." It is basically a process in which two sides sit down to reach an agreement or solution that will leave both sides happy. A successful negotiation is always a win-win situation. Both sides gain out of the exchange of ideas.

Negotiation takes place all the time, every day. Managers negotiate their work schedule with their juniors. Business people negotiate terms and conditions of business with clients. Parents negotiate their ideas about life with their children. When such exchanges of ideas take place in a clear and persuasive manner, the desired results for benefits are created. This is not easy to achieve because you are dealing with perspectives and priorities that are different from those of yours. Thus in a negotiating process, it is how you meet the needs of the person on the other side that is important. Communication researchers have written about the four approaches to negotiation. These are

- ◆ Bargaining approach
- ◆ Lose-lose approach
- ◆ Compromise approach
- ◆ Win-win approach

Bargaining approach. This type of approach basically deals with the strategy of winning against the other party who gets pushed into losing. The winning side has to do a lot of background work about the other party. Information about the party is the most important asset that the winning party can possess. Information can be gathered from personal observation, contacts, research about the party, and on the spot assessment of the communication that takes place. Bargaining takes place when

- Collaboration is not possible.
- Interests are conflicting.
- An 'Us' versus 'them' situation arises.
- Arguments move toward polarization.
- Each side examines the issues only from one's own point of view.

Lose-lose approach. This approach is totally destructive to both parties. The conflict remains unresolved, causing damages to both the parties. This occurs when

- Both the involved parties ignore each other's needs
- One party continuously blocks out the other
- A negative mind set operates on both sides
- Unreasonable demands are rigidly put across

Compromise approach. In this, both sides lose some of their demands to strike a mutually acceptable solution. This approach is adopted when

- Both sides realize that their needs are equally important
- Both sides are tough
- Both are aware of their needs but are not prepared to let go the opportunity to lose out on the demands

Win-win approach. This is the ideal approach to negotiations. The collaborative style makes it a friendly way to deal with the needs. In fact, the focus is not on the conflict at all. It is on how the conflict can be resolved. This positive approach makes it a win-win strategy. Of course, converting a situation into a win-win situation demands a great deal of persuasive communication techniques and a good deal of critical listening ability. Unless a healthy frame of reference is created, neither listening occurs nor persuasion takes place. At the basis of this approach lies a positive mind set. Therefore, one should make an effort in

- Creating genuine interest in the party
- Attempting to understand the need
- Motivating the person to open up and talk
- Listening openly to assess the person (not making unwarranted assumptions, practising wishful hearing, thinking about one's thoughts instead of listening, etc.)
- Not underestimating the other side's intelligence
- Practising the formula of CARESS
- Building a sense of trust and credibility

The win-win formula is an ideal one because it is not the 'Us' versus 'them'. It is 'we' versus the problem that brings the two sides to a healthy dialogue. Both sides recognize the conflict and hence both parties think that a mutual gain is attainable. Transparency on both sides makes them understand each other's point of view. It is this open approach that makes the win-win strategy move toward a long-term relationship. Both task and relationship issues are addressed by this approach.

• The best part of win-win negotiation is that you deal with perspectives and priorities in an open, clear and persuasive style that provides a route to the desired benefits.

The communication pattern in a win-win negotiation is something like the following: Consider the openness of the dialogues that take place. Mark the tone, the words, the willingness to discuss and listen:

"I did inform the people at the top that it would not be possible for me to accept the post at a salary as low as that."

"OK, let's see the work that you are referring to. With your kind of experience, this work seems simple. You don't have to actually go the field and establish contacts. The PR skills that we are looking for are your ability to establish connections with the corporate people so that some kind of understanding and goodwill begin to grow. This work that you need to do can be done from the office itself. Inviting people for lectures and programs, promoting our programs to the corporate are very challenging. We think you are very capable of doing that. Besides, you have the assistants to help you out with the field visits."

"I know I am good in my work. My testimonials and letters of recommendation also support my claim. This is the second time I have come for the interview."

"Well, establish yourself through your work by taking up the responsibility of selling our programs to the corporate and if you are successful at it, recognition will come your way. Our company has the procedure of annual appraisal. Every employee's performance is evaluated. Your performance will also be evaluated. We think you should get a shot at this opportunity. Working with a team of enthusiastic professional will be an exhilarating experience, which you will not regret."

"OK, but can I get a higher salary?"

"Consider the possibility of accepting the opportunity. You can compare our package with any other company for a similar position. Opportunities here are great! We are expanding fast. You can check out our credentials from the market. We have a fair policy. Besides, we are already offering you a higher package than what you were getting previously. What we have offered is very attractive. It's for you to decide."

"OK I am prepared to accept the post but I want it known that handling the corporate will be my job entirely and not the job of the assistants. I will solicit their help as and when needed."

"Sounds fair to us. But, we do think that you'll gain a lot by taking their help. Your work or performance will be separately evaluated if that is what you are worried about. As we said, our policies are very well drafted and applied to employees' performance. You can be rest assured!"

"When do I join?"

All managers have to negotiate with people all the time. The only way they can succeed is to practice the art of negotiating.

COMMUNICATING IN A TEAM

Working with others is a vital managerial skill. Regardless of the work that a manager does in whatever capacity, whether it is task or relationship-focused work, she/he has to practise what has already been written in the section of interpersonal skills of communication.

In order to work effectively and successfully in a team it is imperative that a manager understands the characteristics of groups. The following tips may be of help:

1. It is necessary to recognize the personal goals and the group goals.
2. It is important to deal with the hidden agendas in a teamwork (often the individual goals/interests can overpower the group goals). Personal goals that are not made public are hidden agendas.
3. For congenial functioning of the group, some unwritten norms must be understood and practised.
4. The norms must be established early in the stage of group work.
5. All task roles and relational roles must balance each other for a smooth functioning of the group.

A manager, highly competent in interpersonal communication skills and relations, generally handles teamwork very effectively. Today's management is heavily based on interdependence within the organization. Therefore, collaborative skills are of great importance.

Manager's Telephone Skills

Business telephone etiquette are not trivial. It is very surprising that these daily skills are taken for granted by people at work. People generally think that they are good in their telephone communication. Only those who listen on the other side will be able to tell us whether we are proficient in our telephone skills or not. Very often, you will hear some gruff, cold greetings, and indifferent tone, and also some discourtesies. Certainly, these are not the standard business etiquette for telephone communication.

Since it is an oral form of communication, the vocal quality is the most important medium of communication. Impressions are formed from the words, the tone and the quality of the voice of the speaker. Therefore, if the voice quality is poor and the tone is harsh, the speaker needs to polish up his/her telephone communication skills.

There are books available on telephone conversations. However, a few functional tips it will be useful:

1. Before you dial, ensure exactly what you would like to say. If there are too many points, it is better to make a list and tick them off as you proceed.
2. If you are making the call, hold the mouthpiece at a little distance from your mouth, drop your voice into a warm friendly tone and open your dialogue with "May I speak to ... This is so and so speaking".
3. If it is going to be a long talk, find out whether it is the proper time to talk and also whether the receiver has enough time to listen to what you have to say.
4. Like all effective communication units, telephone communication needs to be properly structured. Short sentences, simple words, precise meanings are of great importance.
5. As you speak, do not hesitate to use gestures like moving your hand or keeping a smiling face or nodding your head. These are after all the illustrators that reinforce your message.
6. It is important to smile while talking on phone; else you may come across as a very stern un-cooperative person.

Finally, it is important to note that "Hello, who is talking" is a most offensive telephone etiquette. It must be erased from a speaker's vocabulary.

Gender Communication

According to gender theorists, women cannot rise up in their professional career because their communication style is less authoritative than that of men. A lot of research has been conducted in this area. Which style is more appropriate is again and again asked—men's style or women's style? However, both styles are important for corporate life. In leadership roles, promotion, recognition, decision making, communication needs a logical and a lateral approach.

According to researchers, men use direct strong language, are blunt and often express preferences directly. They are also poor in reading the non-verbal signals in communications. They interpret aggressiveness as a way to organize and get things done. On the other hand, women are lateral communicators, and are good in decoding non-verbal signals. They prefer to ask questions in order to find out information from others. As they do so, they are given to nodding and smiling as encouragement to the person on the other side.

Both styles have their strong as well as weak points. Business needs rapport building, lateral understanding and motivational leadership. Business also needs reporting or authoritative functioning where tough decisions need to be taken. It is because of this that the modern manager is expected to blend both the styles for their professional functioning. Tomorrow's executive will be known as an androgynous executive, i.e. a professional who will blend both rapport and the report style.

VIRTUAL TEAMS

A new area in communication exerting pressure on today's managers is how far they are able to handle the pressure of virtual team communication across distances and organizational boundaries. In their book *Virtual Teams: Reaching across space, time, and organizations with technology*, Jessica Lipnack and Jeffrey Stamps state:

> Today's trend is tomorrow's reality: In the coming decades, most people will work in virtual teams for at least some part of their jobs.... Electronic communication and digital technologies give people an historically unprecedented ability to work together at a distance... A new form of boundary—crossing team is emerging as the basic working unit of the Information Age Organization. (pp. 1–2)

Today's managers are a part and parcel of this Information Age and they are being driven by the speed and demands that the information technology is exerting on them.

The word 'virtual' came into use during 1990s. It has its root in the medieval Latin word *virtualis*. In its essence it means "not in actual fact". The expression 'virtual reality' means "a stimulated environment which gives the operator the impression of actually being in the environment". The Chambers Dictionary explains the word 'teamwork' as "work by organized division of labour, cooperation, putting together, regard to success of the enterprise as a whole rather than personal exploits or achievements".

The expression 'virtual team' therefore means a team that "works across space, time, and organizational boundaries with links strengthened by webs of communication technologies". (Lipnack & Stamps, p. 7). It is necessary to remember that virtual teamwork is not something like a computer generated game that one plays with a joystick or any other equipment. Virtual teamwork is like teamwork in a real sense. It is a face-to-face exchange of information through a technological medium, the nature of which has to be understood by the virtual team members.

Various communication modes are needed for virtual teamwork. If the team is sitting in one well-equipped room, it will need some of the following facilities mentioned:

1. A computer (the team will sit around it).
2. One of the team members will act as a 'technographer'.
3. The technographer should be able to transmit the team's message on the computer screen across space and real time (known as **web conferencing**).
4. The email server should be kept ready for short messaging or for attaching multiple packages to a letter (for example, project details, business reports).
5. The technographer should be able to speak clearly (voice and speech clarity through audio links) and compose and transmit instant message to the receiving group or sub-groups).
6. The technographer should be able to think quickly, logically, and factually.
7. Tools such as message boards or bulletin boards should be kept ready. Unlike email, these exist on the web and serve the virtual team as a communication tool. This is also known as **knowledge repository**.

Virtual teamwork does need the advanced facility of communication technology to match the speed at which the work has to be carried out. However, all virtual meetings have to be backed up by actual face-to-face meetings. Dennis Roberson, chief technology officer and NCR vice president, observed: "There were lots of meetings. You still need all-hands meetings. With all this wonderful technology and shared information, they still don't replace the need to get together..." (cited in Lipnack and Stamps), *op. cit.*, p. 84.

In the Foreword to Karl Albrecht's *Social Intelligence: The new science of success,* Professor Warren Bennis writes:

> Technological change is rapidly accelerating. We are now beginning an era in which people's knowledge and approach can become obsolete before they have even begun the careers for which they are trained. We are living in an era of runaway inflation of knowledge and skill, where the value of what one learns is always slipping away. The age of "virtual" relationships is upon us, with people changing careers, uprooting themselves, moving their families to follow new opportunities, and constantly forming new but ever more transitory relationships... (p. vii)

The paradox is that despite the nagging areas of clash of egos, power plays, backstabbing, hurt-feelings, low confidence, poor self-esteem, confusion, and inability to keep with the flow of thoughts that can affect the functioning of the virtual team, people will still crave for "personal connectedness".

The reality is that virtual teamwork is here to stay. As Lipnack and Stamps (*op. cit.*, p. 2) say, "Virtual teams are the peopleware for the 21st century."

Social Skills

Another emerging area that challenges today's managers is the need to possess a repertoire of social skills. Exponential growth in modern business has resulted in an increased expectation of desired workplace mannerisms and interactions. These range from "hello" or "good morning" to saying "bye" or "good evening" (to superiors) before leaving the workplace or "bon voyage" (before the boss goes abroad). When these manners or behaviours are incongruent, they do draw attention, and often can cause much embarrassment. Never have human interactions been talked about so much and never have so many books and articles written on the subject.

Mary Mitchell in her book *Class Acts* offers useful tips about good manners in varied business and non-business situations. Knowledge-based economy is bringing people together from across the cultures. Conventional importance given to hard knowledge is now challenged by the gentler art of empathic understanding and communicating one's thoughts and feelings.

Scholars are offering their knowledge about the finer aspects of 'people skills'. Artifactics, listening skills, the art of saying

'No', pleasant conversational dialogues, telephone etiquette and netiquette rules, the power of handwritten notes, public speaking, self-talk, social etiquette, meeting skills, including corporate governance, and meditation techniques are being researched. Mary Mitchell emphasizes how the qualities of self-confidence, virtues of accountability and forgiveness, virtue of trustworthiness, absence of rudeness, and good communication skills matter in modern business. The author describes class acts as an integration of several verbal and non-verbal qualities that have to be internalized, genuinely believed in, and practiced as sincerely as one can. She emphasizes that without a genuine respect for the ideas, integrity, property, and time of others, etiquette rules are hollow at best. Simply knowing the rules of etiquette will not turn someone into a role model for living well.

SUMMARY

In this chapter, we have tried to give a synoptic idea of the basic skill sets that a manager needs to possess for daily functioning. Today's manager has to be rich in people's skills. These skills help the manager to create a healthy and positive communication climate in which employees can function well and feel valued. *Affirmation* is what people look for. An organization that gives respect to people, resolves conflicts and does not impose solutions, is an organization that people feel proud to be associated with. But, such a work environment needs to be created and that can be attained only if managers are equipped with the basic skill sets.

TEST YOURSELF: ONLY ONE OPTION IS CORRECT. TICK IT. DO IT YOURSELF.

1. A manager's effectiveness depends on the style of functioning. Which style should be adopted by a manager?
   - (a) Closed style
   - (b) Blind style
   - (c) Hidden style
   - (d) Open style

2. Indicate which of the four styles refers to the following statement:

   "Do not lecture me please! I know exactly what I am doing".
   - (a) Open style

    (b) Closed style

    (c) Blind style

    (d) Hidden style

3. **Managers with poor interpersonal skills have**

    (a) a blind style functioning

    (b) a closed style of functioning

    (c) an open style of functioning

    (d) a hidden style of functioning

4. **The term 'disclosure' means the person**

    (a) voluntarily discloses information about self to others

    (b) keeps information about self hidden in the closet

    (c) does not bother to share information with others

5. **The term 'feedback' means**

    (a) seeking only positive response

    (b) seeking response from others and not waiting for it

    (c) selecting only the positive response and rejecting the negative one

6. **Handling criticisms *effectively* means**

    (a) criticising immediately

    (b) keeping the 'you view point' in mind

    (c) being judgmental while dealing with the person

7. **A manager is said to have a *closed style* of functioning when she/he**

    (a) does not seek feedback and does not share information

    (b) blocks information and does not allow it to be passed on to others

    (c) wants more information but does not share the information

8. **A manager is said to have a *blind style* of functioning when she/he is**

    (a) high on feedback and disclosure

    (b) neither high nor low on feedback and disclosure

    (c) low on feedback but high on disclosure

9. **A manager is said to have a *hidden style* of functioning when she/he**

    (a) keeps ears and eyes open to collect feedback

    (b) is low on disclosure but high on feedback

    (c) is neither interested in gathering feedback nor in disclosing information

10. **A manager is said to have an *open style* of functioning when she/he**

    (a) gathers feedback and discloses sensibly

    (b) is selective in giving feedback and disclosures

    (c) is indifferent to both feedback and disclosures

11. *Assertive communication style* refers to

    (a) empathetic communication

    (b) sympathetic communication

    (c) apathetic communication

FURTHER READING

Adler, R.B. and J.M. Elmhorst, *Communicating at Work*, McGraw-Hill, Toronto, 1996.

Adler, R.B., L.B. Rosenfield, and N. Towne, *Interplay: The process of interpersonal communication*, 4th ed., Holt, Rinehart and Winston, Tokyo, 1989.

Albrecht, Karl, *Social Intelligence: The New Science of Success*, Wiley Eastern, New Delhi, 2006.

Burnard, Philip, *Interpersonal Skills Training: A sourcebook of activities*, Viva Books, Kolkata, 2002.

Calero H.H. and Bob Oskam, Negotiate the Deal You Want, Dodd, Mead & Company, New York, 1983.

French, Astrid, *Interpersonal Skills: Developing successful communication*, Sterling Publishers, New Delhi, 1993.

Hamilton, Cherryl, *Communicating for Results: A Guide for Business and the Professions*, 5th ed., Wadsworth Publishing Co., Washington, 1999.

Handle, Tim, *Negotiating Skills*, Dorling Kindersley, Moscow, 1998.

Kozicki, Stephen, *The Creative Negotiator*, Gower, Australia, 1993.

Locker, Kitty O., *Business Administrative Communication*, 5th ed., Irwin McGraw-Hill, Toronto, 2000.

Mitchell, Mary, *Class Acts: How good manners create good relationships and good relationships create good business*, Magna Publishing Co., Mumbai, 2003.

Nierenberg, Gerard I., *The Art of Negotiating*, Pocket Books, Singapore, 1981.

Ross, R. Reck and Brian, G. Long, *The Win/Win Negotiator: How to negotiate favorable agreements that last*, Pocket Books, Singapore, 1985.

Part 2

Verbal Communication and Presentation Skills

CHAPTER **4**

Use of Words and Sentences in Verbal Communication

I just wish my prose to be very transparent. I don't want the reader to stumble over me.

— V.S. NAIPAUL

Paul Theroux, writing in "Sir Vidia's Shadow", says:

> He did not, of course, use language casually. He was particular in his choice of words, which made him a demanding listener, too. Any word he used was intended, and considered; he sought simplicity.... Anything that smacked of show, or style, or display, or falsity, anything that was purely for effect, he disdained. Writing must never call attention to itself.... He was a stickler for truth... (p. 296)

It is generally believed that fluency in speaking and writing makes one a good business communicator. Over the years of teaching the subject of business communication, this is the refrain that I have heard. Most management students and young executives, with background of education in English medium schools and colleges, tend to believe that fluency in English language is the prime criterion for qualifying as a good communicator and hence there is no need to learn business communication. This is far from the truth.

Knowing English language is one thing, but to be able to use it for the purpose of communicating a thought precisely and tactually for business purpose is a different skill that one has to learn. Business communication, both oral and written, demands a lot more competency in language and communication skills than one generally associates it with. Language and its nuances, somehow, get no special attention in our country. The sensitive touch to language is neither taught in schools nor developed in colleges. Perhaps, this is why companies keep holding training programs on communication to enable their managers to unlearn, learn and re-learn their skills in language and communication.

Verbal communication refers to both oral and written communication. Oral communication should be as clear, specific, tactful, and precise as written communication should be. Your listener or reader who could be your client, boss, or a customer, may not have endless time to listen to a convoluted oral report or read a long memo or listen to the explanation that you as a sales person may offer for the purchase of a product.

In business, people are expected to communicate clearly, courteously and precisely, which is why the subject is ranked first among all other core business subjects. This chapter mainly deals with the basics of effective business communication, i.e. the rules for expressing one's thoughts in a manner that would impact the receiver in a desired way. Researchers have made extensive study in this area. The principles of effective business communication entail both oral and written communication. However, the two forms of communication have basic differences between them since they are two different mediums of expression. These differences are discussed in separate sections.

In any kind of business or profession, whether it is the finance sector, or the fast moving consumer goods sector, banking or insurance, pharmaceutical or hospitality and tourism sectors, it is absolutely vital that one is proficient in the use of good communication skills, be it oral or written. From customer care to granting of loans or announcing instructions to airline passengers, the purpose of communication should be clear and the message should be precise, both while speaking and writing, according to the nature of business.

TYPES OF COMMUNICATION NETWORKS

There are different kinds of situations in business for which different kinds of communication skill sets have to be used. We have already discussed that there are upward, downward, horizontal, grapevine and external forms of communication in an organization. All of these are important because they enable people to interact and collaborate with one another to work together for the growth of their organization. The communication network in an organization is generally of two types:

- Internal
- External

Internal Network

This includes interaction between the members of an organization, which may be:

1. Shop floor instructions given by superiors for work to be carried out, workshop specifications given to the workers in the tool room, assembly shop, inspection, packaging and dispatch department, and warehouse where finished articles are stored pending and waiting for sale.
2. Administrative communication, i.e. business side of an organization that needs extensive discussions about work to be carried out. Sales, marketing, PR, finance, business expansions, production, market research, general administration etc.
3. Human resource/personnel communication—employee communication, considered to be a vital and sensitive area to manage. Employee needs and satisfaction must be addressed for creating a better environment for work.

Internal communication network involves orders, instructions, sharing and exchange of information, motivating, and explaining matters on hand as and when required. At every point of time such exchanges take place, the three important components of the communication loop come into play—the direct parties involved in the dyad, the message that has to be encoded and the message that has to be delivered well for the anticipated understanding to take place.

External Network

This also forms an equally important segment of organizational communication. An organization has to regularly communicate to customers, suppliers, service companies, other business organizations, the media and the government. If business has to grow, it has to maintain its image and goodwill. Therefore, it is imperative that the organization handles its external communication effectively. External communication is simply not passing on the information to the key stakeholders, but the manner in which the exchange of information takes place.

In today's long hours of operations at workplaces, *social communication* is a vital requirement. But such communication does not take place without personal touch or a sense of genuine warmth. Employees expect a personal touch in communications. This does not mean that one needs to exchange pleasantries by becoming permissive. A personal touch to communication makes a lot of difference to the exchanges that take place. It is important to establish the right kind of environment for fruitful communication to take place.

Equally demanding is *corporate communication*. Quite often, a senior executive has to address the stakeholders in conferences seminars, annual general meeting, and such formal gatherings Both oral and non-verbal communication styles are put to tes when executives have to deliver public speeches. It is then that the clarity and the tone of speaking come under close scrutiny Therefore, one has to pay special attention to these factors.

STRATEGY FOR EFFECTIVE COMMUNICATION: THE USE OF THE SEVEN C'S OF COMMUNICATION

The powerful seven C's of communication govern the compositior of all our messages whether we speak or write. We cannot escape their influence. If we ignore them, we are trapped by the inability to encode and process our message composition. Messages may turn out to be either harsh or incomplete or incorrect. They are explained here with few examples to illustrate how they function in language. A later section will contain more details about the use of the 'C's particularly in business letters.

1. Courtesy

As the word 'courtesy' suggests, one expects the speaker/writer to be aware of the listener's/reader's feelings. In business communi- cation, we not only pass on information but we also share and try to create a harmonious understanding for business to grow and develop and retain goodwill. Courtesy is not merely expressing perfunctorily the much used phrases 'thank you' and 'please', but it is a sincere and genuine expression that stems out of respect and care for others.

The following tips may be kept in mind if you wish to achieve courtesy in communication:

◆ Be sincere
◆ Avoid anger or extreme rapture

◆ Refrain from preaching
◆ Use positive words
◆ Avoid negative words
◆ Avoid all discriminating words

Examples

No	Yes
(a) "Please sign here", said the counter-girl quite surly **(impolite)**	"Sir/Ma'am, would you please sign here?"
(b) "Why do you ask me to ring you up when you are not free to receive my calls?" **(anger/rudeness)**	"I don't mind ringing you up. Will you tell me when I can do so?"
(c) "You failed to confirm the appointment with us" **(negative)**	If you had confirmed your appointment with us, we certainly would have reserved the place for you.
(d) "You must take a note of the piece of advice being given to you if you wish to be successful in your business". "The money you save now will help you to plan your future business". **(Do not preach! Refrain from preaching.)**	We are offering special schemes and if you invest now, you will be able to plan your future.
Readers/Listeners like to be treated as equals and not bossed over or talked down. Indian managers suffer from a bossy attitude while communicating to juniors. All phrases such as **'you should'**, **'you must'**, **'you need'**, must be avoided. It is difficult to retain goodwill if the speaker uses a communication style that does not respect the receiver's feelings.	
(e) "When an unauthorized person enters the security zone, he must be subjected to strict personal checking". (Why only	"An unauthorized person who enters the security zone must be subjected to strict checking".

No	*Yes*

'he'? The person can be a **'she'** also! Avoid being **sexist** in your choice of words/pronouns)

(f) The poetess read out a long poem at the poets' meet. (Why this? **Words have no gender.** Why must you add 'ess' to the word suggesting the profession of writing poetry?)

"Ms. Judith, an upcoming poet, read out a long poem at the poets' meet". (Similarly, use the words for the professions without adding the gender 'suffix-ess'. So you have **sculptor** and not 'sculptress', **lawyer** and not 'lawyer-ess', **author** and not 'authoress'.

(g) "Look at that Indian manager! Doesn't even realize that he is in a foreign country! Why does he speak so loudly?" (Why **stereotype** a person in a **demeaning manner** like this? Can we afford to speak like this in a globalized world where people, culture, and relationships are the twenty first century mantras? Avoid stereotyping by race, nationality, religion, language, and cultural habits. Business cannot grow if discriminations are done through communication by thoughtless and belittling expressions!)

The manager at the counter seems angry. Is he upset?

(h) "Sir, I had sent you the survey form. Did you have a chance to read it?"

"I am sorry I didn't find time to read it. Can I send it to you tomorrow?"

"It's just been *discarded* in the dust bin." (This is how a manager responded to the caller when she asked her question. This is being **rude!**)

(i) Another person said, "We have received it, but we are not interested in filling up the form." (People at workplace **cannot afford to be so rude.** This is a sure way **to lose goodwill and business reputation.**)

"Thank you for sending the form. At present we have no need for it."

In contrast, consider the following expressions. When you hear someone speaking to you courteously, don't you feel nice? Positive words go a long way in building relationships, whether in business or in other areas.

- ◆ I am pleased to meet you.
- ◆ I hope you will be able to meet the deadline.
- ◆ I'll appreciate it if you all cooperate with the new manager
- ◆ May I help you?
- ◆ Could you please let me know when to expect the delivery?
- ◆ If you grant this deferment, we should be most grateful.
- ◆ We are sorry to learn that you were inconvenienced.

2. Clarity

When you choose simple, precise, familiar, right words and short sentences to express your ideas, you succeed in expressing your thoughts well. Clear expression is a fine balance between familiar words and words that are precise. Precision does not mean using jargon. Business requires the use of the right or the expected word and not general words that might cause ambiguity. For clarity, the writer or the speaker must know what kind of words the receiver will accept. So audience analysis or foreknowledge about the audience helps the communicator to use technical words for precise communication.

Examples

No	Yes
(a) "I am sorry I cannot grant you the request unless you submit the statement for payment" **(Which payment? The final or the temporary one?)**	"I am willing to consider your request provided you submit the *invoice* first."
(b) "Will you please ensure that all the necessary machines are kept free to be used for operations?" the young supervisor said to the workers. (Can you edit this sentence by using the business term for the situation?)	"Please see that the *production line* is kept clear."

Several other factors affect the clarity of communication, whether you speak or you write. Of course, in speaking, it is expected that you as a manager know the standard pronunciation of words. It is necessary to remember that when you speak clearly, you impose listening on people. The encoded message has a mirror effect on your listener. This has been explained in the section on oral communication. The factors that reduce clarity in verbal communication are the use of

- ◆ camouflaged words,
- ◆ passive voice,
- ◆ long, convoluted, bureaucratic style of writing,
- ◆ clichés/rubber stamp words, and
- ◆ unfamiliar words.

These points will be dealt with separately in the section on written communication. It is necessary to keep in mind that they form an important chunk of business communication. Effective business communication must be clear and easily understood. Messages that are not clear, or have double meanings or are ambiguous, can result in waste of time, loss of goodwill and finally cancellation of orders. In business, we cannot afford to send confused messages.

3. Conciseness

This is a prerequisite to effective business communication. Time is money in business. *A long winding message is a time robber* and business people reject such messages in no time. Conciseness is achieved by eliminating all redundant words. Conciseness implies that you use only relevant words and phrases.

Examples

	No	*Yes*
(a)	"*I want to take this opportunity* to tell you that we are grateful to you for all the help that you extended when we were in Hong Kong." (Why **ornament** your thought? Say it **clearly and simply.** "Brevity is the soul of wit"!)	"Thank you for your hospitality in Hong Kong/ for being so kind when we were in Hong Kong."
(b)	"When will you submit the report?" "Within the course of next week." (Are you being **clear? Definite?**)	"I'll definitely try to submit it by Wednesday."

4. Concreteness

Clarity and conciseness come with the use of concrete words. Use of figures, facts, names, examples, and vivid nouns add a special touch to expressions. The message is remembered easily. In business communication, we need to be precise and factual. Concreteness means opposite of being abstract or vague.

Examples

No	Yes
(a) "I will send the goods to the upper floor by noon." (But how?)	"The goods will be sent by the *conveyor belt* to the upper floor."
(b) "The new manager seems pretty good in his work. Has an impressive track record." (Exactly how impressive?)	"Mr. Raman, the new manager, has been associated with the *World Bank* and *Government of India* for the rehabilitation of the earthquake affected victims."

5. Correctness

Correct use of grammar, message composition and appropriate words and adapting the right level of communication to suit the receiver's level determine the correctness of communication. Adapting the right tone for conveying a message is basic to the success of communication. Shop floor instructions, for instance, are different from client servicing communication.

Examples

No	Yes
(a) "My dear students, management education is all about strategic thinking, commitment, resource planning, and business process outsourcing! Globalization demands all this from you. Are you ready?" (This was spoken by the head of a management institute to young students at an education fair. The students looked confused and lost. The speaker **failed to adapt**	"Dear students, management education is very demanding. If you have to succeed as the new manager of the new millennium, you will have to be clear about your goal, know what makes global business challenging, and broaden your knowledge about the world of business. Are you ready?"

No	*Yes*
himself to the level of the students who did not know anything about management education. Why could he not be simple?)	
(b) "Since the last two days, I've been waiting for your call." (Very common mistake that most people commit.)	"You poor fellow, you waited for two days for my call?" ('Since' has different meanings. It is used, for example, for a point in time; 'for' is used for a period of time), e.g. we have lived here for 10 years
(c) "I want to use you", said the manager to the secretary. "What do you mean?" said the secretary. "Mind your words." The person immediately corrected himself and said, "No, no, what I mean is that I want to use your services."	"I need your services for my office work."

6. Consideration

This implies that the sender of the message gives due importance to the receiver and composes the message keeping in mind various factors like price, delivery date, specifications, and other benefits from the receiver's side. This kind of a thoughtful approach to communication is also termed as **'you-attitude'**.

Examples

No	*Yes*
(a) "We will not deliver the goods until you have submitted all the documents to us." **(How rude!)**	As soon as you submit the required documents to us, we will promptly deliver the goods to you.
(b) "We are delighted to inform that we have extended shopping time by two hours." (Why use **'we'** so many times? Is it more important than **'you'**?)	"So that you will be able to shop freely, we have extended the shopping time by two hours."

7. Completeness

A business communication message is not complete unless it

adheres to all the seven C's. Completeness does not only mean providing all necessary information, including something extra but also how the matter has been put across to the receiver of the message. The substance and the style of the message must go hand in hand.

Example

No	*Yes*
"I sent you the letter hoping that I would receive a reply by the end of this week. I still have not." (**Which** letter? **What** was it about? **When** was it dated?)	"I sent you a letter dated 2 June, about additional information of the shirt samples that you had sent for approval. I have still not received any reply from you. We are finalizing our order plan. If you send us the information, we will be able to consider your request for placing an order with you."

The power of the seven deadly C's cannot be underestimated as they collectively form the base of any effective communication. It is a power packed approach that lends credence to business communication. A communicator may speak or write fluently but she or he also has to be tactful, thoughtful, courteous, correct and complete in the communication that takes place.

Let us now study the details of the two different forms of communication.

ORAL COMMUNICATION

We have already seen how communication, as a process of exchanging thoughts and ideas, puts demands on the speaker for attaining effectiveness. This is true for oral as well as written communication, both of which are expected to be purposeful and create an impact on the listener.

Researchers tend to put a great deal of importance to written communication and think that it is more difficult than oral communication. This is not true! Oral communication is as challenging as written communication. What makes written communication different from oral communication is that it is permanent and forms a part of documentation that can be referred to as and when required. A letter or a report can always be read over and over again for the purpose of determining the truth so that it helps in the process of taking a decision on an issue.

However, oral communication has its own special characteristics. It is believed by many that good writers may not necessarily
be good speakers. In business communication, however, one has to
make an attempt to master both the forms of communication. Let
us explore the differences between the two forms of communication. In what way does the shop floor supervisor's oral exchange
become as important as the written communication in a memo or a
report?

While it is true that one need not be so finicky about the
correctness of pronunciation, it is vital to remember that in
business and corporate communications, the listener expects the
speaker to have the correctness of standard pronunciation. Also,
the listener expects you to speak at your best. It is a different
matter that one may choose to ignore the incorrectness of the
manner in which the words are spoken. Yet, it is quite a different
matter when one really speaks well. After all, when we speak well,
we force listening on people.

Both the forms of communication depend on the basic
fulfilment of the factors concerning the sender, i.e. the process of
encoding, the message, the channel, the receiver, the decoding and
the feedback.

How do you become a good speaker?

The beautiful aspect of oral communication is that it involves
not only words but also the nuances of voice that acts as a
communication channel. Good speakers are not born; they are
made! This aphorism has been quoted in several books on oral
communication because it is so true! When as a speaker you utter
your words with clarity, feeling, correctness, and you do justice to
the rhythm of the words, your speech begins to sound lyrical,
almost like music. Rabindranath Tagore had long ago said,

> "When music is wedded to words, it signifies much more than what
> the words can ever mean by themselves. Its range becomes wider
> and deeper."

Even if we understand Tagore's statement as an intimate
union of music and words, in the context of his compositions, the
interpretation can be extended to our daily speech. Language is a
combination of consonants and vowels. Words are a mixture of
both. If consonants are hard sounds, the vowels are the soft ones.
When you speak, you have to manage your tongue to produce the
correct sounds. A vowel cannot be enunciated as a consonant. A
vowel demands a glide just as a consonant demands a sharp touch
to the edge of the words.

When we as speakers understand that words have rhythm and a personality of their own, we are in a position to feel the sound quality of the words. We then speak, as we would be expected to utter. Pleasant sounds are enunciated when we do justice to the combination of the consonants and the vowels. Only then, our speech begins to sound like music! All great speakers are pleasant and powerful speakers but they have to work hard to become so!

Factors that Matter in Oral Communication

1. **Projection.** An effective voice is not only clear but also as loud as the occasion and the listeners demand. When you make a presentation to a group, ensure that you are heard even at the end of the room. You are expected to raise and direct your voice to all the listeners by alternating between loudness and a quieter tone. But in interpersonal or small group communications, it is necessary to adjust to the level of the volume required. At no point in time must you be heard as 'yelling' or shouting at the top of your voice. A **loud voice** can be misunderstood, as 'anger' or 'rudeness', and it can be a major point for misunderstanding in a multicultural environment.

2. **Articulation.** It means speaking all the parts of a word carefully. Incorrect articulation occurs because of carelessness on the part of the speakers. It involves:

   (a) leaving off parts of a word (deletion),
   (b) adding parts to a word (addition), or
   (c) slurring words together.

Deletion is the most common mistake that occurs in articulation. Often youngsters are heard speaking incomplete words although they may think that it is quite fashionable to do so. They are heard uttering words like **going** as 'goin', **making** as 'makin', **doing** as 'doin'. This type of deletion occurs with the 'ing' form.

Words ending with '**th**' also are a problem with careless speakers. Words like **with, myth, birth, mirth** and similar ones are spoken as 'wit', 'myt', 'birt' and so on.

Not only the end of words, but also the beginning of some words, is carelessly spoken. For example, **that, this, there, those,** are spoken as 'dat', 'dis', 'dare', 'dose'.

Deletions occur because the speaker thinks of the complete words but does not pay attention to the fact whether the words are spoken completely or not. The speaker assumes that the complete word is spoken.

Addition implies that extra parts are added to words like 'ath-a-lete' for 'athlete'. George Rodman, in his book, *Public Speaking*, provides a list of words that show how speakers take freedom with words by adding extra part to words. **Incentive** becomes (incentative); **oriented** becomes (orientated). He says: "The worst, however, is **anda**. 'Anda' is often stuck between two words when 'and' isn't even needed ... other words that are needlessly added are to the beginning or end of words are 'you know', 'like', and 'right?' To have every sentence punctuated with a barely audible superfluous word (there are others, too, like, 'you see?') can be maddening."

Slurring is caused when the speaker, in a hurry, speaks two or more words at once. Again youngsters are in the habit of slurring, presumably because they think it is a fashion to do so. Thus expressions like **sort of** become 'sorta', **kind of** become 'kinda'.

In India, slurring is mainly noticed in children from English speaking schools and colleges, where the young population comes under the influence of the American style of speaking. Thus, one often hears 'wanna' for **want to** and **that is the way** as 'thatsaway'.

Also beware of 'verbal tics'. Many speakers think that it is quite fashionable to use 'ehs', 'ums', 'errs' in between the words in a sentence or between sentences. They may be prompted to use the verbal tics to buy time so that they can think and then speak. To the listener, the verbal tics do not sound very pleasant. They are scratchy and are jarring to the ear. Hence, they must be avoided. Every word that you speak must be clearly heard and understood. Do not speak fast and swallow your words.

3. **Modulation.** Varying the tone and the pitch of your voice is called *modulation*. Pitch refers to the sound vibration frequency. Pitch should never be too high or too low. Listeners like a controlled pitch. Modulation means the *rise and fall in pitch* and this pattern of speaking makes the voice sound *pleasant and interesting*. If you do not vary the pitch, you will risk being labelled as a monotonous speaker.

4. **Pronunciation.** You are judged by the way you speak the words that your listener expects you to speak. Wherever you go, your knowledge of careful pronunciation will always be an advantage. Pronunciation basically deals

with the stress, non-stress of consonants and vowels and opening and closing of the mouth. Of course, regional or ethnic dialects often come in the way of pronunciation of words. In business or corporate communication, it matters to speak the correct way. Dictionaries offer guidance on standard pronunciation of words. One has to take the trouble of finding out the phonetic sounds of words.

Some of the prominently mispronounced words as spoken in some parts of India are given below:

◆ **Snack** is pronounced as 'snake'—the front unrounded vowel, in a half-open position is uttered as the front rounded vowel

◆ **Hall** is pronounced as 'hole', **Law** is pronounced as 'low'— the rounded back vowel, in a half open and half close position is pronounced as a pure vowel

◆ **Wrapping** is pronounced as 'raping'—the front un-rounded vowel is pronounced as a rounded vowel

◆ **School** is pronounced as 'sa—kool'/'is—kool'—extra consonant sounds are added, breaking the word into two syllables

◆ **Love** is pronounced as 'lub'—half vowel in half close position is pronounced as a closed consonant

When speakers at training programs come prepared, loaded with material meant to fill up two or three hours, it is expected that they be well versed with the pronunciation of words that they have problem with. A mispronounced word hurts the listener's ear, thanks to the power of media these days! Day in and day out, we are bombarded with news and other tailored and customized programs on television. Since such programs on rated channels offer the standard pronunciation, listeners used to hearing such pronunciations, expect only standard pronunciation of words. A slight variation can be passable. But beyond a point, mis-pronunciations can cause not only embarrassment to the speaker but irritation to the listeners as well.

At a conference, I noted pronunciations of the following words:

◆ **Culture** pronounced as 'kol-ture'—half-closed vowel

◆ **First** as 'fa:rst'—the front vowel is stretched long

◆ **Unless** as 'on-less'—half-closed vowel

◆ **Suggestions** as 'so-ggestions'—half-closed vowel

◆ **Mechanism** as 'me-ka-nism'—the second vowel is pronounced with front open mouth and stretched long

◆ **Alternative** as 'el-ternative'—the front rounded vowel is pronounced as an unrounded vowel

◆ **Research** as 're-sharch'—extra consonant sounds are added

◆ **Corporates** as 'kar-porates'—the front rounded vowel is pronounced as an unrounded one

◆ **Automobile** as 'e-to-mobile'—the front rounded vowel is pronounced as an unrounded one

◆ **Mundane** as 'moondane'—the front half open vowel is pronounced as a closed vowel

In *Speaking for Success*, Jean Miculka has presented an interesting list of words that are either pronounced wrongly because they are spoken in a hurry or because it is socially fashionable to pronounce words with a slangy touch. Some of the words are reproduced here:

'Ath-a-lete' for **athlete**—adding vowel sound
'Natcherly' for **naturally**—omitting vowel sound
'Crick' for **creek**—substituting vowel sound
'Sta-stis-tics' for **statistics**—adding consonant sound
'Gover-'ment' for **government**—omitting consonant
'Kaow' for **cow**, 'tauwn' for **town**—nasalizing non-nasal sound

5. **Enunciation.** Enunciation means the care and precision with which you use your tongue and jaw to produce clear speech sounds. While consonants provide sharpness/crispness to sounds, vowels add melody and richness. This is what Tagore meant when he said words must be clothed in music. Since Indians tend to use consonants heavily, their speech sounds less melodious and rich. The Indian tongue is not accustomed to the glides. Hence the word 'glide' is pronounced with a short 'i' and not as 'glaaied' with a longer 'i'. Dictionaries offer phonetic transcriptions and hence one should not hesitate to look them up for the right pronunciation.

6. **Repetition.** The key phrases are used with different vocal emphasis for creating an impact on the listeners. Very often, you might just discover that your listener has missed out some important words or points. By repeating, you help the person to assimilate the thoughts well.

7. **Speed.** The rate and timing of the words when you are actually speaking is called *speed*. People who are in the habit of speaking fast, generally do not time the delivery

of their speech. It is important to bear in mind that we do not speak words in sentences at a stretch. We generally speak in phrases, that is, we group the words and take pauses, just as we use commas to punctuate our thoughts. While commas are used in written communication, we take pauses to punctuate our speech. If we speak very fast, we tend to slur and this amounts to loss of information. In business, we cannot afford to lose out on information by not paying attention to our speech. When you focus on important ideas, you are bound to pause on them. Therefore, search for the important ideas and rehearse them well for the correct rate of your speech.

Because of these challenges, oral communication skills have emerged as an important area for self-improvement. Several communication classes have flourished that promise to correct the tongue. The technology of the tongue has emerged as a crucial component for the study of effective communication. Managers, leaders and professionals are finding the need to perfect the technology of their tongue. It is now being increasingly realized that when you speak well, you force people to listen to you. In today's age of accelerating global change and professional uncertainty, when talents are hunted and challenged, when jobs/careers/vocations demand specific skills, acquiring communication skills has become an essential qualification.

Correct speech stimulates interactions. Imagine those who do not know the correct articulation of the words that the listener would expect the speaker to articulate! Poor speakers inadvertently amuse people with incorrect pronunciation. In social gatherings or corporate presentations, such mispronunciations can result into awkwardness and embarrassment. Very often, one finds the strong influence of regional sounds in the use of English words.

Alan Axlerod, in *Miss Nomer's Guide to Painfully Incorrect English*, talks about VOQ (verbal odour quotient). He brings to the reader's notice that in order to be a good speaker, one needs to pay attention to the correct pronunciation and usage of words. He warns against malapropism, usage errors, mangled pronunciations, misspellings, and homonym snafus "that most commonly torpedo discourse and make the speaker or writer look like a damn fool." A good speaker also has to guard against wrong choice and pronunciation of words. Look up the dictionary to find out the pronunciation and meanings of the following words on p. 86.

Once you master the art of speaking clearly and correctly, despite a touch of regional/dialectical flavour, you will enjoy your

Affect/ Effect	Between/ Among	Ceremonial/ Ceremonious	Foreword/ Forward	Moral/ Morale
Advice/ Advise	Biannual/ Biennial	Classic/ Classical	Hail/ Hale	Naughty/ Knotty
Alludes/Eludes	Bizarre/Bazaar	Clench/Clinch	Human/Humane	Over/Oeuvre
Allusion/Illusion	Breach/Breech	Dissent/Decent	Ingenuous/ Ingenious	Perspective/ Prospective
Already/All ready	Born/Borne	Eminent/ Imminent	Jealous/Zealous	Prescribe/ Proscribe
Altar/Alter	Burglary/ Robbery	Empathy/ Sympathy	Kill/Keel	Register/ Registrar
Seize/Siege	Tamper/Temper	Tenor/Tenure	Urban/Urbane	Righteous/ Riotous
Vain/Vein/Van	Wander/Wonder	Yoke/Yolk	Scent/Cent	Rout/Route
				Sail/Sale

ability to communicate to people who will be all attention for what you have to say. Speaking then becomes an enjoyable experience!

Here is an *exercise* for you to practice. Pronounce every word as clearly as you can and speak with proper pause and intonation. Get yourself recorded on an audio cassette and listen to your own voice after you have spoken out the script:

> **You:** Good morning, Neha. I am ready to meet the applicants for the new job. Do send in the first candidate.
>
> **Neha:** Good morning, Sir! It's Mr. Aurora
>
> **You:** Ask him to come in, will you?
>
> **Neha:** Mr. Aurora
>
> **You:** Do sit down, Mr. Aurora. How are you?
>
> **Mr. Aurora:** Thank you. I am fine. How are you?
>
> **You:** Let me come straight to the point. We are planning to increase our publicity work considerably. Our organization is growing and several new projects are going to be launched. At present, an advertising agency is handling our account but we are not very pleased with their work. We are planning to give our account to another agency. You have some experience in this field and are eager to take up challenging assignments.
>
> **Mr. Aurora:** Yes, I have handled quite a few accounts. I have planned advertising campaigns, coordinated the work of the visual artist, the copywriter, and the typographers. Simultaneously, I was responsible for discussing all details with the clients. What kind of work is it likely to be here?
>
> **You:** Well, you'll report to me for advertising and to Ms. John for public relations. There is a whole lot of work that has got to be done—From getting our company brochures, leaflets, corporate letterheads, and

catalogues designed to ensuring that the press releases are sent regularly to the media.

Mr. Aurora: Do you also advertise on the electronic media?

You: Yes, we do.

Mr. Aurora: Looks like it is going to be very challenging.

How did you like listening to your own voice? Discuss it with your friend. Find out if all the words were correctly pronounced and whether you took the pauses at the right places.

If oral communication throws challenges at the micro level of pitch, enunciation, stress and diction, then written communication too has a long list of minute details that cannot be overlooked.

WRITTEN COMMUNICATION

We have already discussed the power of the Seven C's of communication in the beginning of the chapter. We shall now study the other features that have made business English such a demand today. Throughout your career, you will have to use the written word extensively, besides using the oral channels of communication. Communicating with co-workers, colleagues, juniors, suppliers, creditors, media people, and stakeholders, will test your ability to use words correctly, simply, clearly, and courteously. While we will study letters, memos, reports in a separate chapter, we shall study here the factors that equip you to use your language effectively for business purpose.

Business English

What is business English? Is it the same thing that once upon a time used to be known as *Commercial English*? Many labelled it as 'commercialese'.

The new ones replace the old paradigms. With globalization of markets, mergers and acquisitions, accelerating pace of change in technology, opening up of the Indian economy to global competition, entry of several large multinational corporations into the Indian market, the pressure is on the most vital tool of making business and that is the medium of communication in which it is done.

The more complex and competitive global businesses become, the more the pressure will be on those who conduct these businesses. Communication has to be simple, easily understood, transparent, and pleasant. Business English aims at simplicity, clarity, brevity, authenticity, courtesy and completeness. Simplicity does not mean casual conversation style, for it can be slangy and often vague. Business writing deals with facts and hence language needs to be factual, formal and pleasant.

We will learn more about use of words, phrases, sentences and old style of writing that should be avoided in written communication. Unlike oral communication, where one may occasionally use language in a light-hearted/casual manner, business writing is governed by the rules of formal expression without being impersonal. Correctness of grammar, the right tone, tactful use of technical words, omitting all clichés (overused words), correct punctuations, precise message composition and short messages are the golden rules that govern business writing. Let us explore this fascinating world of writing.

Avoid business jargon

Gone are the days when managers used to think that writing of business letters meant using difficult and heavy words with long convoluted sentences. Foreigners find our style of writing very complex, prolix and underlined by a cringing attitude. Why do Indian business-people write, **thanking you** and **I beg to inform you?** Businesspeople are neither beggars nor commanders who take the reader for granted for fulfilling the request. Business writing supports itself only on the pillars of mutual understanding, neutral tone and respect for facts.

Books on business communication will provide you with a list of business jargon or clichéd expressions. Here is a partial list of such phrases/expressions.

Don't be wordy, be concise

No	Yes
1. Please reply at the earliest (vague; the writer's and the receiver's sense of time may be different)	I'll appreciate it if you reply by the end of this week
2. Thanking you and assuring you of our best attention (avoid all participial phrases. It is a thoughtless and a stereotyped expression so commonly used by our managers)	Thank you for the information. It will be our pleasure to attend to any of your further requests.
3. Enclosed herewith/Enclosed please find (omit herewith and 'finding' implies a search)	We have enclosed a cheque of Rs. 5000/- for the evaluation that you did for our MBA exam.

No	*Yes*
4. Have noted the contents (please omit fragmented/telegraphic sentence constructions, besides perpetuating a stereotyped expression)	We have received your letter and noted the details.
5. Kindly favour us with a reply (Why favour? Why this cringing attitude?)	We shall look forward to your reply.
6. Thanking you in advance, I remain, yours faithfully (omit participial phrases and omit the entire sequence of thought. Never thank someone in advance)	Thank you for your letter
7. We wish to acknowledge the receipt of your letter (please thank straight away. You don't have to ornament your thought)	We received your letter giving the details of the goods that we had asked about.
8. Your early attention will be appreciated (why not say directly?)	We will be happy if you act promptly
9. Your undated letter (you can't write this to a businessperson. It not only sounds like a taunt but you may lose the goodwill also)	We have received your letter dated...
10. Your esteemed favour is in hands/yours in hand (this kind of old language should be discarded at once.)	Please inform us by...
11. We would deem it a favour if you inform us at the earliest. (why make it so convoluted?)	Please let us know if we should...
12. I wish to take this opportunity to thank you (please do immediately)	Thank you
13. We would like to be advised if we should go ahead with the proposal (be simple and direct)	Please let us know if we could proceed with the proposal
14. In accordance with your request (don't make writing so heavy)	As requested by you
15. I would like to point out that we did not like the sample that you sent (omit).	We have received the sample but we regret that we have not approved it.

All bureaucratic phrases and language must be avoided. They make language slow, heavy, and complicated. Business English must be simple and modern.

Read the following passage and underline the difficult phrases and rephrase them into modern English:

> Forms of the interested candidates shall be accepted only if all the rules of the interview as laid down by the organization have been met with. The forms that do not comply with the rules shall be at once rejected and such candidates will not be given any further chances to re-apply for the post. The valid forms that pass the first scrutiny test will then be further examined by the registrar who will then decide who would be suitable for an interview with the managing director of the company.

How do you like the tone of the passage? Typical government tone and unfriendly approach make writing a very unpleasant / un-enjoyable task. Why does the passage sound so threatening and heavy?

The answer is: heavy use of passive voice. If you wish your writing to be simple and easily understood, you have to get into the habit of using active voice.

Avoid using passive voice

No	Yes
1. Your letter of May 2, 2003 was received yesterday. (Why write it in a round about way?)	We received your letter of May 2 yesterday
2. The policy was rejected by the committee. (Bureaucratic way of saying)	The committee rejected the policy.
3. A complete tour of the office building was taken by the president. (Why be so stiff, cold, and awkward in putting across your thought?)	The president took a complete tour of the building.

Business letter writers cannot afford to write dull, stiff, lifeless and awkward sentences by resorting to the use of passive voice. The style of business letter must be vivid, concise, and clear. A reader's time cannot be wasted. The more competitive businesses grow, greater will be the demand for conciseness of writing. Active verbs lend vitality and immediacy to your message, and at once catch the reader's attention!

However, the passive construction cannot be thrown away altogether in the bin. It has its strategic uses. When an unpleasant effect of a situation has to be softened, the emphasis shifts from the doer of the action to the object.

	No	*Yes*
•	Our dispatch clerk did not know the address and by mistake he sent the letter to your old address. (Why reveal who committed the mistake?)	By mistake the letter was sent to your old address.

Avoid repetitions

•	The *responsibility* of preparing a work schedule for the entire month is a *responsibility* that the HR managers must carry out. (Why repeat?)	Preparing a work schedule for the entire month is a responsibility that HR managers must carry out. (It pays to edit your own communication)

Avoid camouflaged verbs

•	*Acquisition* of the property made him very happy (Why use the noun form of the verb acquire? Verbs are action-oriented words and they lend power to language.)	He was happy to *acquire* the property.
•	The *approval* of the merger of Alpha and Beta must be carried out without further loss of time.	The company should *approve* the merger of Alpha and Beta without further loss of time.

Use familiar words

•	John has a tendency to be *verbose and coiled* when assigned with the task of making a speech (Would you speak like this? Business English, both oral and written must be simple, clear and direct. Do not try to impress.)	John's speeches are usually abstract and difficult to understand.

Avoid using vague, abstract words — Use concrete words

No	Yes
• "When will you be submitting your report?	I am late by a day Sir (rephrased reply).

I'm sorry Sir, I'm slightly behind schedule" (avoid).

Similarly, say

- ◆ 25% gain (for significant gain)
- ◆ One of the top 10 (ranked No. 4), for (a leading institute)
- ◆ 80% students have been placed, for (the majority of the students have been placed)

Use Adverbs and Adjectives **sparingly** and **carefully** in Business English: They can be misleading modifiers

• How did you find the lecture?	It was very informative (Rephrased, with controlled tone. There cannot be rapture in business expressions!)
Oh! Very stimulating and highly informative!	

You can avoid the following modifiers and similar modifiers that clutter your sentence but add little to the meaning to your message:

Incredibly, wonderfully well, highly, perfectly clear, absolutely essential, highly demanding, exceptionally good, fantastic, etc.

Not only must you take care of the words that you will use, but you should also ensure that the sentence constructions are correct. One of the main problems that writers commit is to keep the references separate. Effective writing depends on logical and sequential patterning of thoughts. The thought process must be clear. The reader should be able to understand immediately the words that are modified by the modifiers. A modifier is a word that says something extra about the word that is being modified. Correct syntax demands that the modifier and the modified are kept close. Follow the guidelines. These are very common errors that are committed:

Examples

No	*Yes*
1. The students visited the companies where they were absorbed for summer training programme over a period of two months.	Over a period of two months, the students visited companies that had absorbed them for summer training program. (modifiers must be kept close to the words they modify)
2. The new office block furnished recently impressed everybody. (recently furnished or recently impressed?)	The new office block recently furnished impressed everybody. (keep adverbs close to the words they modify)
3. The lady with broken legs wanted to sell away the piano. (who had broken legs? The lady or the piano?)	The lady wanted to sell away the piano with broken legs (ensure that the references are correct, else they will be unintentionally humorous)

Another common mistake that writers commit is **violation of the parallel structure**. This means that when we use phrases and clauses in a sentence, we must ensure that they are uniformly used. That is, phrases and clauses must not be jumbled up as in this following sentence:

No	*Yes*
I rejected the idea of buying the fleet of lorries because of initial expense, problems with petrol, and should consider road-worthiness.	I rejected the idea of buying the fleet of lorries because of initial expense, problems with petrol, and doubts of road-worthiness.

Often, people commit another mistake and that is of mixing up the verb forms in the same sentence:

No	*Yes*
Peter sees the advantages, but reminds Bruce that the new regulations about the road-worthiness were very strict, and has no problem with the police inspectors ordering spot-checks. **(Is there a problem with the tense?)**	Peter saw the advantages, but reminded Bruce that the new regulations were very strict, and had no problem with the police ordering spot-checks. Or Peter saw the advantages and reminded Bruce that the new regulations were very strict. He had no problem with the police ordering spot-checks.

When a writer writes a long, complex sentence, the subject gets separated from the verb. We come across such lengthy sentences in newspapers. In business, readers do not have a lot of time. Communication has to be succinct, clear and less time-consuming. The meaning should be crystal clear. **The subject and the verb must be kept together:**

No	*Yes*
Hector Grant, Managing Director, worried about productivity, and efficiency and output, and keen to introduce particular techniques for better results, decided to engage consultants.	Hector Grant, worried about productivity, decided to engage consultants. He was keen to introduce particular techniques that would produce better results.

Faulty use of prepositions

Prepositions are always used in a phrase. Often mistakes in the use of prepositions occur because we do not know whether to use 'at', or 'in', or 'about', or 'on'. It is assumed that you know some of the commonly used prepositions. You have studied them in school. Some of the sentences given below will acquaint you with the prepositional phrases. When we say that the prepositional phrase is not correct in a sentence, we mean that the preposition and its objects (nouns or pronouns) are not correctly used. In business communication, it is important to pay attention to the correctness of grammar.

Some of the common errors in the use of prepositions are given below:

No	*Yes*
1. She did not ask any questions to him.	She did not ask him any questions.
2. He went away *for doing some* business.	He went away on business.
3. The festival of Deepawali is similar to the Christmas Festival.	Deepawali corresponds to Christmas?
4. He suggested me this.	He suggested this to me.
5. Send this letter on my address.	Send this letter to my address.
6. Our school is built by bricks.	Our school is built of bricks.

To communicate effectively, the correct syntax of a sentence is as important as vocabulary, choice of words, clear thinking, and fulfilling all the C's of communication. It will be advisable to brush up every aspect of grammar. Since this is not a book on grammar, all the nuances of grammatical constructions are not dealt with. Any standard book on grammar will provide you with the basics of English grammar. Business English requires simple and basic constructions.

Inflammatory language

Very often at workplaces, under pressures of work and lack of knowledge about use of words, people communicate in a manner that can stir negative feelings in other people. By now, we know language has the power to stir emotions, a range that includes happy feelings as well as unpleasant or prejudicial feelings in people. In business it is wise to avoid these words. These are essentially emotionally charged words. Inflammatory language includes all biased words and particularly what Adler calls 'trigger words.'

Biased words: These words seem objective but conceal an emotional bias. They are layered with personal/subjective connotation.

	No	*Yes*
1.	How was the presentation? Oh, time consuming! (Long, unedited, hence boring)	The speaker exceeded the presentation time of 15 minutes.
2.	There are too many fingerprints on this beautiful glass door! (Not cleaned/occupants do not know how to keep the door clean)	The glass door has not been cleaned.
3.	The Director has been speaking for a longtime! (Wishywashy)	The Director has been speaking for the last two hours.

Adler says: the "trigger words can refer to specific people...groups or categories of individuals...or other topics." A particular word may be innocuous to you but it may trigger very strong negative feelings in your listener. For instance, people use the word "female" very casually, at workplace and otherwise, quite oblivious that the word also has a strong connotative meaning. It is quite perfect to say "male population" and "female population", but it is derogatory to say, "I met that female at a gathering". Would you say, "I met that male at a gathering?" At workplace, if male employees are addressed as "men", by the same logic, female employees should be called "women".

It is therefore recommended that one uses gender neutral words in order to make one's communication professional and respectable. Some of the words are given in the list below:

No (Gender Sensitive)	*Yes* (Gender Neutral)
1 Fireman	• Firefighter
2. Mailman	• Mail carrier
3. Congressman	• Congressperson
4. Chairman	• Chairperson
5. Spokesman	• Spokesperson
6. Layman	• Layperson
7. Repairman	• Repairperson, mechanic

Words like **layoff, deaf and dumb, old people, handicapped people, juvenile delinquent, laid off, lady doctor, oriental, housewife,** and many more such discriminatory words can be powerful trigger words. One has to be careful with words that violate people's sensitivity. In global business communication, you cannot afford to use expressions that are culturally rejected.

BARRIERS IN SENTENCE CONSTRUCTIONS

Having discussed how different parts of speech (nouns, adjectives, prepositions, adverbs, conjunctions), and the C's of communication that are needed for effective communication, let us see how they can be used as building blocks for forming good sentences. For effective business communication, one needs to know not only the basic structure of subject + verb and object combination, but also learn to give a little variety to the sentence constructions so that the writing attains vividness and interest. Variation in sentence patterns lends power to the writing. Complex sentence pattern and a combination of compound and complex sentence pattern can often cause problems in memo/letter/report writing, or any kind of corporate writing where one has to avoid monotony in expressions.

Complex Sentence

A complex sentence contains two or more clauses—one independent clause and at least one dependent/subordinate clause:

> - *I am going to propose John Martin's name again for President's post* when the elections are held again.

> - *Because there's likely to be a lot of opposition against having our own fleet,* I've postponed the meeting.

Compound/Complex Sentence

As the name implies, it contains two or more independent clauses, making it a compound sentence, and at least one of them has a dependent clause, making it complex. Please note the use of punctuation marks (comma, semi-colon)

1. We need more of wholesale business, but we cannot proceed with our plans *until we have assurances of long credit from our suppliers.*
2. The management trainee, *who has been very efficient in her work,* has unfortunately misplaced the document; I do not know how the matter is going to be discussed now.
3. Counseling sessions, *when conducted by trained counsellors,* can be very useful, but they are risky with untrained counsellors.
4. I asked him about the special class of share; and he said *that he had studied the shares carefully, that they could be bought and sold by employees,* and *that I could also use them.*

A note on the use of comma. The comma is the most frequently used and abused of all the punctuation marks. Note the use of the comma in the sentences given above. Many writers these days have discarded the use of comma, in places where it is not essential, but in business writing the comma has great value. It lends clarity to message composition. The comma basically groups words that belong to the same group and separates words that do not belong to a group.

1. She kept the book, the laptop, and the floppies on the table before beginning the lecture. (separates 'and' from the final item in *a series of three or more*)
2. He did not know what to tell her, and allowed her to enter the premise (separates the clause/s in a compound sentence connected by a conjunction)
3. The seminar was held in a large, ornate, old fashioned hall (separates two or more adjectives modifying the same noun)

4. The athlete, who won the race, was made to go through another test. (the comma sets off a nonrestrictive clause or phrase which, if eliminated, will not change the meaning)
5. The athlete who won the race was made to go through another test. (the comma should not be used when the clause or phrase is restrictive or essential to the meaning of the sentence).
6. The young management graduate, quite a prodigy, is a student of a rural college in India (sets off words or phrases in apposition to a noun or noun phrase)
7. The young management prodigy is a student of a rural college in India (the comma should not be used if words or phrases specify the noun/noun phrase that precedes)
8. May 1, 2003, was Labour day (sets off the year from the month in dates)
9. To the management, the security had become a nuisance (sets off sentence elements that might be misread if the comma were not used)

These are some of the uses of comma, which show that while writing reports, memos and letters, you should take into account the reasons for using and not using the comma. There are many more uses of the comma, which are beyond the scope of this topic.

SUMMARY

Converting language into communication pays off everywhere, whether you interact with people, face-to-face or through the written medium. The word, the tone, the message composition are important!

Speaking well is as important as the structured letter/memo that is well-planned, clear and courteous in tone. These communication skills help a manager to gain respectability, visibility, and recognition at the organizational level, at the corporate level, and at the global level. When managers communicate, they simply do not pass on information. They communicate!

But, to achieve this level of professionalism, they have to pay attention to the details of the principles of communication that make the act of transmission effective.

In oral communication, while managers will have to pay attention to PAMPERS, in written communication, other than the mandatory seven C's, common for both oral and written, managers have to pay attention to structured message composition, correctness in use of words, sentences, and punctuations. After all, written communication can always be improved or corrected.

TEST YOURSELF: ONLY ONE OPTION IS CORRECT. FILL IN THE BLANK. DO IT YOURSELF.

1. We used to get on well...
   (a) and we still keep in touch
   (b) but now we have made it up
   (c) but now we have lost touch

2. Tick the correct expression
   (a) He and me volunteered to go.
   (b) He and I volunteered to go.
   (c) Me and him volunteered to go.

3. Use the correct form of verb
   Rice and *dal*...his staple meal:
   (a) is
   (b) are
   (c) have been

4. Which of the three sentences is a polite expression? Tick the right answer.
   (a) Sign here...please!
   (b) Would you please sign here?
   (c) You must know that you have to sign here.

5. Which of the three sentences has greater clarity? Tick the correct one.
   (a) Admission to you has not been granted because of non-submission of relevant documents
   (b) We could not admit you because you did not submit the original mark sheet at the time you deposited your form with us.
   (c) Non-submission of original mark sheet is a serious violation of our admission rules and hence admission has not been granted to you

6. Which of the three sentences has better conciseness? Tick the right answer.
   (a) Last year the conference was entirely organized by the management trainees who spent late hours working on the details and who went out of their way to spend on the eatables and the decoration so that the event would turn out to be a major success.
   (b) Last year the management trainees worked hard to organize the conference and did not mind spending time and money for its success.
   (c) Last year the management trainees organized the conference by spending time and resources for its success.

7. **What is wrong with the following sentence? Tick the correct option.**

   'We would deem it a favour if you inform us at the earliest'.

   (a) It is a correct expression.

   (b) The sentence lacks courtesy.

   (c) The sentence is wordy and lacks conciseness.

8. **Use the correct preposition.**

   There is no exception...this rule:

   (a) by

   (b) in

   (c) to

9. **Only one word is correctly spelt. Tick the word.**

   (a) Hierarchy

   (b) Heirerchy

   (c) Hieararchy

10. **The phrase *ad valorem* in the sentence**

    "All imported goods are subject to *ad valorem* duty" means

    (a) according to value

    (b) according to quantity

    (c) according to import rules

FURTHER READING

Adler, B. Ronald and J.M. Elmhorst, *Communicating at Work,* McGraw-Hill, Toronto, 1996.

Baugh, L.S., M. Fryar, and D.A. Thomas, *How to Write First-Class Business Correspondence,* Viva Books, Chennai, 1998.

Booher, Dianna, *Speak with Confidence: Powerful Presentations That Inform, Inspire, and Persuade,* McGraw-Hill, Toronto, 2003.

Joseph, Albert, *Put It In Writing,* McGraw-Hill, Toronto, 1998.

Lesikar, Pettit, and Flatley, *Lesikar's Basic Business Communication,* 8th ed., Irwin McGraw-Hill, Toronto, 1999.

Locker, O. Kitty, *Business and Administrative Communication,* Irwin McGraw-Hill, Toronto, 2000.

Mack, Angela, *The Language of Business,* The English Book Store, New Delhi, 1970.

McDowell, H., K.D. Madon, and D.S. Thacker, *Business Letters For All Occasions,* Strand Book Stall, Mumbai, 1996.

Miculka, Jean, *Speaking for Success,* South-Western Educational Publishing, Washington, 1999.

Murphy, H.A., H.W. Hildebrandt, and J.P. Thomas, *Effective Business Communication,* 7th ed., McGraw-Hill, Missouri, 2000.

Sheth, N. and Ajit Sheth, *Tagore: Indian Film and Film Music,* Pankaj Mullick Music Research Foundation, Bombay, 1994.

CHAPTER 5

Presentation Skills

The ability to speak effectively is an acquirement
rather than a gift.

— WILLIAM JENNINGS BRYAN

Our discussion so far has centred around the skills that are involved in making oral and written communication effective at workplace. Both internal and external business situations require managers to interact with people continuously. For decisions to be arrived at and results to be shown, managers have to collaborate, work on their own, and report their work to superiors. A part of regular communication that takes place during the course of daily work is what managers present before the management.

It will not be an overstatement if it is said that managers experience 'discomfort zone' while making presentations either to bosses or to clients. The word 'presentation' brings to one's mind pictures of pairs of eyes staring at the presenter, some smirking, some looking positively disinterested, and others being indifferent. Of course, some members in the audience do encourage the speaker. But they are very few in number. Such mental images work as disincentives and hence the word, 'butterflies' is generally referred to when one speaks of presentation.

Presentations take place all the time in organizations. Generally, presenters have ample time to prepare a presentation. A sequential arrangement of the points gives it a structured shape.

Yet, there are times when a presenter has to make a presentation on the spot. Such a presentation may take an unstructured pattern. Making a presentation to the client for a business deal about products, of course, needs a strong sales pitch about quality, price, reliability and several other factors that are important to position a product as better than its competitor's product. Power point slides supported by excellent oral delivery are called for such a task. But does presentation mean only power point deliveries? What happens when clients show a preference for a face-to-face talk across the table for a discussion about the deal? Would such a communication be different from the power point presentation? When business procedures have to be explained to a newcomer, would it not involve instant presentation skills? Endless, on-going activities that take place in an organization, involve presentations of some kind or the other.

A good presentation is about **effective communication** between two or more persons.

This chapter primarily deals with the various steps and stages that one should follow for making a good presentation. The various stages include pre-presentation jitters, developing a presentation, delivering a presentation, concluding with conviction, and managing questions and objections.

It is important to remember that one might be required to make presentations on various situations, besides the core areas. And each time a presentation is made, the speaker will be under pressure to make it memorable and effective. The competencies of the presenter that will be tested are the verbal and non-verbal communication skills, knowledge of making power point slides, ability to deal with interpersonal skills while handling questions and objections on differences of opinion, and finally a word of thanks on a courteous note.

Effective presentation skills reflect a manager's personality. When things are well explained and presented, the image of the manager is enhanced. Good presentations speak about the manager's confidence, level of knowledge, logical thinking, range of ideas, and application of ideas to practical situations. Presentation demands multiple communication skills. Remember the adage *Small things make perfection, but perfection, is not a small thing!*

Before we study the stages about presentation, it is necessary that you perceive the presentation activity as an enjoyable experience and not one that strangulates you mentally.

PRE-PRESENTATION JITTERS

Misconceptions about Presentation

Although presentations have become vital tools by which organizations assess the performance and expertise of their executives, besides other measures of performance assessment, it is not an unachievable task. There is no need to be mystified by the pressures that the whole exercise builds up on the speaker. Facing people is not as difficult an exercise as people make it out to be. The popular misconceptions surrounding presentation need to be erased. The pre-presentation demands are: you have a clear idea about the whole task and remove from your mind the fears of making a presentation. The following points are worth taking notice of:

- **Good speakers are born, not made!**

  People who speak fluently and smartly do not inherit the gift of the gab. They have to work hard to become good speakers. Winston Churchill spent days to perfect his famous speeches. Good speaking is hard work.

- **I am an introvert. I feel very nervous:**

  This is a common feeling when one speaks for the first time before an audience. A person who is never nervous usually does a mediocre job. It pays to feel a little nervous. Practice makes a man perfect! **The 'P's' of presentation are Practice, Practice, and more Practice.** The more you practice, more you will succeed in taking control of your nerves.

- **I am scared of looking away at the audience. Too many faces make me forget my matter. I fail to present my thoughts:**

  Failure is the stepping-stone to success! When you are married to your matter, you enjoy delivering it to the audience. The strange faces become friendly faces.

- **I am not a fluent speaker. How can I make a good presentation?**

  Presentation is not simply about fluency and smartness. Even people who are apparently unpromising can be good speakers. People who stutter and stammer still make good presentations in spite of the challenges!

- **I have vernacular education background. I find it difficult to express my thoughts in English!**

Presentations are a combination of matter and manner. When you know your matter, the words come to you naturally!

◆ **I must make a perfect presentation every time I present!**

Presentations must be enjoyed. Perfection lies in making your presentation enjoyable to your listeners. Sincerity and involvement are the icing of the cake!

Speaking to a small or a large group demands that you

(a) handle your listeners well,

(b) know your subject well, and

(c) sharpen your skills of speaking.

Presentation is all about how you handle your listeners and overcome your fear.

GETTING READY FOR A PRESENTATION: WHAT IS A PRESENTATION ALL ABOUT?

For making a successful presentation, one simple thing to be remembered is that gathering a lot of information is not the only task. The objective should be to make the points or concepts clear so as to make them comprehensible to the audience. This does not mean that you have to memorize the whole material to be presented.

The following three steps are necessary for you to prepare for a presentation. The initial steps will equip you mentally to anticipate, prepare, and deliver your presentation well.

1. **Developing a Presentation—What is my topic? What is the purpose?**

Like a research project that has to be critically examined for a meaningful study, similarly a presentation topic too has to be looked into depths for a comprehensive understanding of the topic by the listener, who can be the boss or the client or the customer. A written report can run into pages but not a presentation! In fact, the word, 'presentation' has almost become a pejorative word in many business houses where they think a presentation that goes beyond 15 minutes wastes the organization's valuable/productive time. Therefore it is very important to practise the skills of precision and conciseness. Also, the purpose must be made clear at the very outset. Is it about the sales figures of the company's products? Is it about the expansion of the building? Is it about a product launch? Is your purpose to sell/persuade/inform? It is important that you are clear about the purpose of your presentation. You must ask yourself at the end of your presentation, what is it that I want my listeners to carry back with them in their mind? Before you start to make slides or gather data for the presentation, ask yourself very specific questions about the purpose and the relevance of it to your audience.

When you sit down to write out your presentation matter, it is important that you visualize the kind of audience you are going to address and your presentation style.

2. Knowing Your Audience

Who is my audience? Who will be listening to me, my own office people or an interested business party? How large is the size of the audience? Size of the group/expertise of the group?

A part of the planning that you will do is to find out the details of the composition of the audience. Factors like status of the members, their business and professional background, market potential and image, the cultural make up of the group and such other related features, are crucial for your presentation. In the chapter on Cross-Cultural Communication, you will learn about the cultural values of people. You might experience embarrassment if inadvertently you happen to commit faux pas. This is very important particularly in these days of global operations. A large audience requires a more formal and less personalized approach. Other elements like age, gender, culture, country, values, education, and anticipated attitude toward the subject will have to be taken into account. They influence a presenter's delivery style.

3. How Will I Deliver? What Does my Audience want to know from me?

In the first chapter you have learnt that one of the important objectives of communication is that **Communication is message perceived and not message sent.** This is so true of an effective presentation. The entire focus of the presentation has to be on the content and the delivery that must be directed towards the audience. The audience must understand what is said so that they can participate in the listening process and ask questions. Therefore, a good presentation has to be conceptualized well, broken down into separate parts, researched extensively, and concluded convincingly. Some of these questions may be considered:

- How will this topic appeal to my audience?
- How can I relate the topic to practical life?

- How should I deliver so that I am able to hold their attention span?
- How much of figures/statistics/graphics/word explanations/ must I give?
- What does my audience expect from me?
- What does it need to know?

It is essential that you brainstorm this crucial part of your presentation. The success of your presentation will depend on your ability to evoke interest in your audience through indepth study of your matter and an equally integrated style of your delivery. Substance and style must move hand in hand. Matter and manner must be beautifully blended. As you present, the audience must be stirred into thinking "What's in it for me?" **(WIIFM)** (Holliday)

Identifying Your Presentation Style

Find out whether you will be addressing a big group in a big room. If the distance between the speaker and the audience is large, you will have to pay attention to the preparation of the slides and the formal manner of making a presentation. It is then a speaker-centred style where the full attention of the audience on the speaker should be used. The slides will have to be simple for a large audience to quickly follow.

If the group is a structured/focused one, you will then be required to adapt your style to the specific requirements of the group. Although it will be a speaker-centred style, the slides can be more detailed, applied in nature and supported by graphs and charts.

If the group is small, e.g. a supplier's presentation to a small group of buyers, the style should be more interactive in nature and audience-centred, supported by hand-written overheads and customer-relevant visuals.

According to Micki Holliday, the three presentation styles are:

- The Cool Zone
- The Hot Zone
- The Dull Zone

Most speakers belong to any one of these three categories or they have a combination of these styles. A skilled presenter keeps the audience psychology in mind and presents the matter from their point of view. The style helps the presenter to establish a common frame of reference for participation to take place.

A skilled presenter belongs to the **Cool Zone.** The style helps him/her to capture the attention of the audience with clear persuasive skills of thinking. The presentation is a structured one, facts are presented in an orderly manner and the delivery is under control. The pitch, volume, and tone are all under control. The thoughtful manner of presentation makes it a customer-friendly style. The speaker is focused, clear in reasoning, and the arguments are precise. Such a presentation draws maximum attention from the audience. The Father of the Nation, Mahatma Gandhi, Prime Minister, Jawaharlal Nehru, former U.S. Secretary of State, Henry Kissinger, the Prime Minister of UK, Tony Blair, Mr. Nelson Mandela, Prime Minister, Manmohan Singh, and Finance Minister, P. Chidambaram and others who possess the qualities of a cool zone speaker belong to this category. People from the world of academics generally belong to this category. Some of the prominent academicians who have left indelible impression on peoples' minds are late President of India, Shri Radha Krishnan, Nobel Laureate, Amartya Sen, to name a few. Holliday describes such speakers as "analytical, logical, pragmatic, thoughtful, deliberate, rational, restrained, intellectual, and insightful."

The **Hot Zone Speaker** "can blow the roof off a building" says Holliday. Loud voice, rhetorical style, dramatic body movements, and voice inflections describe such a speaker. Because they are driven by passions, their pitch keeps going up and down, the loudness of the voice matching the pitch level, supported by body movement use of hands, darting eyes, and shifting postures. Some audience may enjoy such speakers but others may also get put off because of the dramatic movements. Most political speakers, some of them playing to the gallery, adopt this style of speaking. The adjectives that Holliday uses for these speakers are "emotional, driven, surprising, instinctive, charismatic, creative, impulsive, daring, and disjointed."

However, most speakers operate between the cold and the hot zones. The Nightingale of India, Sarojini Naidu, late Prime Minister Indira Gandhi, former British Prime Minister, Margaret Thatcher, President Roosevelt and President Eisenhower, and many more belong to this category. Variation in the style of delivery prompted by the content and mood behind the thoughts make the speakers alternate the two styles.

The **Dull Zone Speaker,** as the name suggests, makes presentation a boring experience. The lack of pitch variation, unpromising body language, and incompatibility with the audience make the speaker a nervous wreck. Nervous body language, tremors in the voice, poor eye contact, rushing off with matter hurriedly, all put together, make the speaker a dull one. It is equally painful for the audience to sit through the presentation. Holliday calls them "cautious, accommodating, compromising, predictable, neutral, noncommittal, ambivalent, and boring."

Business executives prefer the cool zone Style because business deals with concrete information supported by facts and applied knowledge. There cannot be any room for feelings and emotions in business presentations. A controlled tone, thoughtful approach and fact-based research define a business presentation.

It is important to understand that speech is a part of presentation. Speech is how you use words and the way you express them. Presentation is essentially a multimedia form, for which you use visual aids, synchronize your body language with your speech and the visuals for an effective presentation. In a way, presentation is a total image of your ability to handle all these variants.

PREPARATION AND PRACTICE

Once you have gathered knowledge about the requisites of presentation, it is time for you to start preparing and practising your matter.

How should one go about with the kind of preparation that is needed for a good presentation? The preparation should always begin with an in-depth background research. But the sources needed for the research cannot be identified unless you are clear about the objectives of your presentation.

Presentation Structure

A presentation generally has a few important points around which the text revolves. The idea of making a presentation is to help your audience to recall your matter. Only you can help your audience to remember the maximum by organizing the matter well. What you require to do is to structure the matter in a manner that will give the right message to your audience. Essentially a presentation, like a good report or an essay, has three parts to it, the introduction, the body, and the conclusion. The introduction must begin on the note of the Big Idea. In the chapter on Written Communication you will study about the value of focusing on the important matter to ensure that the listeners, who are the receivers of the message, carry back with them the big idea. The big idea is the essence or the central theme that can be remembered for a long time.

As Hunsaker and Alessandra say:

How you translate your material—your message—into benefits for the audience determines its effectiveness. You need to structure your presentation so that it supports your one Big Idea. Of course, your presentation will contain more than one idea but they should all reinforce the primary focus.

You may choose

- The chronological/historical order
- The sequential order
- Any other order that makes sense.

It is also important to interweave your points to highlight the Big Idea. Once you have structured your matter, you need to find out how you are going to relate the matter to your audience. The audience's attention span needs to be kept in tact. This is not an easy task always!

What you can do is to adopt different styles for different groups

1. If the group is small and informal, use a **narrative** style, interspersed with **anecdotes**, a bit of humour, in a lighter vein. Often a factual delivery can make the presentation very dry and monotonous. At such moments, a relevant story or an anecdote from life or a metaphorical idea can add sparkle to the presentation.
2. If it is a business presentation to a small, knowledgeable group, a **deductive** approach can be used to save time. But then, for such presentations, too much of compactness also may not interest the audience. If there are detailed facts and figures to be given, a better way is to give away hand-outs which the audience can read at leisure. The actual presentation should be kept lively and interactive.
3. You may also use a **descriptive style** that enables you to describe the details of the topic (sales/marketing/market survey, etc.) Whichever style you choose, you must make it a point to get accepted by your audience.

How to find the material and which sources to follow?

A good presentation always demands the right sources that have to be tapped for background research. This is a tedious part of the work. In today's time of information explosion or information overload, one is flooded with information/data. From articles in journals, magazines, newspapers, books to the Internet, one has opportunities to explore various sources. The various sources are:

1. Newspaper agencies/documentation archives for newspaper cuttings
2. Documentation archives/public libraries/college libraries/ institute libraries for various articles
3. Bibliography section in well-written books for relevant references
4. Company reports, government reports by personally approaching them
5. Professional journals
6. Interviews with professionals/friends/personal contacts
7. Other sources such as Internet, CD-ROMs, videos, audios.

How many slides to use? Are there any rules to follow?

A presentation is a multi-media work. Slides are a part of a good presentation. The question is about the number of slides that can be used. Often, a presentation is marred by too many slides. It is as though the presenter has decided to hide behind the slides and has allowed the slides to do the talking for him/her.

---

1. The number of slides will depend on the matter that you wish to present. But each slide must be a comprehensive one. It must contain only the minimum text in support of what you have to say; 6–8 words per slide seem a good number because they will not clutter the slide. Please remember, the audience has come to listen to you, not for a visual demonstration!

---

2. Let your slides be a combination of powerful visuals and powerful verbal, one supporting the other. The elaborate explanation of your matter should be spoken by you and not included in the slide. Many poor slide makers include too many words/long sentences in the slide. This must be avoided. According to Anthony Jay and Ros Jay, "The verbal slide is a slide consisting of whole statements, sometimes several of them numbered sequentially on a single slide. It is a killer."

---

3. Avoid abstract nouns/too many adjectives/adverbs and Passive constructions.
4. Use action oriented words/verbs. They lend power to your thoughts.

---

5. Ensure that the font size is readable—not too small.
6. Use a consistent style—bullet points, font size and colours (Times New Roman and Arial).
7. Use Caps only for the headings.
8. Use diagrams/charts/graphs wherever possible, but keep them simple.

GETTING STARTED

Practise before You Present

Before you actually go to give your presentation, it is necessary that you practise or rehearse the presentation seriously. Synchronizing with your visual aids is a crucial requirement; otherwise, a lot of your valuable time as well as that of the audience will be wasted. The practice sessions will give you a chance to smooth over the difficult edges. These could be pronunciations of difficult words (many speakers do not pay attention to this aspect of presentation at all), emphasizing key words or ideas, pausing at specific places for repetition of important ideas, and most importantly, visualizing the audience and their responses and preparing to give answers to anticipated questions.

A part of your practice session should be devoted to the way you would establish eye contact with your audience, smile and keep a pleasant face and simultaneously handle the delivery. If all this is not done naturally, your delivery will soon project a stiff body language, wooden voice quality, and generally an un-interesting style. All these points will go against you. Therefore, a few points need to be kept in mind. Rehearse for

◆ confidence,
◆ spontaneity,
◆ synchronization with your visual aids,
◆ interaction with your audience, and
◆ inviting questions and answering them.

Take Care of How You Dress/Look

It is necessary to look well turned out for making a presentation. Looking well doesn't mean dressing up to kill the audience. It means the speaker must be well groomed for the presentation. Impressions always have a lasting impact on an audience and that too the first few seconds! All corporate presentations must meet the corporate standards reasonably well. Try to build an idea about your dress, your gestures, and your 'speaking face'. The expressions on your face are of great importance to your audience.

What is important is that your audience should be able to identify with you. A business/corporate world make demands on appropriate dress, manners, posture and gestures and a pleasant disposition. Of course, if you are to make a presentation to a group of social workers or factory workers, you may make the necessary changes in your dress code. The end viewers must be able to identify themselves with you.

Writing Down the Presentation

You may choose to write out the entire speech or just the outline. In the beginning, when you are not used to making presentations, you may have to write out the entire manuscript. However, it is essential that you write down the detailed sub-heads or lengthy matter and practise it well.

Putting it all together.   Clarify your topic; make sure that you know exactly what it is you will be speaking about. Develop a comprehensive plan that pinpoints issues and desired outcomes.

Identify your theme.   This is the message around which you will weave your content, the thread that connects all your points. The theme must connect all the pieces of the content, must flow logically from concept to concept.

Choose your words well.   The words must accurately express your thoughts. Do not use difficult words or jargon to communicate. Every word must be visually powerful and accurate. The audience must feel convinced.

Emphasize the important points.   The key concepts must be cleared in the allotted time which must include the

- Transition (link ideas, through theme)
- Anchor (grab attention, draw participation)
- Benefits (constantly noting in real-world terms what is in it for me. WIIFM)

Avoid pretence.   A put-on accent or behaviour is a sure way to mar your presentation. You need to be yourself!

Edit ruthlessly.   Time-bound presentations need concise and precise expressions. Superfluous words/phrases/sentences/paragraphs, must be removed.

DELIVERING THE PRESENTATION

Once you have visualized that your presentation is going to be successful because you have researched and practised your matter well, you should be able to stand before your audience confidently and raring to go ahead with your presentation. However, no matter how well prepared you are with your presentation, the first few minutes have to be under your firm control to avoid having butterflies in your stomach. Hence, the first few minutes as you focus your attention on the audience, let your mind take control of the butterflies. And how do you do that? Here are a few tips:

1. **The introduction.** Open your presentation with words of thanks both for the chairperson and the audience. Be courteous and sincere in doing so (for a formal or large gathering). In case you are introduced with flowery language or exaggeration to the extent of causing embarrassment, deflate the comments by being a little humorous and without embarrassing the person who introduced you.

By now the audience has begun to scan you. The expectation has set in. Announce the topic clearly and concisely. Come straight to the point because the audience does not like wasting time.

2. **The body language.** Deliver your speech not simply through words but also through your body. It is very crucial to work on yourself for an effective delivery that is a combination of verbal, vocal and the visual. The following tips will help you to enhance your body language in a presentation:

◆ Stand straight, hold your head high, and keep your shoulders straight and not drooping.

◆ A straight standing posture will make your spine straight and help you to pull your stomach in. This in turn will help you to breathe well. A deep breath helps you to release your tension, activate your mind and enable you to focus on your matter. It makes you feel relaxed and confident.

◆ The correct standing posture makes you distribute the weight of your body equally on both legs and not one. Standing firmly enhances your stature and gives you tremendous self-confidence.

◆ It also helps you to use your hands well. An open palm gesture integrates well with an open body language.

The common errors that you should not commit:

(a) Putting your face down
(b) Showing awkward gestures (crossed arms, tilted body, eyes down, and no smile)
(c) Making the body stiff (give your body a bit of movement to add a little variety to your speech and let the audience be a part of your presentation)
(d) Talking too fast/too slow
(e) Not speaking in clear and audible fashion

Note on voice and tone. Use a well-controlled tone of voice. If it lacks confidence, people won't give much credence to your ideas. If your voice is too gruff—(cocky, deep and harsh, unfriendly), people will turn you off.

Rate/speed. Volume, emphasis, inflection, raising and lowering of voice, and slowing down for important points, are all equally important for the speed at which you speak. The preferred speed is 125 to 250 wpm. This rate helps the listener to concentrate well, listen for facts and the intended meanings, and research the meaning. A good listener practises CARESS for a good presentation. If the rate is too fast, the audience will get frustrated. High voice and talking fast indicate nervousness. A slower, lower tone indicates confidence and expertise, which can only be attained with a lot of preparation.

THE POWER PAUSE

A very important and yet often overlooked aspect of delivering a presentation is the dramatic pause that a speaker needs to take to give an additional effect to the speech.

James C. Humes in his book Speak Like Churchill, Stand Like Lincoln says,

> Before you speak, try to lock your eyes on each of your soon-to-be listeners. Force yourself before you begin your presentation to say in your own mind each word of your opening sentence. Every second you wait will strengthen the impact of your opening words. Make your Power Pause your silent preparation before any presentation you make. Stand, stare, and command your audience, and they will bend their ears to listen.

QUALITIES OF A SKILFUL PRESENTER

A speaker needs to have a few basic qualities in order to be a good presenter. The delivery of a presentation is as much important as the content of the presentation. A good delivery originates in a groomed/trained mind. The following qualities are expected of a good presenter:

1. **Self-control**—not feeling nervous
2. **Poise**—in good command of body language
3. **Awareness of people, time and place**—full knowledge of the audience, time and the venue
4. **Tact**—the ability to blend with the audience and the matter
5. **Decisiveness**—being clear about the matter

6. **Persuasiveness**—the ability to make the audience see your point of view

7. **Enthusiasm**—never losing sight of the objective of the presentation and hence keeping up the spirit of the presentation

8. **Honesty**—not faking knowledge or information

9. **Flexibility**—not being rigid if there is a different point of interpretation from the audience

CAPTURING AND MAINTAINING ATTENTION

All presentations have a broad framework. The main objectives are to inform, persuade, inspire, and convince. Many speakers try to blend their presentation with a bit of fun or humorous remarks to break the monotony.

As you deliver your presentation, use illustrations, facts and figures, and references to continually move toward your predetermined conclusion. The following points should be kept in mind:

1. Begin confidently by speaking slowly and less loudly than you usually do. Keep your voice under control. The pitch and the rate are crucial because they can tilt your presentation either way—against you or in your favour.

2. Watch the tone of your voice. Do not speak in a demeaning manner. A good presenter does not talk down at the audience. She/he talks to an audience. The idea is to carry the audience with oneself. A soft, mumbling voice/preachy tone, will make you lose your credibility.

3. Deliver with confidence and humility—no one likes to listen to an arrogant speaker. No matter how knowledgeable you are, you need to make your audience feel comfortable with you and your message.

4. It is important that you choreograph yourself well with the visual aids and the audience. How do you do this?

5. As you speak, you should not only smile and sustain your focus on your audience, but you should also know how to manage your thoughts, the aids and the delivery. Use a pointer or a laser torch to point out the text that you wish to be read by the audience.

6. Do not memorize your matter. If you forget, you will tend to panic over it leading to nervous body language. Focus on the key points, learn to develop them on the spot, and string your thoughts for a harmonious presentation.

7. An introduction, body, conclusion should be the format of your presentation.

8. If you jump-start confidently and clearly, your audience will love it and be willing to listen to you for the rest of the presentation.

9. A good presentation has a mix of humour and real matter so that the audience is made to experience the seriousness without getting bored of the facts and the technical matter.

10. Once you are confident of your matter, you will prefer to stay in the cool zone, for the matter flows from your mind in a systematic manner. A structured presentation helps the audience to understand the content.

11. The audience will also look for what is new in the presentation. The presenter must keep WIIFM (What's in it for me?) in mind. When the presenter delivers from the audience's point of view, connectivity with the audience is on a higher level. Full knowledge of the audience and their expectations help the presenter to tailor the presentation well.

The following questions are important for consideration:

(a) What does the audience **need** to know?
(b) What does the audience **want** to know?
(c) What are the possible benefits for the audience?
(d) What questions might the audience have?

BRINGING YOUR PRESENTATION TO A CLOSE

A well-structured presentation has to reach the peak before it begins to climb down for an end. This is where you will seize the opportunity to make the conclusion memorable. It is a part where you clinch the purpose of your speech. The audience should be able to see clearly how the introduction, the middle, and the conclusion are beautifully tied up to form a chain. To progressively move toward this achievement is not easy. It is an intense task and it has to be done well. A good presenter does not blow away his/her chance.

The conclusion is an important part of the presentation because it is the part that the audience will carry back with them. A quick recap of the points that you have developed throughout can be reviewed. The impact is all the more intense when it is packed with an anecdote or an analogy. At the end, do not forget to thank the audience for listening to you. The audience will like to be thanked.

HANDLING QUESTIONS: 'THINKING ON FEET' SKILL

An insightful and intelligent presenter always anticipates questions from the audience. 'Thinking on feet' means the presenter should be able to handle the questions calmly and confidently. A responsive audience not only practises CARESS but also notes down the questions that they would like to ask. Often, there may be hostile or resistant listeners and they are likely to ask intriguing or ambiguous questions. These need to be handled well. Never allow yourself to be ruffled. Here are a few tips for handling questions from the audience:

1. *Encourage the audience to ask questions*—be forthright about it and do not mumble. A confident presenter enjoys answering questions. Say, "I would love to answer if anybody has any questions to ask."

2. *Listen to the questions very well*—an exhausting presentation may leave the presenter tired and hence a little disoriented. But the task of presentation is still not over till the last question has been answered. Effective listening helps!

3. *Do not blurt out an immediate answer.* Practise the technique of power pause. Absorb the question and arrange your thoughts in an order. Frame your reply in your mind. A hurried answer may indicate that you have not fully heard to the question. This might hurt the person who asked the question. As James Humes says: "A deliberate pause before you talk adds weight and wisdom to both your actual answer and your audience's perception of it. You're perceived as having really listened to the questioner instead of rushing in with a stock, or canned answer." (p. 3)

4. Somebody who has asked a good question must be complimented. It encourages others to ask also. Successful handling of questions establishes a good rapport between the presenter and the audience.

5. Those who ask questions for the sake of asking only should be tactfully handled. If questions are repeated, tactfully edit the questions and club them well with the previous questions and remind the audience about the answer you had made.

6. Do not let only a few members dominate the question-answer session. Encourage others also to ask questions.

7. A sincere attempt at answering questions is always appreciated by the audience.

A Quick Recap of Things that You Should Not Commit in Public Speaking

- ◆ **Content**—poorly researched matter
- ◆ **Speech**—talking too rapidly/monotone/lack of speech clarity/over accentuation/wrong pronunciation
- ◆ **Voice**—high pitch, talking down at the audience, speaking in a mumbling/muffled tone, lack of voice modulation, wrong intonation/inflection
- ◆ **Face**—unsmiling face/poker face, poor/no eye contact
- ◆ **Gestures**—fidgeting behaviour/hands in pocket, arms crossed across the chest, tilting body weight
- ◆ **Language**—poor grammar, long sentences, using slang/colloquial expressions
- ◆ **Style**—lack of confidence, indirect communication, beating about the bush, no proper introduction, body and conclusion of the speech, but repetition, and talking much without actually saying anything!

Speech-Presentation

Very often managers are required to present reports orally, without any visual slides. That is, they are expected to make a short speech explaining, for instance, a project proposal, or why a visit to the plant is absolutely necessary. Not always do managers sit down to make visual slides to deliver the message. In such situations, the ability to make *impromptu* speeches is of great help. An impromptu speech demands that the speaker has knowledge of the subject, the appropriate vocabulary to support the ideas, and the presentation skills that will help the him/her to blend the matter with all the powerful vocal cues. Here is an example that gives some ideas about what can obstruct a speaker from delivering a short speech presentation:

This is the story of a senior manager, Shashank Tripathi, who was asked by the top management to explain why his visit to the plant in Jamnagar was absolutely necessary. Shashank was one of the twenty people sitting around a conference table. In the audience were also present three vice presidents, and four senior general managers. They were all seated around the table. Shashank too was sitting at the table with his papers in front of him. When he was asked to begin, Shashank dug into his sheaf of papers and began:

"I think I must visit the plant because I need to find out why there has been a pilferage of materials from the warehouse which has been happening for some time. I have the figures with me... ." (and then Shashank began to shuffle his papers for exact figures.) As time elapsed, Shashnak could sense the palpable impatience among the listeners. He felt distracted and annoyed with his own clumsiness. Consequently, he forgot all the facts that he had gathered. His mind was suddenly overcast with clouds of unrelated data. The blank look on his face startled the top management and Shashank felt embarrassed. Anyway, Shashank had to continue which he did but in a dragging manner with a lot of time lag, vague statements and rambling information. He could see some of the audience were playing with their pens and pencils—a sign of clear disinterest. With a great effort he concluded. But he knew he had messed it up.

What went wrong with Shashank?

1. Did Shashank come prepared for the oral presentation?
2. Did he come straight to his point of view?
3. What facts did he put forward? Did he suggest any solution?
4. Did he speak every word clearly and correctly?
5. Did he take his power pauses to add dramatic effect to the urgency of his need?
6. Did he sit straight? With his shoulders in a square shape, and eyes focused on the group?
7. Did he slouch? Sit in a casual manner, with hands stretched out on the table?
8. Did he mumble? Did he fail to lift his voice to reach all the listeners?

A speech presentation is a high powered presentation. It is significant because the speaker becomes the main focus of attention. Since the speaker is the multi-media of expressions, listeners are bound to pay attention to every nuance of words spoken, supported by the complementary accompanying body language of the speaker. The lesson to learn is "Never take a presentation casually. Do not be cool about it!"

SUMMARY

A good presentation needs a careful preparation and must not be taken lightly. Practice and more practice only can drive away all the fears that one associates presentation with. From perfecting body language to writing out the script, a presentation requires good research, well-made visual slides, use of correct language, use of proper voice and tone, adapting the right presenting style (the cool zone), synchronizing oneself with the visual aids and the audience, capturing and maintaining attention, and dealing with difficult members who may be in the habit of asking hostile questions. By handling the question-answer session assertively and courteously, you help yourself to carry back pleasant memories about the audience as much as you help the audience to think warmly about your presentation. The purpose of making a presentation seems to be then fulfilled!

TEST YOURSELF: ONLY ONE OPTION IS CORRECT. TICK IT. DO IT YOURSELF.

1. **The popular understanding of the word 'presentation' is that it**
   (a) has to be a power point presentation
   (b) must have colourful slides
   (c) must have many slides

2. **The term 'speech presentation' refers to**
   (a) a long speech
   (b) instant oral presentation
   (c) a power point presentation

3. **What makes a power point presentation memorable are**
   (a) well made power point slides
   (b) sincerity and articulation with which the presentation is delivered
   (c) A combination of oral communication skills and well designed power point slides

4. **The acronym WIIFM means:**
   (a) 'What's in it for managers?'
   (b) 'What's in it for most?'
   (c) 'What's in it for me?'

5. **The presentation style that applies to corporate executives is the**
   (a) cool zone
   (b) hot zone
   (c) dull zone

6. **Choice of a presentation format (narrative, descriptive, deductive) depends on the**
   (a) presentation matter

    (b) kind of audience attending the presentation

    (c) venue where the presentation is to take place

7. **A power point slide is perceived as a 'poor slide' when it has**

    (a) too much of textual matter

    (b) loud colours and ornamental fonts

    (c) a combination of all the three

8. **The body language of a presenter should be**

    (a) closed

    (b) open

    (c) diffident

9. **Which of the qualities of a presenter, according to you, are important during presentation? Tick the right ones:**

    (a) Enthusiasm

    (b) Involvement

    (c) Audience-focused

    (d) Self-control

    (e) Monotone

    (f) Addressing only a select section of the audience

    (g) Flinging arms

    (h) Keeping arms across the chest

10. **'Thinking on Feet' skill in handling Q&A means**

    (a) standing on feet

    (b) standing and thinking simultaneously

    (c) answering the questions calmly and confidently

FURTHER READING

Alessandra Tony and Phil Hunsaker, Phil, Communicating at Work, A Fireside Book, New York, 1993.

Bender, Peter Urs, *Secrets of Power Presentations*, 6th ed., Macmillan India, New Delhi, 2000.

Booher, Dianna, *Speak with Confidence: Powerful presentations that inform, inspire, and persuade*, McGraw-Hill, Toronto, 2003.

Jay, Antony and Ros Jay, *Effective Presentation*, Universities Press, New Delhi, 1999.

Hamilton, Cheryl, *Essentials of Public Speaking*, Wadsworth Publishing Co., Washington, 1999.

Handle, Tim, *Making Presentations*, Dorling Kindersley, Moscow, 1998.

Holliday, Micki, *Secrets of Power Presentations*, 2nd ed., Career Press, Franklin Lakes, NJ, 2000.

Humes, James C., *Speak Like Churchill, Stand Like Lincoln—21 Powerful secrets of history's greatest speakers*, Three Rivers Press, New York, 2002.

Osborn, Michael and Osborn, Suzanne, *Public Speaking*, AITBS Publishers & Distributors, New Delhi, 2002.

Scott, Bill, *The Skills of Communicating*, 2nd ed., Jaico Publishing House, New Delhi, 2002.

Part 3

Non-Verbal Communication

CHAPTER 6

The Power of Non-Verbal Communication

The medium is the message.
— MARSHALL McLUHAN

HUMAN BODY—THE MEDIUM OF THE MESSAGE

The popular notion of communication is that the more one speaks, the more the person is communicating. Such has been the predominant impact of words on the human mind! Books on written communication will tell you that the written word is more important than the spoken word. And books on oral communication point out that spoken communication is as difficult and challenging as written communication. Researchers certainly have a right to put in perspective the importance of their individual area of study but it is for the reader to put together the different areas in order to evolve a complete picture of the significance of communication skills for day to day interactions.

In this chapter you will learn that non-verbal communication also forms a vital part of the process of communication that an individual goes through daily. And that individual is you—a student of management, tomorrow's manager, and the multiple roles that you will play in the course of your professional career and your life. When you understand the mysterious power of non-verbal communication, you will be able to comprehend better how a manager conveys disapproval through the shrug of shoulders or the language that eyes or the face or the body speak in meetings that can be time robbers!

Ever since Charles Darwin published his scientific study *Expressions of the Emotions in Man and Animals* in 1872, considerable amount of interest has been generated in the study of body language. Albert Mehrabian, R.L. Birdwhistle, E.T. Hall and others have significantly contributed to the study of body language, i.e. silent or unspoken communication. According to Mehrabian, one of the foremost experts in non-verbal communication, transmission of message is effective only when all the three aspects of communication—the verbal, the vocal, and the visual—are in tandem with one another. However, since it does not happen that way all the time, owing to human limitations, the impact of human message occurs in the following manner:

Verbal—7% (words)
Vocal—38% (intonation, pitch, volume)
Visual—55% (gestures, postures, all physical movements).
See Figure 6.1.

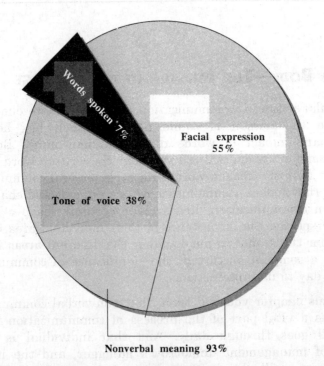

FIGURE 6.1 Elements of Oral Message.

The study of body language will help you to look beyond the words that people speak to convey what they really mean, or silence that substitutes words that do not get spoken. Peter Drucker said, "The most important thing in communication to **hear** what isn't being said."

WHAT IS NON-VERBAL COMMUNICATION?

When we communicate our thoughts without using words, we communicate non-verbally. The popular aphorism "Actions speak louder than words" holds a great deal of meaning when it comes to understanding the essence of non-verbal communication. Any skilled communicator, whether the person is a negotiator, or a public speaker or a business person, knows very well the power of the unspoken language and how to hear the unspoken word.

Non-verbal communication is the way in which we express our feelings, emotions, attitudes, opinions, and views through our body movements. In verbal communication we use words; in non-verbal communication we use our eyes, hands, face, and other body movements to express our thoughts. The body and its movements substitute words.

It is astonishing how scholars, researchers, writers, and even ancient wise men have pronounced observations about the subtle power of non-verbal communication. Some of these quotations are provided here to give an idea about the interesting manner in which people have made their observations:

1. Watch out for the man whose stomach doesn't move when he laughs.
   — CANTONESE PROVERB

2. The eyes of men converse as much as their tongues, with the advantage that the ocular dialect needs no dictionary, but is understood the world over.
   — RALPH WALDO EMERSON

3. Learning is acquired by reading books, but the much more necessary learning, the knowledge of the world, is only to be acquired by reading men, and studying all the various editions of them.
   — LORD CHESTERFIELD

4. Communication is like a dance, with everyone engaged in intricate and shared movements across many subtle dimensions, yet all strangely oblivious that they are doing so.
   — WILLIAM CONDON

5. Mortals can keep no secret. If their lips are silent, they gossip with their fingertips, betrayal forces its way through every pose.

— SIGMUND FREUD

We go to school to undergo a formal training in cognitive skills of learning. Yet, when it comes to noticing sadness, anger, envy, love, fear and such emotions, we do not think of undergoing any kind of training to decode these emotions. Yet, since the time of Charles Darwin, researchers have conducted in-depth study of relationships between the non-verbal channels of communication.

It will do you a world of good if you ponder over the statements and raise a few questions in your mind about the way you communicate with people even when you are not using words.

- How much of your hands do you use when you talk?
- Do you look at people in a conversation or do you also stare at them?
- Does your stare make people feel uncomfortable?
- When you make a presentation, do you stand with your hands interlocked in front at the fig leaf position?
- Do you often keep your arms crossed while talking?
- Do you know what 'conversational overlap' is?

There are a whole lot of such small gestures that we use all the time without our conscious realization. All these gestures, put together, form the language that your body speaks. When you express well through your body language, people take a notice of you and admire you for your well-controlled hand gestures, your standing posture, the colours that you wear, the way you sit, the way you walk and several other positive body language indicators. But, if our body speaks a loud language, people may not feel inclined to admire us.

Body language is certainly not a new phenomenon. Since the beginning of time, human beings have used body gestures to make their needs and desires understood by other people. Body language was used as a tool of communication long before language developed as a communication tool.

NON-VERBAL SIGNIFIERS ARE LIKE WORDS

In body language, there are single gestures and cluster gestures. Single gestures like the nod of head are equivalent to single words like, 'yes', or 'don't know'. Cluster gestures like standing, talking and using hands to make our point, are equivalent to arrangement of words in a sentence for a meaningful message. If we want our message to be effective, we know that we have to select the right words, arrange the words in a proper grammatical structure, supported by the right tone. If we do not do this, we will be branded as a poor communicator. Similarly, in body language, the gestures have to be appropriate to convey the meaning that we have in mind. An angry face may put off people from approaching you, or a raised voice might suggest that you are either annoyed or disapprove the other person's conduct.

In real life, however, verbal and non-verbal communication cannot be separated. Our oral speech is accompanied by the movement of eyes, use of hands and pitch of our voice. In written communication, the non-verbal communication signifiers are the use of white space, proper margins, right kind of fonts, right length of sentence, length of paragraphs, and line spacing. A page that has matter condensed closely is usually skipped by the reader or it is rejected. A poor visual appearance of a proposal or a resume will prompt the reader to reject it. The details of the non-verbal aspects of written communication will be discussed in the chapter on business communication writing.

Non-verbal Communication Sub-disciplines

Last three decades have witnessed researchers working in the sub-disciplines of cultural anthropology and linguistics. Since the time Albert Mehrabian (1972) made known his views about the three 'Vs' of communication, human behaviour has come under a close scrutiny and scientific study has been made in the following sub-disciplines:

◆ Kinesics (K)
◆ Occulesics (O)
◆ Paralanguage/Paralinguistics (P)
◆ Proxemics (P)
◆ Artifactics (A)
◆ Chronemics (C)
◆ Tactilics (T)

Registering the different kinds of body movements under the label 'KOPPACT' will help you to associate the nuances of each skill and its relation to the total synchronization of body language. Normally, human gestures come in clusters and it is these clusters that we need to study for an overall meaning of human behaviour and oral communication. Human interaction at the micro level can be both an interesting and a frustrating experience. It certainly is not an easy task to study peoples' body language, complicated that they can be with personal feelings, emotions, attitudes expressed through a series of gestures, consciously or unconsciously accompanied by spoken language. Nonetheless, the vast volume of literature available on it enables us to explore ourselves critically. In today's global multiculturalism, knowing others as well as knowing one's own non-verbal cues have become essential.

ACTIONS SPEAK LOUDER THAN WORDS

All our thoughts are accompanied by some kind of body movements. The more conscious we are of our body movements, more prepared we will be to face any situation, to the extent of masking our feelings in unwanted situations. However, it may not be possible to mask our feelings and expressions always. Working on body language will help you to handle questions in job interviews, seminars, conferences, social gatherings, travelling in public transports, public places like airports, hotels, railway stations, hospitals banks and places wherever you may have to interact with people of varied cultural groups.

Kinesics

The different ways in which people move their bodies that include postures, gestures, head nods, and leg movements, are called Kinesics.

Gestures have been classified into three categories:

1. Emblems	These have direct verbal translations, like nodding of the head for 'yes', shaking the head for 'no' or waving hand for 'hello' or saying 'bye bye' They are used in place of words.
2. Illustrators	These gestures naturally accompany our speech and accentuate what we say. Very often, we tend to close our palm in a fist formation or bang the table to suggest our mode of thinking, often for the purpose of emphasizing our points. These gestures have a dramatic effect.
3. Adaptors	These are unconscious movements of body that originate from the nervous state of our mind. In an interview, when the candidate is nervous or uncomfortable with the questions asked, she/he may unconsciously crack knuckles, shake legs, or tap the foot.

All these three types of gestures are natural accompaniments of our speech. However, when we are in a formal situation like our workplace, it is important to keep in mind that we cannot afford to show nervous or diffident behaviour. A manager, in day to day work, has to make presentations, offer oral reports or talk on telephone, or entertain clients. Can she or he afford to show nervous gestures? If managers show adaptor gestures in such situations, they will get evaluated as diffident, insecure or confused. At an interview, the candidate will fail to convince the interviewer with confident answers.

Similarly, in social situations, when people are not trained in social skills, they exhibit cross-cultural patterns, often showing confusion and nervousness.

Here is what happened to an Indian gentleman at the de gaulle airport, Paris, a few years ago. I was a mute observer to the whole incident.

The security officer at the airport was on his duty. A meticulous examination of all boarding passengers had to be done, because of the threat perception and the global sensitivity of travelling these days. He was engaged in physical checking of the passengers before they were permitted to proceed to the aircraft.

The long queue had nationalities from all countries—Indians, Malaysians, Chinese, English, Americans and others. We were in a desperate hurry to catch our flight back to Mumbai by Air France as the connecting flight from Schiphol, Amsterdam, had arrived late. Yet, our security check had to be conducted. As tired passengers, we somehow wanted to get over the ritual and board the flight and have a good rest. But that did not seem to happen for a while. We had to hold on to our patience.

In the meantime, a drama seemed to be going on with the French security officer engaged in verbal and visual enactment with the Indian gentleman. What seemed from a distance was total breakdown of communication between the two. They both did not understand each other. Perhaps it was a language barrier. But the visual impression that the confused behaviour of the Indian passenger evoked in the onlookers was not very pleasant. The security officer said something which was not understood by the Indian gentleman. He did not know how to negotiate the situation and make himself understood. I saw him going in circles, anticipating the officer to examine him and the officer looking away at him in desperation. Perhaps the officer felt pushed into a situation. The whole drama went on for few valuable moments. The situation became more embarrassing for the Indian passenger as he was being started at. He grew all the more self-conscious and nonplussed.

I said to myself. "Only if his company had oriented him with the airport rules and regulations, or groomed him socially with a few inputs on cultural norms of the land from where he was going to embark, or a few functional words in French, this embarrassment would not have been caused."

A lot of literature is available on different gestures of the body. Research provides us with the knowledge of different gestures. Some of the prominent ones, as observed in presentations, interviews, social meets, and training programs are cited here. In group meetings, official meets like interviews, and other interactive situations, it is essential that we understand the medium of our body well:

Hands: See Figure 6.2.

FIGURE 6.2 **A good business handshake shows professionalism!**

1. Clenched hands	In a sitting position—the gesture has many meanings. It can mean emphasis, determination, 'I know it all', nervousness as in an interview.
2. Hands interlocked at the crotch level	The fig leaf position is only meant for statues and should be avoided.
3. Slashing/jabbing the air with hand	Something very culturally specific to the Indians is **slashing/jabbing the air with hand** and pointing someone with the forefinger.

Palm gestures

1. Open palm gestures	Is associated with openness/frankness, particularly valued in presentations.
2. Slapping the palms	A common sight with people in a joyous mood, but must be avoided in presentations.

Handshakes: See Figure 6.3.

FIGURE 6.3 **'My God! He doesn't even know how to shake hands!'**
Fingertip handshake is nonprofessional!

1. Handshakes	*Normal handshakes* determine good grip and professionalism.
2. Knuckle grinding handshake	Should be avoided particularly in social situations. It belongs to the 'rough and tough' guy.
3. Fingertip-grab handshake	Diffident people and those socially not groomed do not know how to shake hands. They offer only the tips of their finger and keep the person at arm's length. Many Indian managers, not knowing how to shake hands with ladies, often commit this error.
4. Dead-fish handshake	These hands are sweaty, flaccid and lifeless, like a dead fish. The hand is cold and clammy, and the person with such hands is considered weak or ungroomed and, therefore, unpopular. Shaking such hands gives a damp and uncomfortable feeling. All managers must learn how to shake hands professionally.

Finger movements: See Figure 6.4.

FIGURE 6.4 'Didn't I ask you to bring ... why don't you listen?'
An unpleasant gesture! Should be avoided.

1. Pointing index finger	As a natural accompaniment of speeches, the movement of the finger may not seem offensive. But very often when it accompanies heated arguments, it sends a negative signal to the onlooker. The finger pointing is associated with authority, politicians, parents, and preachers. But pointing it out as an accusation should be avoided.
2. Steepling fingers	The term was coined by Birdwhistle (1971). According to him, it suggests "the confident and sometimes smug, pontifical, egoistic, or proud gesture." The gesture communicates that the person is very sure of himself. The gesture essentially is indicative of a superior attitude and often gets reflected in a superior-subordinate relationship. The raised steeple indicates 'giving opinion' and the lower steeple indicates 'listening.'
3. The OK gesture	The tips of the thumb and the index finger are brought together to form an 'O'. Allan Pease (1993) has provided many interpretations of the non-verbal symbol. In all English-speaking countries, including India, it suggests that 'all is correct.' However, in Japan, it means 'money', in France, it means 'zero', and in Brazil, it means 'insult.'
4. The "V" sign	The gesture was used by Sir Winston Churchill during the Second World War days. He popularized it as a sign of victory. The sign is popular in our country too and we often see our leaders flashing their fingers in the 'V' form after emerging victorious in elections.
5. The neck scratch	It is a symbol of **doubt** or **uncertainty**.

Arms: See Figure 6.5.

FIGURE 6.5 'Don't they believe what I said?' An example of crossed arms, clenched teeth and serious face ... clearly the person is on the defensive.

1. **Crossed arms across the chest**	This kind of gesture indicates that the person is on the defensive; has a made up mind and a fixed position on a subject. The gesture also means a protective guard against threats. Sometimes when the person is on the defensive, the gesture might combine with clenched teeth or red face.
2. **Partial arm cross**	A diffident gesture, this is commonly seen in people who are with strangers.
3. **Arms crossed behind the back**	A person disturbed mentally often takes this body position. The locking of the hands is virtually like locking one's mind over a situation.

Postures

Gestures are a part of postures although for our understanding, we will study some of the postures separately. Often in interviews and group interactions, you will be judged by your postures. When we make a presentation, we stand and do it. When we report to our bosses, unless asked, we do not sit down, but stand and report. When we sit and listen to someone in a meeting or a lecture, our sitting posture indicates whether we are interested in the talk or not.

Postures form an important chunk of kinesic behaviour that communicate a person's responses to different people in different situations. Scholars have critically studied postures and offered their analysis. These days of quick-learning finishing schools, a lot of emphasis is given to deportment. Our everyday interactions with people at work matter a great deal. Do we fling our hands while talking? Do we stand straight or we tilt our body weight in presentations? A cluster of such postures that accompany our gestures indicate whether we are liked or kept at a distance.

Wainwright writes: "We each have a repertoire of postures that we characteristically use though these repertoires are quite limited. It is possible for us to recognize people we know at a distance from the postures they typically use. Posture can be a clue to personality and character. The person who usually holds his body erect often has a quite different temperament from the person who slouches about with rounded shoulders."

Standing posture. In presentation, it is necessary to have an erect posture with weight evenly distributed on both legs. Tilted body weight gives a clumsy/casual impression to the presenter. It is a negative posture. A person with drooping shoulders and sagging body gives a poor impression.

Yet, a person with arms loosely held down by the sides of the body, is interpreted as an open and friendly person.

Sitting posture. In interviews, if you sit with one hand on the table and support your face with your palm, in a typical cheek-and-chin gesture, with a look of boredom, or attend a seminar in a similar posture-gesture combination, you would be viewed very negatively by people. It is a gesture cluster that doesn't invite pleasant comments.

Also, if you lean backwards in a sitting position, you may be considered a hostile person.

Occulesics

This is the science of the movement/grammar of our eyes and of facial expressions. The interest in the science of occulesics began with Charles Darwin when he published his scientific study *Expressions of the Emotions in Man and Animals*, in 1872. Since then, it has generated great interest in researchers to study perhaps because the eyes and the face are the most potent vehicle of communication. It is claimed that in the science of body language, there are 7,50,000 signals, of which 15,000 come from the face alone (Richard Denny).

The power of our eyes

The study of facial expressions begins with the eyes because they are the most powerful medium of communication we possess other than words. Poets, writers, artists, and film makers have spent considerable time imagining the beauty and grace of human eyes and the subtle power that they possess. Isn't it often said "People speak through their eyes?" Eyes are said to be the windows to our soul and mirror of our heart! In literature, you will come across phrases like 'loving eyes', 'laughing eyes', 'piercing eyes', 'steely eyes'. Of all the parts of the human body that are used to transmit information, the eyes are the most important and can transmit the most subtle nuances. (Julius Fast)

In your daily life, at your place of work/college/social meets, have you ever felt that somebody is staring away at you? Or someone talking to you does not establish eye contact and continues to either look down as she or he is talking? At the same time, another person while talking may be engaged in the process of thinking, and in doing so may be moving his/her eyes sideways, or upwards. A great deal of fascinating study has been done in this area. The dynamics of our eye movement have been labelled as 'eye grammar' (Wainwright) and the research unfolds the micro-power of our eyes. The main ones according to Michel Argyle and other researchers are:

Eye grammar

1. **Staring eyes**	Too much eye contact that either shows superiority or lack of respect, a threatening attitude or a wish to insult.
2. **Too little eye contact**	It has multiple interpretations. The gesture indicates dishonesty, impoliteness, insincerity, and also shyness.
3. **Withdrawal of eye contact**	This is considered as a sign of submission.

| 4. **Frequently looking away at people from a distance** | This is generally an extrovert's behaviour, interested in knowing reactions, or to dominate or to influence or scrutinize. |
| 5. **Scarcely looking at a person when in close proximity** | An introvert shows this kind of behaviour, when discussing intimate or difficult topics, or dislike for the other person. |

At workplace, our body language dynamics are constantly evaluated by people with whom we interact. If an employee has a fixed facial expression, with eyes caught in a thinking pattern, that is, looking upward or sideward, then perhaps the employee is engaged in the mental act of making decisions. Thinking eyes need time to be understood. Research indicates that people either look left or right, depending on what thoughts dominate their mental activity. Left lookers are considered more emotional, subjective, and suggestible. The right lookers are more influenced by logic and precision.

The Face

"You can read his face like an open book" is a common remark made about people whose facial expressions show a lot of transparency of expressions. Emotional people have a demonstrative face that shows the feelings of anger, envy, happiness, sneers, dislike, tension and sadness, as the thoughts enter their mind. However, there are also people who are described as 'poker faced'. At workplace, you will come across such people who do not like to show their feelings often, as researchers say: "sometimes facial expressions are guarded in order not to betray a position prematurely by expressing a nonverbal opinion."

(ALESSANDRA AND HUNSAKER)

Paralinguistics

This is the science of the vocal cues that accompany our speech. Some scholars separate it from the study of body language and call it 'paralanguage'. However, the vocal cues are an integral part of non-verbal communication and hence it has been included in this section.

The science of paralinguistics refers to the volume, pitch, tone, intonation, modulation, and the rate of speech. In the chapter on

'Use of words and sentences in verbal communication,' you have already learnt about the meanings of these paralanguage factors. Accent, stress, rate of speaking, pitch and volume help us to judge people's age, sex, attractiveness, educational background and level of confidence in the voice, Often these subtle micro factors influence us to think whether we should trust a person or not. A voice that has tremors or diffident tone will not make you feel very positive about the person. A high speed of talking in interviews or negotiations or presentations will not instill confidence in the interviewers or the audience. Rhetorical speeches, therefore, never succeed in convincing intelligent listeners. The raised voice, high pitch and tone are exploited by politicians to play to the gallery and earn quick applause. In business, the strategy does not work.

Alternatively, when pauses are taken, words are emphasized, or pitch is kept low, the speaker is definite to show a lot of confidence and maturity in his or her communication.

People with speech disability might think that errors in their speech might affect their performance in interviews or presentations. If the speech errors are a normal way of speaking, the evaluator may empathize with the person. But, if they are not, then the errors may be understood as signs of diffidence or nervousness.

The non-verbal importance of paralinguistic skills, hence, can be seen as extremely influencing skills when we communicate with people. An awareness of the subtle nuances of vocal qualities will help you to understand working relationships. Speaking to co-workers, employees, higher management, clients, and customers needs different uses of vocal behaviour. The sooner we understand the power of our vocal intonations, the better we will be at our interpersonal relationships at workplace and in life. Our credibility improves and the payoffs are worth the try.

Proxemics: The Cultural Iceberg

It is the study of the distance between people and objects. In international business, proxemics has emerged as an important area owing to cross-cultural factors. Different countries have different cultural patterns. When people with conflicting cultural patterns interact, problems do get created in understanding one another giving rise to delayed decisions or rejections of orders in business. **Proxemics,** the science of space, is an important area of study in non-verbal communication.

It was Edward Hall, an American anthropologist, who first coined the term 'Proxemics', and defined the four space zones as

◆ The intimate zone—(0–.5 m)
◆ The personal zone—(.5–1.2 m)
◆ The social zone—(1.2–3 m)
◆ The public zone—(3 m)

The language of space is important in the context of business as we are always involved with human interactions of a high speed nature. Except for the public zone, very often, the mix up of the other three zones can create problems at work. Every person is surrounded by an invisible space, a personal territory that belongs to him or her. This personal territory, called the space bubble, when invaded, can result into a 'bubble burst', causing irritation and displeasure.

For instance, people at work are not always free to attend to queries or requests during work hours as they may not find time due to the pressure of work. If they are drawn into discussions, face-to-face, across the table against their willingness, they might feel intruded upon as their space is invaded. It is important for an individual at work to find out from the non-verbal cues of the person whether she/he is free to attend to your request.

In the chapter on cross-cultural communication, you will learn about the non-verbal aspects of behavioural dynamics in a multi-cultural group. Examples of cultural traits of nationalities from different countries have been included to give you an idea why it is important to keep in mind the cultural factors of business interactions. Every country has cultural space that is well defined, and people operating in a certain cultural environment need to know this. Violation of spaces whether personal, social or public, can create a wrong impression and lost business opportunities.

Personal Space must be Respected

Personal space is culture specific. In the low-context cultural countries, the definition of personal space, in formal situations, can be quite different. In India, at work place, we are sensitive about our personal space, which is why any intrusion by another person can cause great disharmony and the person can be looked upon with suspicion. This is again gender specific. Women in high context cultural countries, which include India, are sensitive about the use of intimate and social space at workplace.

Every person prefers a surrounding personal space also known as spatial bubble. The space is used as a buffer against intrusion from others. Different cultures have different notions of personal space. The social behaviour of people will indicate the culturally/socially accepted spatial requirements. In social situations, when we feel uncomfortable, we prefer more personal space. And where we feel comfortable, we do not mind less personal space. See Figure 6.6.

FIGURE 6.6 'Hey, you're violating my space!' An example of intrusion of space. The girl in the picture is not liking it! Avoid it.

In multicultural groups, one needs to quietly observe the accepted proxemics of different groups and interact accordingly.

Different perceptions of personal space can be a problem in organizations, particularly with different cultural groups. It is therefore a sensible thing to find out what the accepted boundary is between two persons or in a small group. The bubble-burst can cause irritation and result into discomfort zones in interpersonal relationships. People from high-context cultural countries generally prefer to keep greater distance while interacting with others, whereas those from low-context cultural countries are more care free and casual. In an organization, the personal-space expectations of multicultural groups must be recognized and respected. The ignorance of it can lead to serious cross-cultural problems.

Other than the cultural factors, researchers have enlisted a number of other factors in the category of proxemics. It also refers to peoples' responses to the environment in which they live and work. Referring to this aspect of space as **'territoriality'**, Gary Kreps writes, "People are territorial about their 'possessions' or objects for which they claim ownership. These objects can range from clothing and books to homes and automobiles. People generally protect their territory vigorously and become quite angry if it is limited or their possessions are taken away from them."

The language of space is also reflected in the way meetings are arranged. A round table formation encourages participation among members rather than an arrangement where one member has to crane neck to address somebody's point.

In organizations people are also touchy about their seating places, furniture, and equipment.

Another important aspect of space is the architectural design of buildings. The trend today is to have open office spaces and not closed spaces/rooms. The explanation given is that open offices induce increased communication that results into instant feedback and better interpersonal relationships. As Kreps says: "small offices with low ceilings and no windows can cause people to feel boxed in and make them sullen and depressed. ..."

Most well-designed office complexes these days pay a great deal of attention to organizational proxemics such as landscaping, colour schemes, ergonomically designed furniture, and furnishings that are soothing and pleasant. The idea is that people should feel comfortable during their long working hours in offices.

Artifactics

The non-verbal message signals that an individual sends across through appearance, clothing, style, perfume, personal objects like pens, cell phones, briefcases, etc. belong to the area of artifactics. These form a part of your total personality. Very often, a person is associated with the use of certain choice of brands, or perfumes or even the automobile that the person owns.

In interviews or presentations, it is said the first thirty seconds are crucial for making an impact on the interviewers or the audience waiting to listen to your presentation. Before the candidate or the presenter gets ready to speak, an impression is already formed in the mind of the interviewer or the audience. In both these cases, your artifactics do influence the prospective interviewer's perception of you or the audience's perception of you.

Globalization has brought the multicultural environment at workplace. The pressing demands for personal grooming and personal hygiene, till now neglected, have become important to a manager for his/her professional image. Several things like clean finger nails, laced shoes, sober/conservative colours, well-brushed hair, no dandruff on collar/jacket, no smelling mouth, no smell of hair oil, a touch of deodorant (to prevent body odour) are considered important. Every micro detail that is necessary for you to project a clean image of yourself must be observed.

It will be to your advantage if you pay attention to personal grooming.

Chronemics

The concept of time and its impact on people is the science of chronemics. Like proxemics, chronemics too is culture bound. People from low-context cultures have a precise sense of time-keeping in stark contrast to the time keeping sense of people from high-context cultural countries that include India. Time-keeping, of course, does not mean 'looking at your watch' and keeping time. It means several things:

◆ Have you taken an appointment if you wish to meet someone for business purpose?
◆ Do you inform that the meeting is likely to be of certain duration?
◆ Do you limit your meeting to specific points?
◆ Do you intervene and hijack the talk?
◆ Do you keep people waiting if someone has come to see you?
◆ Are you punctual for your appointments?

Ask yourself about your time keeping habits and what you are doing to improve yourself.

Of 168 hours per week or 10,080 minutes a week, how do we plan and manage our work? The way we use our time tells others about our sincerity of purpose, our dedication to our work, and how serious we are at work. The way we use time tells others about our personality like our clothing, personal hygiene, and personal habits do!

Time in India is very flexible. Appointments are not kept within a time frame and very often unpunctuality is taken for granted. Unfortunately it is socially accepted. In a country where time is stretchable like an elastic band, plenty of time robbers also exist. Unscheduled visits, long telephone chats, absence of time log books, long memos, and mixing up personal work with office work are major time robbers. Time robbers reduce our efficiency at work and result into poor time management. The more we get competitive and professional, more pressure we will have on ourselves to respect time.

Today's fast paced business world is a slave of time. Time management has emerged as a vital factor in organizations today.

Tactilics

Humans do not only communicate through words and eyes, but also through the language of touch, something that they have learnt from the world of animals. *Tactilics* is the science of touch language. It includes touching self, others, and objects. Research shows two kinds of touch language:

- ◆ Bodily contact
- ◆ Touching with hands

Bodily contact refers to touches that are accidental and unconscious and any part of the body may be involved in it. In overcrowded buses and trains, like in India, back-pushes or elbow rubbings, stepping on someone else's feet, are so common.

Touching implies that the actions are deliberate, conscious, and made primarily by hands. As Wainright says touching has the 'connotation of a more active involvement of the person doing the touching.'

The language of touch can have great therapeutic value. A mother's touch on the shoulders of her worried child can be a source of solace. A worried friend can find assurance when patted on the back by another friend. Researchers have stated that humans consciously or sub-consciously express through the language of touch because it fulfills physiological and sociological need. (Montagu 1971). The needs can be social, sexual, or psychological.

Various kinds of touch are:

- ◆ *A pat on the shoulder* (assurance/encouragement)
- ◆ *Holding hands and arms* (social gesture of goodwill/ goodbye)
- ◆ *Stroking hair* or *face/Caressing* (in a close relationship, usually sexual one)

Michael Argyle has identified many of such touch behaviours, of course, in western cultures.

In India, the touch language is restricted to people known to one another and that, at best, is the pat on the shoulder from a senior to a junior or touching both palms together to greet a visitor or a person, or touching the feet of elderly people to show respect. Tactilics as a subject is a new in concept in India and hence needs to be explored. However, one has to be careful while using the touch language. As Wainright says, "bodily contact is a highly sensitive area of body language which is fraught with dangers with the careless and the unwary."

GESTURE CLUSTERS

Gesture clusters are a series of non-verbal signals that a body speaks at a point in time of communication. Judging a person's gestures in isolation or separate from the rest of the gestures at the point of making an analysis of the person's body language should be avoided. No gesture operates in isolation. One gesture is wired to the other at any given point in time during an act of communication. They are a combination of different body gestures. While interpreting gesture clusters, one has also to examine a person's state of mind.

Meanings Attached to Certain Gesture Clusters

Certain combinations of gesture clusters have been identified as reliable indicators of a person's feelings. Some of them as pointed out by researchers are:

1. Open palm, hands, leaning slightly forward in the chair while in conversation/discussions, a good handshake, broad, natural smile	are congruent gesture clusters indicating openness/transparency.
2. Crossed arms, rigid body, minimal eye contact, clenched fists, tense face	are all indicators of defensiveness.
3. Mouth guards, side glances, smirk smile, shifting body, rubbing nose	are indicators of suspicion, doubt, secrecy and dismissal.
4. Head tilted on one side, hand under the chin, hand-to-cheek, leaning forward	are indicators of evaluation.
5. Steepling fingers, feet up on the desk, hands interlocked behind head with chin thrust upward	are indicators of superiority/ authority/ confidence.
6. Sound of jingling pocket change, tapping fingers, shifting body weight from one foot to the other	are indicators of nervousness.
7. Wide eyes, extended arms, open hands, broad smile	are indicators of enthusiasm.

While reading body language, focus on gestures that make the clusters congruent. However, there is what is called incongruent gesture clusters. If an angry person has a smile on his/her face and the tone is shrill and loud, the gesture cluster is incongruent. Smile indicates a happy state of mind while a shrill/ loud pitch indicates anger or irritation. Similarly, a nervous laugh, a fidgeting body and lost eyes, make an incongruent gesture cluster, because the laugh indicates a mind that is under strain and is preoccupied.

The study of body language is endless. The world of micro body language pointers makes the study a complex and challeng- ing one. Often the interpretation of gesture clusters goes wrong because a lot of conjecture is involved in the study of body language. Yet, some functional knowledge and the proficiency in reading gesture clusters at workplace is essential for enhanced interpersonal communications.

NEURO-LINGUISTIC PROGRAMMING (NLP) AND THE POWER OF THE NON-VERBAL

Today, the study of body language has received a boost from the on-going research on NLP. A great deal of study has been done on neuro-linguistic programming or NLP. It is a science that deals with the way human beings think and process the outer world through their senses. The science of NLP has proved to be a power house of limitless energy that human beings possess. It is a revolutionary approach to human communication. Ever since Richard Bandler and John Grinder, the original code developers of NLP, made known their path breaking work about the hidden potential of human energy, many researchers and scholars have added their research to reconfirm how human beings think, and how they can transform their own thinking pattern in search of excellence! Managers have a great deal to gain from the study of NLP.

NLP has the power to modify your thought process and behavioural patterns to suit your projected goals. Marketing and sales executives, financial analysts, corporate directors, educa- tionists, athletes, students and a whole lot of people have gained from the practical lessons of NLP which literally 'reprograms' the learners/individual's mind for faster learning, better relationships and greater success, in professional as well as personal and social life. You as a student manager and prospective efficient manager for challenging assignments will be able to contribute substantially if you equip yourself with the power of NLP.

The word, 'neuro' refers to our nervous system, the mental pathways of our five senses by which we

1. hear,
2. feel,
3. taste,
4. see, and
5. smell

consciously or unconsciously, and translate our thoughts into experiences.

The word **linguistic** refers to our ability to use

◆ language,
◆ specific words and phrases to mirror our mental worlds,
◆ 'silent language' of postures, gestures, and habits that reveal our thinking styles, beliefs, and opinion.

Our language and non-verbal patterns are expressions of who we are and how we think and behave.

The word **'programming'**, borrowed from computer science, suggests that our thoughts, feelings and actions are simply habitual programs that can be changed by upgrading our 'mental software.' Programming is a coding experience and constitutes a series of steps designed to achieve a specific result. The results we want to achieve are the direct consequence of our personal programs.

In any kind of situation, business or non-business, the ability to build understanding with people is a strong indicator of our personal efficiency. In NLP, this is called 'rapport building.' Apart from the use of words in human interaction, we use our non-verbal communication skills. We have already studied how the non-verbal elements naturally accompany our gestures in our communication and enable us to create a better frame of reference.

In NLP, we talk about 'instant rapport'. The techniques of rapport building need to be practised in every interactive situation.

How to Achieve Rapport

NLP prescribes the techniques of:

◆ Matching
◆ Mirroring
◆ Pacing

Matching can be consciously used to establish and increase rapport. Matching means to observe the behaviour of the person on the other side and match the same. You can match literally any behaviour you can observe. Posture, facial expression, rate of breathing, voice tone, tempo, eye movement, and pitch can all be matched.

Mirroring is the act of watching the non-verbal gestures of the other person. You then make it a point to mirror the body dynamics of the other person in such a way that you almost begin to look like the other person.

Pacing is the manner in which you match and mirror. Imagine you have gone to meet someone in the office. It is a business meeting. As you sit with the person, you begin to notice how the person is sitting, the body posture, and how she or he is using the hands. You then slowly begin to adjust your body to match, mirror, and pace his or her body movements. If the person's head is tilted on one side or the eye moves in a certain angle, very slowly you too adjust your behaviour. If you suddenly adjust looking like the other person, you might be just misunderstood mimicking him or her, and that will break the rapport.

Things to match, mirror and pace

1. **Voice**	match pitch, tone, volume, rate,
2. **Language**	words that are used (this has been explained below)
3. **Posture**	sitting position, tilting of head, leaning forward or backward, standing
4. **Breathing**	rapid or slow speaking
5. **Emotion**	expressed in voice, face, eyes
6. **Values and beliefs**	challenging people's values and beliefs will break your rapport. Extreme caution has to be used in this regard
7. **Gesture movements**	movement of fingers, face movement

Calibration skills. The success of matching, mirroring, and pacing depends on how successfully we calibrate through our senses and make contact with the world/people with whom we communicate and interact.

Pattern of Language Used by Speakers: How NLP Can Help

There are five different language patterns that are used by speakers. NLP teaches us how to get into a person's frame of reference by studying the language patterns:

1. *Visual*—thinking in visuals/pictures/images	"It is important that students *see* the logic of the argument."
People in this mode frequently use words like **see, visualize, look, watch,** and **vision.**	"*Watch* for the reactions of the audience when the play is on."
2. *Auditory mode*—thinking in sounds/words/voice	"The *loud* exchange of words made her *speechless*."
People in this mode use words like **hear, sound, loud, shout,** and so on.	"The audience was *mesmerized* by your *speech*."
3. *Kinesthetic mode*—thinking in feelings/emotions	"He just doesn't have a *grasp* on the subject."
People in this mode use words like **grasp, touch, feel,** and **handle.**	"The security officer could not *handle* the crisis at the plant."
4. The least common language patterns are olfactory and gustatory.	
Olfactory mode—thinking in terms of smell	"Don't consume garlic before meetings. Your mouth will *smell* of garlic."
People in this mode use words like **aroma, smells stinking,** and so on.	"The building looks nice but the staircase *stinks* in corners."
5. *Gustatory mode*—thinking in terms of food/taste tasty	"The banquet hall was full. People enjoyed the *delicious* food."
People in this mode use words like "tasty, delicious, sumptuous", etc.	"Don't *eat* a lot of junk food. It will cause obesity."

Note: You need to note that when a person interacts with you in a certain mode (visual, auditory, kinesthetic, olfactory or gustatory), you must respond back in that particular fashion (style of mode/wording) because the person is using that pattern to process his/her thoughts/reality.

Rapport Helps Influence People

As a manager you will need to ensure that you are not only understood by others but also help yourself to influence others. In negotiations, rapport building has a great value.

The dictionary meaning of rapport is "A relation of harmony, accord, or affinity." The definition itself shows the importance of rapport in an effective communication process. When we speak of rapport we mean:

◆ Trust
◆ Confidence
◆ Participation

Within the parameters of these three factors, we can see why and how people freely respond or do not respond.

The advantage of rapport is that we create 'sameness'. It helps both parties to move through discussions and relationships.

When the factor of 'sameness' decreases in communication, it gives rise to 'difference'. In that case, rapport is broken/lost and understanding suffers. **Difference is the basis of poor rapport**.

Rapport is established when there is a degree of mirroring, matching and pacing. "Notice that when people are in rapport, their communication takes on a pattern of dance, it is rhythmical, their bodies, as well as their words, match each other ... smoothly and easily. When people are in rapport, they unconsciously match, mirror, and pace each other."*

Andreas and Faulkner tell us how achievers have consciously or unconsciously used NLP at work.

> Famous achievers like Lee Iacocca and Mary Kay know the importance of relationships. Iacocca is often described as open and immediate. He makes personal contact, and he is liked and trusted. People feel good being around him. Mary Kay's tremendous success is directly attributable to her primary business concern—treating her employees with respect. Ask her about management and you'll hear about her people. She says: 'Treat others the way you want to be treated-on and off the job. Listen closely to others' concerns and show that you value them.

According to scholars, NLP has shown that many high achievers develop liking and appreciation very rapidly. They naturally make people feel comfortable around them and demonstrate a concern for others' values. Those who are marginally successful or unsuccessful typically lack these abilities.

According to Ribbens and Thompson, people from the West are said to 'think' primarily in terms of pictures, sounds and feelings, whereas in the East they think in terms of smell and taste. They also state that "roughly 45% of the population has a primary preference for thinking in terms of feelings (kinaesthetic), compared with 35% in terms of visual images and 20% in auditory form.

---

*(Dr. William D. Horton, Founder-President, National Federation of Neuro-linguistic Psychology, USA).

The Final Word on Body Language

Although a great deal of study has been carried out on the fascinating area of non-verbal communication, researchers still consider body language to be an inaccurate science. They say this because there are occasions when people, well groomed in the art of body skills, can mask their feelings and pretend to look agreeable and pleasant even when they are really not interested. Often we cross our arms in a conference hall or at a party not because we are on our guard and on the defensive but because we may be feeling cold and a little uncomfortable or when we are physically tired.

However, it is important to know the different aspects of body movements as the knowledge allows us to speculate/guess/read a person's gestures and postures. The advantage of the prior knowledge helps us to keep reconfirming our impressions about the person's behaviour on a minute to minute basis as we remain engaged in a communication loop, and speak to ourselves in our mind about the possible indications that the gestures might suggest Paying attention to clusters of gestures helps us to decode the total meaning.

Prior knowledge of body language also helps us to know about **'body leakage'**—the non-verbal signals that a person subconsciously sends out because the person may just be unable to control these movements. What is important to note is that these leakages give out clues to the real truth.

How to know when people tell lies?

Albert Mehrabian made the following observations when he investigated the behaviour of people who indulged in speaking untruthful messages:

- The person talks slowly and talks less; commits speech errors, and has slow body movements
- The person blushes and perspires
- The voice has tremors
- The person may gulp and shake
- The person may play with pencils or spectacles

Wainwright adds to the list of a liar's body movements:

- Shuffling the feet
- Twitching the toes
- Crossing and uncrossing the legs
- Touching the eye
- Licking the lips
- Drumming the fingers and gripping the arm rest

The point is that the body language of a person who tells lies contradicts the spoken words. One has to look for the mismatch between words and body movements. As Judi James says,

> Studying body language will not make you a mind-reader or give you power over people by being able to analyze their deepest-hidden thoughts. What a person's body language will do, though, is speak to your subconscious—and that is why it is such a powerful communication.

Non-verbal communication skills help you to be a people's person

In the world of business, you need to have command on both your verbal and non-verbal communication skills. In today's increasingly, competitive business environment, professional touch is expected in any work that we do and more so in the area of customer care where polished communication skills are expected.

The high speed at which you need to adapt your body skills to the demands of customers can be sometimes challenging, but that is where a person skilled in the art of combining the vocal and visual skills with the verbal can attend to customers satisfactorily. The head nod is as important as the eye contact. Listening has to be established with eyes, ears and the mind. Even if a customer appears to be demanding, negative emotions cannot overtake the positive ones of care and genuine concern. The customer's bubble burst can be a serious issue. As Judi James says,

> Even in this electronic age it still holds true that when prices and products become less diverse, it's people skills that create success and failure of a business.

SUMMARY

What we have studied in this chapter is that in order to be good in one's work at workplace, it is important to pay attention to our multiple mediums of communication. That our body has multiple channels that we can successfully use to communicate our thoughts must be utilized fully. We need to develop proficiency in understanding our own gesture clusters and also interpret the gesture clusters of others so that our interpersonal relationships and communication do not suffer. We know that today's demanding workplace depends on how we sensitively scan the environment and adapt ourselves to work without causing disruption or breakdowns. Good verbal and non-verbal communication skills are assets and we must capitalize on them.

TEST YOURSELF: ONLY ONE OPTION IS CORRECT. TICK IT. DO IT YOURSELF.

1. **Non-verbal Communication means:**
   (a) Absence of verbs in our communication
   (b) Presence of action in our communication
   (c) Communicating through body movements

2. **The adage 'Actions speak louder than words' means:**
   (a) Actions are more important than words.
   (b) Actions are like words we speak.
   (c) Body language has a greater impact than words.

3. **Match the pairs:**
   (a) Kinesics   • Science of the movement of our eyes
   (b) Occulesics   • Science of space
   (c) Paralinguistics   • Concept of time
   (d) Proxemics   • Language of touch
   (e) Artifactics   • Pitch, tone, modulation
   (f) Chronemics   • Postures, gestures, head nods, etc.
   (g) Tactilics   • Appearance, clothing, personal objects

4. **The expression 'gesture clusters' means:**
   (a) A universe of people
   (b) A combination of different body gestures
   (c) Gestures that are clustered

5. **Match the following pairs**
   (a) Open palms   • Indicate defensiveness
   (b) Crossed arms   • Indicate superiority
   (c) Mouth guards   • Indicate evaluation
   (d) Tilted head, hand under chin   • Indicate suspicion
   (e) Steepled fingers, feet up on the desk   • Indicate openness
   (f) Tapping fingers, shifting body weight   • Indicate nervousness
   (g) Broad smile, wide eyes   • Indicate enthusiasm

6. **Which of the following dimensions refer to the human body and its appearance? Tick them.**
   (a) Posture   (g) Gestures
   (b) Volume   (h) Touch
   (c) Space   (i) Seating Arrangement
   (d) Height   (j) Tone
   (e) Dress   (k) Rate
   (f) Interior décor   (l) Pitch

7. Which of the following dimensions refer to the human voice? Tick them.

(a) Modulation   (e) Pitch
(b) Intonation   (f) Time
(c) Handshake   (g) Volume
(d) Posture   (h) Articulation

8. The term NLP stands for:

(a) Neural-Language Processing
(b) Neuro-Linguistic Programming
(c) Non-Linear Programming

9. Establish the relationship between the matter in the left column with the matter in the right column

(a) Matching   • To act of observing the behaviour of the person on the other side and match the same

(b) Mirroring   • The complete integration of matching, mirroring, and pacing

(c) Pacing   • The act of watching the non-verbal gestures of the other person

(d) Calibrating   • The manner in which you match and mirror

10. State true or false

(a) A speaker whose voice has tremors and may gulp and perspire could be concealing the truth.
(b) Hands interlocked at the crotch level indicate confident body language.
(c) Pointing index finger at someone is a negative behaviour and should be avoided.
(d) A person who shuffles feet, lick lips, and drum fingers could be a liar.

FURTHER READING

Alessandra, Tony and Phil Hunsaker, *Communicating at Work*, A Fireseide Book, Singapore, 1993.

Andreas, Steve and Charles Faulkner, *NLP: The new technology of achievement*, Nicholas Brealey Publishing, London, 1998.

Denny, Richard, *Communicate to Win*, Kogan Page, New Delhi, 2002.

Fast, Julius, *Body Language*, Pan Books, London, 1971.

Harris, Carol, *NLP: An introductory guide to the art and science of excellence*, Element, Victoria, 1999.

James, Judi, *Bodytalk: The skills of positive image*, Excel Books, New Delhi, 1996.

Knight, Sue, *NLP at Work: The difference that makes a difference in business*, Nicholas Brealey Publishing, London, 1998.

Lewis, Hedwig, *Body Language: A guide for professionals*, Response Books, New Delhi, 1998.

Nierenberg, G.I. and H.H. Calero, *How to Read a Person Like a Book*, Pocket Books, New York, 1975.

Quilliam, Susan, *Body Language Secrets: Successful social life*, Thorsons, London, 1996.

Ribbens, G. and R. Thompson, *Body Language in a Week*, Hodder and Stoughton, Oxford, 2000.

Wainwright, G.R., *Body Language*, Teach Yourself Books, London, 1985.

Part 4
Written Communication

CHAPTER

Written Communication

---

*The source of bad writing is the desire to be more
than a person of sense—to be thought a genius.
If people would only say what they have to say in
plain terms, how much more eloquent they would be.*

— SAMUEL TAYLOR COLERIDGE

We have already discussed about the principles that govern the use of words and sentences in oral and written communication. In this chapter we will continue with the study of effective written communication, considering the importance that it now finds among managers and top executives in business organizations. Top executives are reiterating the point that managers should be made to learn the functional importance of effective business writing. Persuasive letters are important. And so is the routine one, e.g. writing an application for leave, or explaining a situation that has gone wrong through a letter or a memo.

In business deals, precision of writing and clarity of meaning are extremely important. Time is a valuable factor and those who can save time through precise communication, will be able to use time as an asset for the organization. In the shortest possible time, the right kind of information can be passed on, thus restricting information overload. An organization that values time and values communication is bound to gain benefits out of their sagacious use of communication skills.

In 1979, *Fortune Magazine* interviewed many successful executives about what business schools should teach. Their question was: "What kind of academic program best prepares business school students to succeed in their careers?

The answer from the corporate executives was: *"Teach them to write better."*

Here are two letters from two 'B' school students who wrote them as a part of their class assignment. The letters prove, beyond any doubt, why business school students need to pay attention to their writing skills. Please note the errors in spelling, grammar, and organization of points, poor sense of courtesy, and correctness and completeness.

Example 1

January 12, 2007

To,

Customer Service Executive
XYZ Company
Mumbai

Dear Sir,

Subject: Delay in Payment of Mobile Bill

With reference to your Bill No. 1543 dated November 1, 2006, I would like to apologise for payment of bill.

I must genuinely thank you for being so patient and giving me the required reminders at the appropriate time. However, I could not pay up because I had certain out station commitment and could not find the necessary time to make the payment. I apologise for the same.

I would make the necessary payment by February 19, 2007, when I would be in Mumbai. Sorry to keep you and your company on a hold.

Thanking you for being so patient

Your's Sincerely

ABC

Example 2

To,

Mr. A Paul
Customer Service Executive
XYZ Company

January 12, 2007

Dear Sir,

Ref: Customer No. 12856

My mobile phone (number 1111111111) has been temporarily suspended due to non-payment of bill.

I have been a valued customer of your mobile service for the past 5 years. But unfortunately due to busy schedule, I have been unable to make the payment on the last month's bill on time.

I am extremely dependent on this mobile service for all my business activities. It would cause me a great deal of trouble if this mobile phone is disconnected.

I would request you to reactive my mobile connection with immediate effect. Be rest assured that I will be making the payment on the bill within 7 days.

With Regards,

ABC

A revision of the power of the seven C's of communication and several other uses of grammar will enable you further to understand how to use these words and sentences in business letters, memos, reports, resumes, cover letter and e-writing.

Penrose, Rasberry and Myers, in the first edition of their book, observed:

> We are drowning in a sea of letters, memos, report, printouts, and faxes. We stand corrected: We are now drowning in a sea of e-mail, voice mail, cell phone calls, and letters, memos, reports, printouts, and faxes.

The communication revolution has given rise to a business world that regales in storing massive data in small hard disk drives, reproduce information with high-speed copy machines, and transmit information to the whole world through e-mail and internet. Apparently, today's world is mesmerized by the magical power of information technology and the business world has gladly allowed itself to be loaded with the towering inferno information.

What today's competitive business organizations need is not words, information, or data storage, but precision of information, data, and also precision of thinking.

What has earlier been said is repeated here:

◆ Focus clearly on your message for **Clarity**
◆ Check all facts, including grammar and language, for **Correctness**
◆ Check all relevant data for **Completeness**
◆ Build and maintain goodwill through **Courtesy**
◆ Express and impress through **Conciseness**
◆ Avoid vagueness in expression through **Concreteness** of choice of words, phrases
◆ Maintain old business relationship and build new ones through **Consideration**

We have also studied that modern business English is not full of business jargons like 'your esteemed favour', 'for your kind perusal', 'at your earliest convenience', 'beg to inform', and such other old-fashioned expressions. It has also been discussed how commercialese or jargon makes writing heavy and impersonal. The language of business communication is not a different or a special language. It is the same language that all educated people use for clear understanding of a message. One does not need a vast vocabulary to write a good business letter/memo/report.

A few more aspects of business writing have also been included here to give an idea of the kind of attention to writing that is needed. Respect for the receiver of the message rules supreme in business writing. Words once written cannot be taken back. Words arranged well give rise to a positive tone in communication. Effective communication is about using various communication tools thoughtfully and wisely. Effective business writing is about using plain English. Business English is not 'gobbledygook.' Business writing has acquired a great deal of importance in recent times, and hence the need to know as much as is possible about nuances of effective communication. A few more such examples are given here:

Use of polite/courteous words or phrases helps build rapport and understanding with our listeners. Some of the words and phrases are:

• 'Please', 'Thank you'	'Would you *please* help me?'
'That was a *delicious* dinner!'	'*Could* you pass on this information to her?'
• 'The resort rates are pretty *attractive.*'	'*May* I request all of you to ask me questions at the end of the presentation?'
• 'The place has a *superb* ambience',	'You may *reconsider* your decision of resigning'
• '*Thank you* for a *pleasant* stay'	'Would you mind helping the student?'
• 'That was a *delightful* talk'	'I am *sorry* that I am not able to find that copy. Can you help me *please?*'

Action words. Being positive and pleasant by avoiding angry, rude and discriminating words always helps in bridging understanding. Rude words lead to a negative tone.

• I *appreciate* the hard work you have put in	You *tried very well* emphasizing that point
and not	*and not*
• Your work is sloppy in spite of the long hours you took to complete it.	Your explanation was garbled

Avoid camouflaged verbs (a verb used as a noun). It leads to loss of message. Message must be clear and less time consuming for the reader. A reader's time must not be wasted.

• Compulsory **attendance** effected a full auditorium
Rephrased
• The auditorium was full because everybody attended the programme.

Avoid clichés. Modern Business English does not use clichés or jargon. These are old fashioned expressions/phrases or overused expressions that sound stale and stilted. The use of *commercialese* or jargon makes writing heavy and impersonal. Business messages must be expressed naturally and not by resorting to stale expressions. There must be a personal touch to one's message. Some examples are given here:

Enclosed herewith please find	At your earliest convenience
Your esteemed favour	Beg to inform
For your kind perusal	Yours in hand
Factor in	Thanking you in advance
In view of the fact	We beg to inform
The fact of the matter is	At this moment in time
As per our agreement	Level playing field
Pursuant to	The bottom line
A whole new ballgame	Drill down

Use simple, familiar, short words for big words. Short words are of great value in business communication. The reader enjoys the advantage of understanding the message quickly for taking a decision. The objective of business communication is to obtain a result. Words play a major role in this process. Short words do make a bigger impact; their readability index is very high.

Anticipate	= expect	Eliminate	= remove
Indication	= sign	Regulation	= rule
Subsequent	= later	Initiate	= start
Utilize	= use	Juncture	= point
Reiterate	= repeat	Articulate	= explain
Culmination	= end	Comprehensive	= total
Solicit	= request	Initiate	= begin
Gamut	= scope		

Use abbreviations, technical words and acronyms cautiously. The rise in information overload, the need to communicate faster, and meeting deadlines are forcing managers to resort to written mechanisms that would save their communication time. Hence, managers from every field of business such as accounting, production, marketing, information system, advertisement, and operations use technical language and abbreviations of their own. It is true that abbreviations of all kinds save a great deal of time, space, and help people to remember long and difficult names. However, the reason why one has to use them cautiously is that sometimes the receiver of your message may not understand all the abbreviations, including the technical language. This may lead to either miscommunication or loss of message and this loss could be vital. However, it is expected that important abbreviations are known by people in business. Some of the terms regularly used are:

Abbreviations
1. **NSE** (National Stock Exchange)
2. **BSE** (Bombay Stock Exchange)
3. **SEBI** (Securities and Exchange Board of India)
4. **NPA** (Non-Performing Asset)
5. **RBI** (Reserve Bank of India)
Business Terms
1. **Break-even point** (neither profit is earned nor loss incurred)
2. **Amortization** (repayment of a loan by installments)
3. **Cold Call** (a visit without a prior appointment)
4. **Cartel** (a number of persons grouping together to monopolize)

Here is a piece that uses technical language heavily (Produced with permission):

> Realisibility of the funds advanced affects the profitability of banks. Banks always try to minimize their NPAs, either by being precautious in extending loans or by expediting recovery action of existing NPAs. Bank of XXX has given special emphasis to recovery of their outstanding dues under NPAs. The Bank has established branches for Asset Recovery in various zones. One of them is Asset Recovery Management Services (ARMS) Branch. These branches are directly governed by Asset Recovery Department (ARD) situated at the Head Office of the Bank. The Bank is giving utmost priority for reduction of NPAs. Suitable measures were initiated to augment recoveries and minimize slippages in order to reduce NPAs....

Words have personalities. Do not reduce the importance of the main word by adding extra words to the main word for emphasis. The extra words are redundant and hence are not necessary.

New innovation (all innovations are new)
Revert *back* (the preposition is not needed)
Proceed *further* (proceed means to go ahead)
Let's cooperate *together* (cooperate means to work together)
Future plans (plan refers to future)

Communicate without bias: Avoid all discriminatory words. People in today's world of multi-culturalism, gender-neutrality, and equal rights have developed an increased awareness of their self-respect. People have become sensitive about their race, ethnicity, religion, age, class, personal looks, intellectual ability, and factors that would hurt their esteem. Words therefore carelessly used in such an environment can offend people and hence lead to embarrassments, misunderstandings, and loss of goodwill. One has to remember that business demands a sense of professionalism and sophistication in the use of language. Business persons need to remind themselves of this unwritten rule of today's changing environment. Do not typecast people with disabilities/physical problems/diseases:

No	Yes
• Deaf	• Hearing impaired
• Blind	• Visually impaired
• Person short in height	• Vertically challenged
• Dumb	• Mute
• Persons with AIDS	• Those suffering from AIDS

Avoid sexist words

No	Yes
• Air hostess	• Flight attendant
• Chairman	• Chairperson
• Manpower	• Human resources
• Headmaster or headmistress	• Head
• Old people (above sixty)	• Senior citizens

Use short sentences. Maximum length is 17–20 words. Short sentences emphasize content and quick understanding of the message. Suzanne D. Sparks in her book, *The Manager's Guide to Business Writing* has given the following chart. The chart has been published in *Communication Briefings*.

• up to 8 words	– very easy—**90% readers reached**
• 11 words	– fairly easy—**86% readers reached**
• 17 words	– standard **75% readers reached**
• 21 words	– fairly difficult—**40% readers reached**
• 25 words	– difficult—**24% readers reached**
• 29 words and up	– very difficult—**4.5% readers reached**

A paragraph must have one topic/idea. Each paragraph should move an additional step toward the goal. The example cited below illustrates the point:

Seeking a Place in the Sun!

Idiomatically it means working toward a favourable position that allows scope for development. Professionally it means seeking recognition only through work like the whales do in Whale Done!

All businesses make a demand on the resourcefulness of the employees. The more creative, intellectually disciplined, hard-working and socially empathetic ones succeed in facing challenges. Today's competitive employment market is replacing the minimum acceptable employable skills with higher standards. And the higher standards that they are specifying are what they call "soft skills."

Soft skills refer to the cluster of personality traits, social graces, personal habits, cheerful nature, empathetic attitude, sensibility, and careful use of language. It also means absence of arrogance, cheating on others, manipulating to gain one's favour, self-glorification, and deriding others. Persons who rank higher in the cluster of positive skills are generally the people who are endowed with soft skills and whom most employers prefer to hire. Soft skills complement the hard skills, which are the technical requirements of a job. People need to be made aware of these skills, some of which may be latent in them, while others need to be aroused. Very often, the absence of simple courtesy-expressions like "please", "thank you", "excuse me" or "may I help you" or "I am sorry if I have hurt you" in daily interactions at workplace can sour relationships. People without such manners may get branded as lacking in finer qualities.

Why simple words should be used in business writing

Letters, memos, and reports are written to achieve desired business goals. They could be written for inviting quotations, enquiries for products or services, seeking appointment for potential customers, persuading customers and clients to accept a business proposal or buy a product, and generally maintaining good business relations with members of public.

For business writing, one needs to possess a clear and concise style of writing. One also has to adapt to the receiver's level of understanding a message. The receiver could be a layperson, a business person, or an expert. If you wish your message to be accepted and understood completely, then it is necessary to know what is **readability index**.

Readability index refers to the reader's ability to understand a message fairly well, not so well, very difficult to understand, and hence time consuming. In business, time is valuable, and no wonder, therefore, it is said "time is money". A long time spent on comprehending a message is equal to losing out on business opportunity elsewhere. Therefore, it is recommended that business messages must have a high rating on business comprehension.

Many managers seem to think that if they use big words in their communication, they will impress their clients and, therefore, have a better chance of obtaining business deals. This is far from the truth. What they do not realize is that they end up fogging their message, making their writing less effective.

Fog Index

Robert Gunning and Douglas Mueller in their book *How to Take the Fog out of Writing* have suggested the following steps that will help writers to remove the fog from their writing. A caring writer adapts the message to the reader's level of understanding.

1. Select a sample of your writing. Note the total number of words in the sample.
2. Divide the number of words in the sample by the number of sentences to arrive at the average sentence length.
3. Now count the number of words with three or more syllables in your sample. Do not count proper nouns (names), compound nouns (dark-haired, travel-agent, non-resident, short-term, long-term).
4. Do not also count verb forms that have three syllables because of a suffix (informed, hated, concerned, instructing, persuading, examines, encourages).
5. Now divide the number of long words by the number of words in your sample to get percentage of long words.
6. Now add the average length (from step 2) and the percentage of long words (from step 4), dropping the percentage sign.
7. Now multiply the sum by .4 to find your fog index.

Writing with a high fog index makes reading ability difficult. In business writing, it is therefore suggested that the fog index is kept low, which is fairly easy for the reader to grasp the meaning without much difficulty. Hence, alternating between 7 and 17 is a good way of striking a balance between short and medium length sentences.

In recent times, a lot has been said and written about the language used in business. New York-based Deloitte Consulting, for instance, sent a clear message to corporate America to **"cut out the bull"** (June 17, 2003, CNN *Moneyline with Lou Dobbs*). The authors, Fugere, Hardaway and Warshawsky, write:

... Business today is drowning in bullshit. We try to impress (or confuse) investors with inflated letters to shareholders. We punish customers with intrusive, hype-filled, self-aggrandizing product literature. We send elephantine progress reports to employees that shed less than two watts of light on the big issues or hard truths...Bull has become the language of business (pp. 1–2).

An example of a message that has more of esoteric stuff than factual truths is given by the authors to illustrate the point that a lot of business people use jargon to confuse buyers. The following example is self explanatory:

Platform Symphony™ is a leading enterprise-class software that distributes and virtualizes compute-intensive application services and processes across existing heterogeneous IT resources creating a shared, scalable, and fault-tolerant infrastructure, delivering faster, more reliable application performance while reducing cost.

In short, what we have learnt is that a business letter writer must avoid using big words and stiff, unnatural expressions. While big words only impress people and not express, stilted or stiff expressions make writing artificial and jaded.

We have also studied the requirements of language for using it as an effective medium of communication. Despite the phenomenal growth of communication technology, business people still depend a great deal on the use of the written form for transacting business. Buyers and sellers have to carry out their decisions of taking orders, fixing prices, making bargains, adjusting complaints, collecting overdue payments, sending proposals for future business developments, and above all, building good business relationship. Besides, the written form of business communication can never be replaced by the oral ones for the simple reason that they serve as records for future reference.

Apart from the grammar and punctuation requirements, that are a must for business communication, what is now required is your knowledge about

- ◆ Formatting business documents (letters, memo, reports)
- ◆ Strategic approaches to dealing with business communication, for example persuasive approach for unpleasant situations
- ◆ Miscellaneous letters for different business situations.

BASIC REQUIREMENTS OF A BUSINESS LETTER

Most business letters have the following basic parts:

1. Letterhead
2. Dateline

3. Inside Address
4. Reference Lines (Attention, Personal and Confidential, Subject)
5. Salutation
6. Body of the letter
7. Complimentary close
8. Signature
9. Stenographic Reference
10. Enclosures/Copies

Please note carefully the way the details are mentioned against each part of a letter:

1. Letterhead	Company's name & full address
2. Dateline	May 12, 2003 (American style)
	12 May 2003 (British style)
	In India, both styles are used. It depends on the organisation as to which style should be followed
3. Inside Address (with open punctuation)	Professor Wilfred John Senior Advisor Athens Institute of Management Studies 403, Empire Enclave Nariman Point Mumbai 400 001 (This is in Full Block Form. This form is generally used by all business organizations)
4. Reference Lines (Personal, Confidential, Attention)	(a) Personal & Confidential Ms. Aruna Nadkarni, Vice President Securities Department ABCD Bank, Nariman Point Mumbai 400 001
	(b) Human Resource Department XYX Company 123 Main Street J.P. Road, Andheri (W) Mumbai 400 058 *Attention:* Ms. Shreya Dalal Placement Manager

(c) Ms. Anita Deshmukh,
Manager
Blue Heaven Resort
Khandala Hills
Khandala, Maharashtra

Subject: Delivery of Kitchen Wares

5. *Salutation:* These are the courtesy-titles written before the addressee's name. The salutation is followed by a comma.

- Dear Mr. John Pinto
- Dear Ms. Karen D'sa
- Dear Sir/Madam
- Gentlemen/Sirs/Messrs/ Mesdames (company headed by women)

Often letter writers use a professional title like

- Dear Executive/Professor/ Manager

In a situation where the name of the receiver of the letter is confusing (that is, you do not know whether the receiver is a 'he' or 'she'), it is advisable to address the person by the first and the last name:

- Dear Candido Gonsalves
- Dear Sapan Mehra

6. *Body of the Letter:* Usually a business letter has three paragraphs:

- Para 1: Introduction of the matter (catch the reader's attention with a 'you' approach)
- Para 2: Expansion of the points mentioned in the first paragraph. (Show your interest and what service you can offer.)
- Para 3: Courteous end to the letter. (Show the action that would be beneficial to the reader. Stress the goodwill part.)

7. *Complimentary Close:*

(a) The preferred complimentary close today is "Yours sincerely", "Sincerely", "Yours truly".

	(b) Letter writers in India still continue to write "Yours faithfully" when the salutation is "Dear Sir/Madam".
Signature	The writer of the letter must sign in ink in the space between complimentary close and the typed name.
	Sometimes, you may have to sign for someone else or use a stamped signature. In such a case, ensure that you put your initials after the signature and on the same line.
Stenographic Reference	• These initials refer to • The typist • The person who is sending the letter
	The sender's initials are typed in all capital letters followed by a slash and the initials of the typist in lower case as • LS/ra
Enclosures or Copies	This appears one line space below the stenographic reference line. It can be indicated in the following manner: • Enclosure: (1) • Enclosures: 3. Copy of the appointment letter 4. Map of the location of the company

A survey of managers indicated that they would prefer to replace 'Yours faithfully' with 'Yours truly' or 'Yours sincerely' even when the salutation is 'Dear Sir/Madam'. The explanation given is that letter writers do not like to think of themselves as 'slaves'. Just as business jargon or clichés are not welcome in business writing, similarly, outdated patterns of closing a business letter must also change, they say. International business communication has brought about this shift in thinking and it is surely a welcome change!

An example of a business letter will give you an idea about the layout and the agreement between the parts of a business letter. These days most business letters are written in Full Block Format although other formats like Semi block and Modified block are also used. The advantages of using Full Block Format are that it is easy to use, there are no indentations involved, and all lines are flushed with the left margin. It saves a great deal of business time.

Example 3: *A business letter in full block form*

Venus Manufacturing Co. Ltd.
418, Grand Hotel Road, Prabhadevi, Mumbai 400 025
Maharashtra, India

January 12, 2007

Ms. Manisha Joshi, Graphic Designer
Colourful Printers
123, Highway Road, Goregaon (E)
Mumbai 400 063

Dear Ms. Joshi,

Thank you for sending the quote for the design of our brochure. I am pleased to inform you that we found your quote competitive and hence decided to accept your bid to carry out the design of our company brochure in three-colour combinations.

We would like you to submit the complete layout/design of the brochure by May 31, 2007, as our company directors would like to have a preliminary view of the brochure. We consider this assignment an important one and hence attach a great deal of value to its perfection.

This new business venture should be a rewarding experience for both of us. We look forward to working with you on similar assignments in future.

Yours sincerely,

REENA MEHTA
Corporate Manager

Example 4:   A memorandum

X Y Z Company (name of the company)

To: All Employees
From: Mike Mehta, Managing Director
Subject: Year End Bonus
Date: May 12, 2003

I am pleased to inform you that in appreciation of the spirited work that all of you have put in for the growth of the company during the year 2002, the management has decided to offer bonus to you all.

In less than a year, the profit of the company has increased by 40 per cent. This has also resulted in earning a good name in the eyes of the shareholders. The achievements of the company have been extensively covered by the national television and will also be telecast next month on June 12, from 8.00 pm to 9.00 pm.

Bonus will be calculated on the basis of employees' salary and period of service as indicated below:

Period of service:	Amount
5 years and above	Half of monthly salary
1 year to 4 years	One fourth of monthly salary

The management hopes that you will continue to excel in your work and contribute further to uphold the reputation of the company, which you have helped it gain. The bonus cheque will be issued this month along with the regular pay cheque.

The format of a memo is different from that of a letter. You can see the differences. The order in which the parts of a memo appear may differ from company to company, depending upon the in-house style. But the five parts remain constant. These as you must have noticed are

- Name of the company
- Sender's name
- To whom the message is sent
- Dateline
- Subjectline

Second to phone calls, memos, both in hard copy or e-mail transmissions, have emerged as the primary means of in-house communication in most business houses today. They are used for almost all kinds of business requirements—information, clarification, reminder, and authorization etc. The everyday importance of memo/e-mails makes one realize the increased value of concise communication for fast reading and quick grasping. Therefore, no jargon, no clichés, no roundabout sentences!

Like business letters, memos/e-mails also have to follow rules of communication. Research on memo or e-mail writing indicates that both the forms are casually taken by managers. The common errors pointed out are:

◆ Garbled language
◆ Half-formed sentences
◆ Mistakes in spelling and grammar
◆ Poorly organized message
◆ Always sent in a hurry (poorly organized message)
◆ Poor proofreading

Arthur Bell and Dayle Smith in *Management Communication*, recommend the following tips for writing a good "in-house correspondence":

◆ Give in-house writing your best effort
◆ Exercise judgment in sending in-house communications
◆ Use positive language to produce positive results
◆ Use appropriate procedures for transmitting, routing, filing, initialing, and presenting in-house communications
◆ Send the whole message when you send a memo.

It is ironic that while letter writers are conscious of the fact that a business letter must avoid rude tone, negative words, long sentences, and other flaws of language, the same letter writers almost forget that in-house writing also has to follow the same rules.

Much as the importance of plain business English has been emphasized, one can hardly overlook the need to know the ethics of in-house writing.

While writing a memo/e-mail, it is imperative to use appropriate procedures for routing the memos. Good writing skills may get one noticed in your organization, but poor sense of discretion of language or channel, may mar a person's image. Courtesy demands that you make it a point to bring to the notice of your immediate superior that you wish to send your memo to a larger group within the company. At the same time, you need to guard against the careless approach in selecting words and tone in framing your message. Pressing the 'Send' key can be done in a jiffy, but irretrievable damage can occur in terms of hurt feelings and humiliations. Workplace ethics caution you against the use of the 'heat-of-the-moment' emotional comments. All responsible managers must understand this.

It is also customary to initial above your typed name. Initialing is important because the notation suggests that you have read over your own communication and have approved the typed copy.

A study of memo writing in a private firm indicated that memos were flying in all directions, with allegations and counter allegations flung at one another. Understandably, the firm got caught in a messy pool of employee-dissatisfaction and frustrations. The careless handling of this powerful medium of communication fanned the grapevine to become active. The situation became so bad that some neutral employees remarked that the memo writers had found a vent hole in the memos. Because the memos began to carry unpleasant messages or hate messages, the employees soon began to use the word 'infamous' for the memos that were being written in their organization.

Once you are clear about the basic format requirements/parts of a letter, a memo, and e-mail, you need to understand the mechanics of message composition. While the parts and the agreement between the parts of a letter/memo/e-mail, are essential components, the content of a business document is of great importance.

Mind Your E-mail and Memo Manners

1. Do not contribute to email overload
2. Keep messages short
3. Use short paragraphs
4. Limit each message to one subject area or purpose
5. Use a subject line
6. Proof read each message
7. Do not use all capital letters
8. Remember email is not private

This chapter will now focus on the strategies that must be used for dealing with routine and non-routine business messages. The strategies are common to e-mail messages/memo and letters.

ORGANIZING YOUR THOUGHTS: THE PROCESS OF WRITING FOR BUSINESS PURPOSE

Behind good writing lies the power of clear thinking. Writing becomes cluttered and is devoid of clarity of meaning when the thought process goes awry. Clear thinking leads to clear writing. Managers need to understand the importance of clear writing. We may summarize that the process of writing begins with:

- A clear purpose
- Who the reader is
- What is to be conveyed
- What is the scope
- What action/result is expected

Barbara Minto in the preface of her book *The Pyramid Principle*, writes,

> For the average business or professional writer, producing more literate memos and reports does not mean writing shorter sentences or choosing better words. Rather, it means formally separating the thinking process from the writing process, so that you complete your thinking before you begin to write. It is the order in which you present your thinking that makes your writing clear or unclear, and that you cause confusion in the reader's mind when you do not impose the proper order. Imposing the proper order means creating a comprehensive structure that identifies the major ideas and their flow, and organizes the minor ideas to support them.

The reader's limited time forces the writer to fulfil the demands of logic in thinking and organizing thoughts and hence she says: "the structure will always be pyramidal in shape, hence the Pyramid Principle." The following points need to be analysed by the writer before the process of writing starts.

1. **Clarity of purpose.** Ask yourself the following questions for determining your purpose:

   - Why am I writing this letter/memo/e-mail?
   - Is it an order that I expect? An explanation from my supplier? Is it an extension of payment date? Is it rejection of a request? Is it a denial of what your colleague may have stated in his/her memo? (Depending upon the nature of your work, frame suitable questions.)

2. **Know your audience.** Adapting yourself to your audience will help you to compose your message in a manner that will have a higher possibility of acceptance. It is important to know what motivates your reader. Most receivers of letters like being addressed by their professional titles. These days when there is fierce competition amongst the players, personal touch to communication is most essential. A little bit of extra effort in finding out the relevant details about target audience will enable you to frame message in a coherent manner.

3. **What is the scope of my letter/memo/e-mail? What do I convey?** Having established the purpose, you now need to be clear about what should be written and what should be left out. A routine, short letter does not need any elaboration. A letter of inquiry for service or product information should be brief and to the point.

   This may not be so with a letter where you have to reject goods because their quality is not satisfactory. You will have to gather your thoughts and arrange them in proper sequence for a clear communication.

   In the case of a sales letter, you need to adhere to a plan that will include all the steps for attracting the attention of the reader who may get converted into a prospective customer.

4. **What action do I want?** Ask yourself "Do I want an order?" "Do I want a favour?" "Do I want a job?" The more you research your subject, more focussed you will be on your specific need, and you will begin on a definite note. The picture should be clear and concrete in your mind. A good letter is like a necklace where the starting and the ending points meet.

Once you have processed your thoughts, the next stage is to put your thoughts into an order. Usually, a letter has three parts.

1. The opening paragraph
2. The middle or the body
3. The conclusion

All the three parts have separate functions to perform although they are connected to one another. As you read the explanation of the points, please refer to the previous letter and the memo and analyze them from the point of view of message composition.

The main function of the **opening paragraph** is to catch the reader's attention and evoke sufficient interest so that the entire letter is read at one glance. It is an opportunity that cannot be lost. All the tips given on communication skills of keeping writing concise, correct, courteous and coherent must be practised. If reading of the first paragraph does not arouse enough interest, the opening, understandably, needs a revision.

The **body** of the letter/memo is a continuation of the ideas included in the opening paragraph. The body must develop the ideas in order to cement a clear understanding. This needs to be done carefully with facts and data to support what has been earlier said. The style must be simple, to the point and concise. Long sentences or a roundabout way of saying would put the reader off. In such a case, the letter is sure to find a way into the dustbin. Readers do not like to be insulted with irrelevant information and circuitous manner of communication. The aim is to lead the reader gradually to the closing.

The **closing** is an indication of your ability to conclude on a clear note of what action you would like the reader to take. The action will depend upon the purpose indicated in the opening paragraph. If you have applied for a job, you might then ask for an opportunity to be given to you for an interview.

If you have supplied information about a specific service, you might ask whether you could be of further help. The end must also be as specific as the beginning. The reader has a better grasp of what you have indicated.

Here is a letter that you can study from these three angles

December 6, 2006

Dr. Francis D'souza
Associate Professor
Department of Management and Marketing
The University of Madhavpur
170 Red Street
Vadodara 390016
GUJARAT

Dear Dr. D'souza,

Doctoral Programme for Naresh Jhawar

Naresh Jhawar was a student of mine for an entire semester when he was pursuing his studies in Masters in Marketing Management at NIIM. In the course of my teaching the subject of "Effective Communication" for business executives, I discovered in him a perceptive mind that was prepared to understand the intricate factors that often make business unnecessarily complex.

His assignments included analyses of varied areas in sales, marketing, manufacturing and general administration with focus on communication barriers and solutions to these barriers. His grasp and insightful explanation of these factors added depth to his assignments. His proficiency in both written and oral skills of communication can be determined by his ability to express succinctly and clearly. I believe this kind of ability to write has a great research value.

He comes from a family that has valued education and the reason why he is so keen to pursue his doctoral programme.

I highly recommend him for the doctoral study at your institute. I think you will have an exceptional student who would be able to put into his research study his eighteen years of work experience.

With best regards

Yours sincerely,

T.D. Prasad
Professor of Business Communication

STRATEGIES FOR WRITING BUSINESS LETTERS

Business writing is functional writing. As Paul Timm says, "The difference between literature and business writing is like the difference between culture and agriculture. In business we are concerned with the yield." The result or action is the yield. But the yield is not automatically produced. Efforts in the form of planning, organizing and executing ideas can lead to a fruitful yield. All business letters have one central idea—the 'big idea'. The other ideas are related to the central idea. The whole process of thinking revolves around the big idea.

In business, there are pleasant and unpleasant situations. Both need to be handled differently. There are two approaches followed in business writing:

- ◆ Direct approach
- ◆ Indirect approach

Direct Approach

All routine or pleasant messages begin directly on the note of the good news that has to be shared. **Timm calls this a BIF approach.** The acronym **BIF** stands for **Big Idea First**. If your reader expects a communication from you and if it is good news, then why not mention it right away? In such situations, "there should be no beating about the bush", says Timm. The big idea is the central idea of the message.

Steps to follow for a BIF approach

- Put the big idea first and let your reader know the purpose of your writing.
- The details should follow in the subsequent paragraph.
- Do not put unnecessary details in the letter. This will neutralize the effect of the good effect that has been created.
- Only select points should go into the letter.

Advantages of the use of BIF

- A direct approach saves the reader's valuable time. In India, where letters or resumes generally run into pages, and the style is circular in fashion, applying the BIF formula makes a good deal of sense.
- It helps the writer to focus on the central idea and organize the thoughts briefly. In a way, this helps the writer to be concise and to the point.
- The writer also experiences less of the 'writer's block' fear.
- This kind of approach works very well for all employee relations and public relations.

Disadvantages of the use of BIF

- Directness must not lead to curtness or insensitive way of communicating a message. '(We have received your letter and are happy to favour you with an order).'
- Directness does not mean that the writer alone enjoys the freedom of communicating a message the way she/he wants it. The message also has to be received without any confusion.

Example 5:   A BIF formula

Dear Ms. Joshi,

We are happy to inform you that our directors have approved the design and the lay-out that you submitted for our company brochure.

We now want you to submit in a week's time the design in a final form. We plan to give the design to our printer soon after you submit so that the printing work can begin immediately. Our new plant is starting on the 1st of June and we want to distribute a copy of the brochure to all our workers.

We expect to receive similar kind of quality work from you in future for all our publicity material.

Yours sincerely,

Is there any strategic approach to handling an unpleasant business situation? How does one say "No"?

Communication experts suggest indirectness for bad news and persuasive situations. The approach that Timm suggests is the formula of **BILL**. The acronym stands for **Big Idea a Little Later**.

All business letters have a big idea. If the big idea is emotionally sensitive or a negative one and if the writer feels that a direct reference to the idea will hurt the feelings or sentiments of the reader, then such a reference should be delayed a little bit. An immediate expression of a negative idea has the potential of ruining goodwill and future business prospects.

Timm says: "The effect of positioning the big idea a little later is to prepare the reader for action or conclusion you are requesting."

It is important to bear in mind that not all business letters convey information that the reader is anxious to know. Here is a non-business situation that needs to be understood:

For instance, thousands of students in India and abroad sit for the entrance examination for management courses in top business schools. It is well known that these preparations take a lot of time and money as well. There are always intelligent students and students who are mediocre and below average. But they all have stars in their eyes! They all aspire to get admitted to the best institutes and make it big in life!

When they await the results of their performance from various institutes, they all experience a very high level of anxiety and stress. And not all qualify to get into the institutes of their dream. A letter that simply, in a perfunctory manner, states that the student has not been selected because there were other better students, causes immense harm to their psyche.

The following letter is an example that illustrates an insensitive and anti-reader attitude of a premier management institute in the country.

Dear Mr...

We are sorry that you have *failed* in the personal interview and hence have not been selected for admission to ...

....
(Registrar)

I have known students who, on receiving such letters have psychologically and emotionally broken down. All they said to me was, "Ma'am, why can't they be a little gentle and considerate?"

A revised draft of the same letter may be as given in Example 6.

Example 6

Dear Mr./Ms. ...

Thank you for taking interest in our institute and deciding to pursue management education under the guidance of our illustrious professors.

This year we experienced an unprecedented rush for entrance examination. With limited number of seats, you can imagine how rigorous the selection process becomes for us at the institute. While you scored well in the written examination, the performance in personal interview pulled down your overall score. A little more preparation in this area will surely help you next time.

> Should you require any clarification, please direct your letter to Ms...of the administrative section.
>
> We encourage you to remain focussed and prepare well for management education.
>
> Best wishes
>
> Yours sincerely,
>
> (Registrar)

Note: A little touch of compassion and empathy can have such a strong counselling impact on millions of our students. Management institutes and organizations need to remember that an emotionally sensitive letter needs to have tact, as there is a human mind at the other end. The reader has feelings too!

Structure of a Letter Conveying Bad News: BILL

A typically bad news business letter could be about refusal of a favour, refusal of extension of time for delivery of goods, refusal of adjustment to a claim, complaint about poor service, warning a bank account holder about the closure of the account, etc.

In business, although readers might get used to receiving curt letters containing bad news, survey shows that readers welcome bad news conveyed at a later stage in the letter because it softens the impact of the news on their frayed nerves. Business always has its share of ups and downs, and a bit of that turbulence can get neutralized through strategic positioning of the main idea in a sensitive letter.

Strategy

1. **The opening paragraph must function as a buffer/ shock absorber paragraph**—the primary function is to psychologically prepare the reader. A polite sentence of 'thanks' or 'acknowledging the reader's interest in your organization' can act as a base. "This buffer is designed to get the reader into the rest of the letter and to avoid a premature turnoff before getting a chance to explain the reasoning behind the refusal. It should **cushion** the blow." **The opening should be neutral or vaguely positive.** (Timm) The letter should not begin abruptly.

2. **The buffer paragraph should naturally flow into the next paragraph with proper, reasoning—reasoning must be logical and courteously presented.** Now that you have drawn the reader's attention to this important paragraph of the letter, you need to organize your points in a clear and considerate manner. The 'you attitude' is an important factor. Sometimes bad news does not sound bad when it is presented in a factual, simple, and considerate manner, with the tone under control. If the reader is able to see the light of your reasoning, you stand to gain. You do not lose the goodwill or the credibility.

3. **The BAD NEWS has to be conveyed.** All that the reader expects is your explanation of the 'No'. This has to be carefully worded because an insincere/condescending tone might mitigate the good work you have done in the earlier two paragraphs. Stating the 'No' in active voice might put the onus on you and hence it is best to code the thought in passive voice. The doer of the action becomes less important than the thought itself. An important point that Timm underlines is that the writer, while giving explanation for the refusal, must not hide behind company policy. All policies are based on reasons and they need to be explained.

4. **The letter must end on the note of Goodwill—the end must be an optimistic one.** Having explained with the support of facts and carefully chosen words so as not to hurt the feelings of your reader, you can end on a firm note. At the end of the letter if your reader is convinced why you have refused a favour, the reader is unlikely to feel hurt or get turned off.

This is an example of the BILL formula where the supplier declines to cancel a part of an order. He writes to the buyer thus:

Dear Mr. Doshi,

We received your letter of May 10 asking us to cancel a part of your order of February 12 for office stationery. You had indicated that you needed the items by end of May.

Making a request for cancellation at this late stage comes as a surprise to us. Our past records show that our services were appreciated by your organization each time you placed orders with us. It has always been our constant endeavour to see that our customers' needs are fulfilled. The items that you had ordered are nearing completion and will be ready in a week's time.

We generally listen to the requests of our regular customers. I regret, this time, it will not be possible for us to keep your request.

Had you made the request within the first week of placing orders with us, we would have considered your request for cancellation. In future, if you need to make changes in your order or cancel a part thereof, please do give us sufficient time to make necessary adjustments at our end. I do hope you understand why this time we have to hold you to your initial order.

Yours sincerely,

....

THE DEBATE OVER THE USE OF DIRECT/INDIRECT APPROACH FOR BAD/NEUTRAL MESSAGE

People are sensitive to the way words are used in negative situations. A rejection/refusal/cancellation can always mean changes in business patterns, and not always such situations are liked by business people.

Communication analysts provide us with different approaches that the writers can adopt for the negative situations. Penrose, Rasberry and Myers comment, "A decision that is often difficult is whether to use a direct or indirect approach to carry information with negative content. ... Many people prefer all job rejection letters, contract denials, and negative information to follow an indirect order." Your challenge, then, is to find answers to these three questions:

1. Does this information or occasion justify a direct approach?
2. Does this person prefer a direct approach?
3. Is this a routine message, one that is "business as usual?"

In Chapter 8, we will study cross-cultural communication which details the characteristics of people from high- and low-context cultural countries. In the Western countries, yardsticks for measuring efficiency at work are accuracy, directness, no beating about the bush, clear communication, and not wasting anyone's time which is considered a valuable factor in business. Directness in communicating negative thoughts in business is accepted since the reader's time is saved. Once readers know why and where things have gone wrong, they can immediately take corrective measures. Therefore, the authors say: "If your answer to all three questions are 'yes', use the direct approach. If you are unsure of the answers, you are probably safest with the indirect approach."

In high-context cultural countries like India, the indirect approach dominates even when the letter is a routine one. The letter writer apparently enjoys the freedom of detailing the thoughts by building up the preliminary ideas but the question is whether the reader finds it rewarding. The big ideas in a 'good news' letter, as well as a 'bad news' letter, are hidden under unnecessary details. The indirect approach, of course, has to be used for all negative situations where it cushions the negative impact of the letter. However, in business, time cannot be wasted and therefore precision has to be practised well.

REPORT WRITING

One of the most challenging communication exercises that managers face at workplace, is to write reports. Virtually every aspect of a manager's job involves report writing, from meetings with clients/customers, employee grievances, monthly sales reports, annual reports, quarterly production reports and project reports, to extensive analysis of facts and figures that run into pages. Reports are a fact of life in today's business environment.

In the beginning, report writing may seem an overwhelming task. Gathering data, putting the matter in an order, making it clear and easily understood, demand attention during the entire thought process to enable the writer to put it in a formal report structure. The length of a report also may vary from a page or two to lengthy manuscripts as in the case of special project reports or government report. The whole process of writing a report can be a tiring experience but with practice and knowledge, one learns to deal with the vast body of data by separating it into parts for a well-written document. Report writing is a tenuous task. Whether managers like it or not, they simply have to get used to the habit of organizing data for writing a good report. Report writing is mandatory for a manager and the quicker it is learnt the better it is for the manager to be recognized by bosses. It is often said that promotions get blocked because of a manager's poor report writing skill. Good organizations pride themselves for taking logical and practical decisions based on sound reports.

What is a Report?

The British Association for Commercial and Industrial Education has defined a report as

> "... a document in which a given problem is examined for the purpose of conveying information and findings, putting forward ideas first and sometimes making recommendations."

A good business report has been defined as

- ◆ an orderly arrangement of factual information
- ◆ that is objective in nature
- ◆ that serves some business purpose.
- ◆ that is functional and aims at solving organizational problems.
- ◆ that is designed to give a complete picture of what has taken place at a distance from the reader who does not know about it but gathers knowledge about it from what the report writer writes in the report.
- ◆ that is logical, clear, and comprehensive.
- ◆ that gives information, helps the process of decision-making, and helps in clearing the jungle of information, and clear doubts.

Last but not the least, it has to serve some business purpose.

Features of a good business report. A good business report must be

- Factual (not imaginative). The words should enable the reader to visualize distinctly what has been written (use of concrete words).
- Objective (no personal opinion/no bias, no prejudice, no criticism, no gripes)
- Orderly/structured in a predetermined fashion
- Comprehensive (concise and complete)
- Detailed (all relevant information included)
- Logical (sequential)
- Clear (accuracy and clarity)
- Coherent (devoid of all clichés)

Types of Report

Reports are of different kinds. They depend upon the organization's business requirements. There are as many types of business reports as there are business situations. Broadly, they can be classified as

1. **Routine/Periodic/Progress reports.** These are the most common types of reports written at regular intervals. These may be weekly reports from the sales/production/ operations/customer service personnel. The reports facilitate monitoring of work and decision making.

2. **Informational reports.** These are reports that examine business situations/problems and provide factual information.

3. **Justification reports with recommendations.** Often managers have to justify a decision that arises out of the facts gathered and relevant to the problem. In such cases, managers offer recommendations based on the analysis and the interpretations.

4. **Situational reports.** Managers are also expected to submit reports about their office trips, conferences, and seminars to keep the organization informed about what they have gained from these activities. Such reports do not follow a formal order. Since they are informal in nature, letter/memo format is generally used.

5. **Feasibility reports.** All business projects may not appear profitable. Therefore, based on analysis and interpretation of cost, benefits, disadvantages, and future possibilities, managers have to point out whether it is feasible to proceed with the project.

6. **Research reports.** Research is the backbone of an organization. Decisions about growth depend so much on research that it has to be continuously carried out. Often, business houses commission research studies that must examine the real problem objectively and completely.

7. **Business plan/proposal.** These are persuasive reports that attempt to secure new business. They answer all the basic questions that the investor might want to know. The report writer must write convincingly.

How to Become a Good Report Writer?

Since report is a management tool, responsibility attached to report writing is immense. Report writing style is different from the style of writing business letters.

The following qualities are essential for a report writer:

1. Sound knowledge of English language and grammar
2. Ability to use intuition to probe into the vast body of data and gather relevant information

Business letter writing style	Business report writing style
• Business letter writing style is personal and informal.	• Report writing style is formal, detached, and impersonal.
• A personal touch to information establishes an instant rapport with the reader.	• There is no room for personal favours or subjective decisions.
• The letter writer enjoys the freedom to persuade the reader with favourable business propositions.	• The more factual and restrained the tone, the more believable the report.
• The business goodwill is a key factor.	• It is a clinical approach to writing which should be precise and coherent.

3. Good judgment of facts (ability to sieve facts from fiction, assumptions, biases)
4. Ability to write accurately, concisely, clearly, correctly, and simply (describe facts and place them in perspective)
5. Ability to think logically and objectively
6. Ability to perceive facts in totality and not in isolation

Good judgment on the credibility of the facts is of crucial importance in report writing. Reports are business documents and they can always be produced in a court of law. Therefore, it is of utmost importance for the writer to consider the legal implications of the report before it is finalized.

Reports can be written in

◆ Letter format
◆ Memo format
◆ Formal/Manuscript format

Constructing a Long Formal Report

Formal reports are usually long and hence they have several parts. The parts can be divided into four sections:

SECTION I

The Prefatory Parts
• *The Title Fly* (only the title). This is only far formality. It appears again on the following page. The title should be carefully worded. At one glance, the reader should know what the report covers. A good title answers the five W's (what, why, who, when and where).

EXAMPLE: A Survey of Cellular Phones: Market Potential in Mumbai.

- *Title Page* (The title, the receiver's name, The writer's name, date)

A Survey of Cellular Phones: Market Potential in Mumbai

Prepared for
Tentron Telecom Ltd
April 22, 2001
Presented by
Masseh Khatib and Pankaj Jha

- *Letter of authorization.* The person who has authorized the research and has asked for the report to be submitted should write the letter. The letter should mention the purpose.
- *Letter of transmittal.* It is a different letter from the letter of authorization, and is addressed to the audience/reader of the report.
- *Table of contents.* It gives the report outline and lists all the topics and material used for the report. It mentions the topics against the page numbers. It is easy for the reader to find out the relevant page(s) for quick reference.
- *Executive summary.* Also called synopsis, it is a report in a miniature form. The summary gives a concise overview of the report. It is generally one page in length.

SECTION II

The Body of the Report

Introduction. The report writer must mention

- Why the report has been authorized
- What is the purpose/the goal/the objective of the report
- What is the scope of the report, i.e. the boundary within which the research has been carried out (economic segment of population, geographical boundary, etc),
- What are the limitations (obstacles faced by the reporter; for example, some crucial information from an organization is not available)
- Which are the sources for data gathering
- Methods of collecting data (secondary and primary research)
- Explanations/definitions of terms/usages.

It must also give a brief description of the organization of the report material. As in all forms of writing, the introduction should arouse interest in the reader.

Main text. This part includes:

- All the details of the report—a comprehensive analysis of the data examined. In fact, this is the soul and the heart of the report. All the hard work that the reporter has put into the work, culminates in this part of the report.
- This contains charts, graphs, and illustrations, in support of the written explanation.

The main matter is divided into separate parts and appears under sub-headings for clear understanding of the analysis offered.

Conclusion:

This is another important part of the report. Very often, busy executives, having limited time at their disposal, head straight for the conclusion to know what the end result of the data is. They are eager to know the indications/directions that the report offers. Hence, it is very important that

- the conclusion is written clearly, concisely, correctly, and completely.
- one keeps to the authenticity of the logical conclusions drawn. For example, "Masseh and Pankaj have concluded in their report that there is an overdependence on MNC segments for business communication systems".

Recommendation

- It is included only when it forms a part of the report.
- Often there are reports where this may not be a required part.
- But most often, the authorizer would be interested in the recommendations.
- They may be interested in knowing how the conclusion can lead to suggestions or recommendations.

So the authorizer of the report may ask the reporter to recommend further steps for action, such as asking the question: "How can this report help in the expansion of the business communication system's market in Mumbai?"

Note: Informational/Descriptive reports usually end with a summary of the report.

SECTION III

Appended Parts

Generally, the appendix contains information that indirectly supports the report.

- These may be official letters from an organization, questionnaires and responses, charts/graphs
- They may not get included in the main body.

- The inclusion of the appended parts adds extra importance to the report.
- Many reporters prefer to incorporate the charts/graphs in the body of the report.
- Many get included in the appendix.
- Whatever it is, since the graphical representations of information is a primary means of communication with clients, inclusion of them in the body as well as the appendix of the report adds value to the report.

SECTION IV

Bibliography

A researcher refers to many sources for data gathering. These may be books, magazines, journals, and newspaper articles. The reporter also refers to other sources like the websites, talks, interviews, and seminars and conferences. This section lists all sources that have been used for the report.

The convention of listing the referred sources such as books, articles in magazines/journals, reports, etc. must be followed. Many researchers take up this part of report writing very casually. The authenticity of the work without a proper list of sources can be doubted. Such violation does not speak very well of the serious involvement of the reporter.

For books, the order or style, for example, is:

Lesikar, Raymond, V. and Pettit, John D., Jr., *Report Writing for Business*, 10th ed., Singapore, Irwin McGraw-Hill, 1998.

For articles in magazines/journals, the style generally followed is:

Robert V. Roosa, "Coping with Short Term International Money Flows", *The Banker*, London, September, 2001, p. 15.

Formal reports have a structured approach to report writing and can be quite expensive to produce. Reports can also be informal/semi-formal in style, which do not include all the parts of a formal report. They may be for a smaller readership.

All reports include graphs and charts. They are a composite part of a good report. These days a lot is heard in the business circle about the McKinsey way of presenting reports. Ethan Rasiel in his book speaks about the significance of graphs and charts that are followed at McKinsey. He writes,

> "McKinsey relies on charts or graphical representations of information as a primary means of communicating with its clients....The Firm uses charts as a means of expressing information in a readily understandable form. It adheres to the cardinal rule of **one message per chart**."

He emphasizes:

"The more complex a chart becomes, the less effective it is at conveying information. Use charts as a means of getting your message across, not as an art project."

RESUME WRITING

An important aspect of written communication that managers need to pay attention to is the way they compose their resumes.

Crafting good resumes for jobs is a skill that has to be learnt. All recruiting executives expect to scan well-written resumes. But most often what they get are pages after pages that contain irrelevant, fudged information about 'self.' A typical story of a human resource manager could be something like this:

Sandeep Gupta, the senior human resource manager of ABC Company, was a worried man that day. Last two days he and his colleague had to spend hours on scanning resumes of candidates before calling them for the interview. With every passing day, he worried about the onerous task of reading lengthy resumes! He simply shuddered at the thought of going through such an ordeal. Yet the job had to be done. He murmured in his mind 'why can't people be taught how to write resumes?'

He couldn't help thinking that way. Each time he attempted, he was full of expletives for the candidates. Puffery at its height! Impression! Each thought he/she was the best. He did not feel connected with the resumes he held in his hands. Thousands of words and not one that told him succinctly why the candidate thought he/she was suited for the job. He wanted the best and could not settle for the mediocre. Somewhere at the back of his mind he had that nagging feeling that some of them could perhaps be called for the interview but strictly going by their resumes, they seemed so confused and lacking in confidence and focus. He felt quite frustrated and hopeless too!

He kept rejecting the resumes, which he didn't like doing. But could he help? His company was going to invest in the candidates' training. Sandeep was a frustrated man that day!

What lessons can we draw from Sandeep's experience? At best we can ask, "What are the qualities of a good resume?" "How can I draw the human resource manager's attention?"

Here are a few tips that you can follow while constructing your resume:

- Your resume is a marketing tool. Market yourself well. "It is not an autobiography that chronicles all your experiences." (McDonald and Narang)
- A resume is an extension of your personality.
- A cluttered resume will replicate a cluttered personality in the mind of the scrutinizer.
- A resume is not an inventory of your qualifications.
- Communicate clearly and completely, without making it an assortment of your abilities/accomplishments.
- Choose only the relevant. Outdated information will not interest the evaluator.
- Eliminate accomplishments that are more than 5 years old.
- Your evaluator would like to know the latest and the best of your accomplishments.
- Hence, grab the attention in the top 1/3rd of the page as newspapers do.
- All redundancies must be omitted.
- The preferred length is one page
- The idea is to make your resume concise, and focused for a quick understanding of your knowledge and talent, and not disorganized, irrelevant, or vague.
- Keep it simple, and not fanciful or overdone, and crammed.

Parts to be Included in a Resume

1. **Your name followed by your full postal address** in a single-line-centred format as illustrated in the sample format. Don't include too many telephone lines in the address. That could send loud signals about your being overanxious to be called or noticed. It is always better to practice restraint and balance. The single line containing name and address saves a lot of space and looks neater. The space saved can be used for information about yourself.

2. **Two lines/sentences about career objective.** The objective must not be a paragraph. The career objective indicates the focus that you desire in making a good career. Examination of several resumes reveals the use of the pronoun 'I' in the career objective line. Please avoid this. The objective is more important than the 'I'. And do use action words/verbs. Lesikar says, *"Verbs are the strongest of all words. If you choose them well, they will do much to sell your ability to do work."*

3. **Education** must give the formal degrees/diplomas/ certificates that you have earned. The section also includes

the non-formal accomplishments like short courses/seminars and conferences that you have attended.

4. **Work experiences** must be specifically mentioned and elaborated and not fudged to make yourself appear a super-human. Most of the resumes examined show the kind of puffery that writers indulge in. This section must include

   (a) Company's/Employer's name

   (b) Exact employment dates—from the date of joining to the date of leaving the job. The recent job must get prominence in the resume. Employers want to know how you can be of use to them with your latest knowledge and experience.

   (c) Title of the job held—in what capacity did you execute responsibilities.

   (d) Job responsibilities must be specifically mentioned. Most resumes contain a list of items of various kinds of work that the candidate has done. This should be avoided. It is a meaningless way of writing about oneself. A list doesn't say anything about you specifically till you explain in few words how exactly you have contributed. What you write must convince the evaluator about your potential. A good resume always explains the job responsibilities.

5. **Personal details**—Apart from the details of job responsibilities that you mention, you must also include some data about yourself. Employers attach a great deal of importance to this column these days. The more emphasis is given to the emotional quotient of a person's nature these days, more is the need to know about the person's reading habits, social habits, personal development, awareness, and general interest.

6. **Professional membership**—Names of professional bodies give an idea about your interest in the work that various professional bodies keep doing. This column adds to your total personality as it emerges from your resume.

7. **Should references be included?**
   The trend today is not to include them. The two specific reasons for this are

   (a) They take away a lot of valuable space of resume that you can use for details about yourself

   (b) You can always give references at the time of interview.

In case the organization insists, take prior permission of the reasons whom you would like to include as references. That is a part of protocol that you have to observe.

Types of Resumé

Resumés can be written in different forms. The usual ones are

◆ Chronological/traditional resume
◆ Functional resume

The traditional or the chronological resume is formatted in the reverse chronological order, that is, you begin with the recent achievement first along with the date. Please note the details of the parts in the sample resume. This format is preferred when the candidate has had a steady career growth, and therefore would like to highlight the advantages of a successful career. It includes education, employment history, job titles, company names, and dates of employment. Here is the sample of a one-page resume of a candidate in a reverse chronological order:

Chronological Resume

JYOTI SRIVASTAVA

Greenfields, 1131 Wing 1B, Lokhandwala Complex, Andheri (W), Mumbai 400 053 · Tele: 26367891

Summary: Eight years of responsibilities in the HR area. Focused in the services sector.

Experience: XYZ Company as   1995–present
HR Manager

Responsible for recruiting and managing consulting staff of ten. Organized the entire recruitment process including the selection and hiring of consultants.

Additional Responsibilities:

• Coordinated with PR and advertising agencies
• Developed brochures for the industry and other corporate publicity material.

Experience: ABC Company   1994–1995
Manager, Administration
Responsible for managing the general office in northern India. Trained the staff of twenty for daily office administration and operations. In addition, set-up office policies for the functioning the entire set-up in northern India.

Education:	Excellent Institute Management, Chandigarh	
	Master in Business Administration	
	Specialization: HR	1994
	St. Xavier's College, Delhi	
	Bachelor of Arts (Economics)	1992

Functional Resumé

A candidate prefers to use the functional format when she/he has changed jobs quite often gathering work experiences or wishes to highlight challenges, handling problems, and showing results. A changing career, jumping from job to job, and returning to career after a gap make a candidate choose this format.

Here is a sample of a functional resume:

Functional Resumé

JYOTI SRIVASTAVA

Greenfields, 1131 Wing 1B, Lokhandwala Complex, Andheri (W),
Mumbai 400 053 • Tele: 26367891

Objective:	To take up challenges in the HR area of training, recruiting and leveraging on corporate relations for the business expansion of the company.
Recruitment:	As HR manager, at XYZ Company, (1995–present), recruited and managed consulting staff of ten. The work entailed organization of the entire recruitment process including the selection and hiring of consultants.
PR and Corporate Work:	Coordinated with PR and advertising agencies and developed brochures for the industry and other corporate publicity material.
Manager Administration:	Was responsible for managing the general office in northern India. Trained the staff of twenty for daily office administration and operations. In addition, set up office policies for the functioning of the entire setup in northern India.
Experience:	XYZ Company, (1995-present) HR Manager

	ABC Company, 1994–95	
	Manager, Administration	
Education:	Excellent Institute Management, Chandigarh	
	Master in Business Administration	
	Specialization: HR	1994
	St. Xavier's College, Mumbai	
	Bachelor of Arts (Economics)	1992

All resumes must be accompanied by a short cover letter. The purpose is to draw the evaluator's attention to your capabilities and the reasons why you have applied for the job.

A Cover Letter to Resumé:

JYOTI SRIVASTAVA

Greenfields, 1131 Wing 1B, Lokhandwala Complex,
Andheri (W), Mumbai 400 053 · Tele: 26367891

May 21, 2003

Miss Amrita Pande
Senior HR Executive
Blue Nile Ltd.
1365 Bandra–Kurla Complex
Mumbai 400 060

Dear Miss Pande,

It was wonderful to listen to you on "Consumers Expectations" at the Oberoi Hotel, on May 11, 2003. For young managers like us, with limited exposure to the market, your insightful tips meant a great deal to us.

I have been working for Alpine Interiors as a business analyst for the last three years. The work has been very enjoyable and a great learning experience. I have gained a lot in terms of understanding customer satisfaction and meeting their demands.

Unfortunately, the company is now contemplating a change in their business plan and may not continue in the interiors business for long. I am looking for a change. Your talk has inspired me to write to you and tell you that I am available for a marketing executive's post. I will be very happy if I could meet you for an interview on any day suitable to you. I would like to talk to you in person about my experiences.

My resume will provide you with the details of my educational background, interests and career goal. I shall look forward to receiving an encouraging reply from you

Yours sincerely,

Jyoti Srivastava

Miscellaneous Letters

Managers are also required to write letters of general interest to various target audience. These may be letters of 'thanks for an invitation that could not be accepted', 'inviting speaker to conference', 'hotel booking', 'requesting an appointment', and such other situations that are not directly related to business. A polite tone characterizes these letters. The social relevance of these letters makes them important. A manager's social image is important as the business one. Many times managers fail to connect with people at the social level. A courteous "No" and a pleasant "Yes" are very important for today's networking style for a growing business. Globalization also is exerting pressures on managers to be culturally more accommodative.

A few samples are provided here:

1. Letter declining invitation for a talk at a conference

Dear Ms Nazareth,

I am very pleased to receive your letter of May 20 inviting me to be the theme speaker at the education fair to be held at Hotel Oberoi on June 1, 2003.

I would have been more than happy to accept the invitation, for education is a very topic dear to my heart. Unfortunately, I have to attend another programme on the same day. I am therefore not in a position to accept your invitation. I am indeed very sorry for it.

Next time if you let me know well in advance, I shall most certainly accept your invitation. I wish you great success for your program.

Yours sincerely,

2. Letter of request for conference accommodation

Dear Mr. Dave,

Our company is planning to hold a two-day conference on Friday and Saturday, 23rd and 24th May, 2003, from 9.30 am to 5.30 pm. We are looking for a suitable centrally air-conditioned accommodation for

- 100 delegates
- Conference room with a theatre-style seating arrangement
- Space for displaying our promotional literature, instruments and accessories
- Screen for power point presentation
- A small reception area for welcoming delegates
- Break-time tea and coffee at 11.00 am
- A buffet lunch from 1.00 pm to 2.00 pm
- Afternoon tea and coffee from 3.45 pm to 4.15 pm

We will be happy if you let us know by the end of this week if the facilities we are looking for are available in your hotel. Please let us know the total cost for two days and if any concessions are available. We will also be happy if you could send us the menu for a buffet lunch.

We hope to hear from you soon.

Yours sincerely,

3. Letter of thanks after the event has taken place

Dear Ms Nazareth,

I must thank your organization for the wonderful arrangement made for the talk I delivered on May 23rd. I enjoyed sharing my thoughts with the managers.

Human resource development is my favourite subject that both excites and grabs the interest of the audience because of its relevance to their everyday lives. And I do look forward to present new ideas and practice on human resource management. However, next time, please let me know a little bit in advance so that I can schedule my other appointments accordingly.

Thank you very much once again. I wish your organization great success for all the developmental work that they are engaged in.

Yours sincerely,

SUMMARY

What you have learnt in this chapter is how to process your thoughts about pleasant messages as well as the unpleasant ones. While handling routine or pleasant messages do not put pressures on the reader by including irrelevant details, it is advisable to use the direct approach. Unpleasant messages require a great deal of tact and persuasiveness. These are difficult to handle. All managers have to master the technique of writing a 'bad news' letter by using the indirect approach. By doing so they will be able to keep the goodwill of the customers/clients/employees.

The two formulas mentioned are BIF and BILL that Timm wrote about in his book *Managerial Communication*. They both clearly explain the points that one has to remember for dealing with business and non-business partners/clients. The acronym BIF stands for 'Big Idea First' for all pleasant letters. Receivers of 'good news' letters expect to read the good news first. Hence it must be mentioned first. With the unpleasant ones, the big idea must presented a little later (BILL), and hence the need for the buffer para-graph in the beginning. The chapter also covers the importance of report writing, formatting job resumes, and other miscellaneous letters that managers must know how to write.

Advanced business communication demands tactful approach to writing business letters and other documents. Simplicity, courtesy, clarity, correctness, completeness, consideration, concreteness, and conciseness are the hallmarks of effective business communication.

Sloppy writing instantly reveals the sloppy mind.

— JAMES KILPATRICK

TEST YOURSELF: ONLY ONE OPTION IS CORRECT. TICK IT. DO IT YOURSELF.

1. Clarity in written communication is achieved by using
   - (a) exact words
   - (b) complicated words
   - (c) jargon and clichés

2. The expression 'Kindly favour us with a reply' should be redrafted as:
   - (a) 'Please reply...'
   - (b) 'I want you to reply...'
   - (c) 'You must reply...'

3. The expressions "man hours," "policeman", "fireman" are
   (a) Gender specific
   (b) Gender neutral
   (c) Non-gender

4. Use of active voice makes sentences
   (a) slow and stretched
   (b) dynamic and forceful
   (c) ambiguous and complicated

5. "I communicated the message to him" is in
   (a) active voice
   (b) passive voice
   (c) neutral voice

6. In business, we must
   (a) speak at the customer
   (b) speak to the customer
   (c) speak over the customer

7. The sentence "We will be pleased to deliver your order by the end of this week" is poorly drafted because the
   (a) customer is not so important to the writer
   (b) writer is more important than the customer
   (c) writer respects the customer

8. The tone of the sentence "Items desired should be checked on the enclosed form" is
   (a) rude
   (b) polite
   (c) threatening

9. All e-mail messages must be
   (a) short because they save bandwidth and cause less strain on the reader's eyes
   (b) long because sometimes situations demand long e-mails
   (c) both short and long

10. Tick the characteristics of effective business writing
    (a) Clear writing
    (b) Impossible to read quickly
    (c) Familiar words
    (d) Colourful tone
    (e) Ambiguity
    (f) Courteous and complete
    (g) Simple and plain language
    (h) Short, clear sentences
    (i) Concrete expressions
    (j) Jargon and big words

FURTHER READING

Baugh, L.S., M. Fryar, and D.A. Thomas, *How To Write First-Class Business Correspondence: the handbook for business writing*, Viva Books, Chennai, by arrangement with NTC Publishing Group, USA, 1999.

Bell, A.H. and D.M. Smith, *Management Communication*, John Wiley & Sons, Toronto, 1999.

Booher, Dianna, *E-Writing: 21st Century Tools for Effective Communication*, Pocket Books, Singapore, 2001.

Brittney, L., Sending e-mail and Writing Business Letters, Infinity Books, New Delhi, 2001.

Elgin, S.H., *Business Speak*, McGraw-Hill Inc., Toronto, 1995.

Fein, Richard, *Cover Letters*, Jaico Publishing House, Mumbai, 1999.

Gartside, L., Revised by S. Taylor, *Model Business Letters*, Pitman Publishing, London, 1996.

Guffey, M.E., *Business Communication: Process and product*, 3rd ed., South-Western College Publishing, Toronto, 2000.

Joseph, Albert, *Put It in Writing: Learn How to Write Clearly, Quickly and Persuasively*, McGraw-Hill, Toronto, 1998.

Lesikar, R.V., J.D. Jr. Pettit and Flatley, M.E., *Lesikar's Basic Business Communication*, 8th ed., Irwin McGraw-Hill, Toronto, 1999.

Locker, Kitty O., *Business Administrative Communication*, 5th ed., Irwin McGraw-Hill, Toronto, 2000.

McDonald, Sandy and S.K. Narang, *Writing the Perfect Resume/ Bio-Data*, BlueGrass Publishers, Haryana, 1998.

Minto, Barbara, *The Pyramid Principle: Logic in writing and thinking*, Pitman Publishing, London, 1987.

Penrose, J.M., R.W. Rasberry and R.H. Myers, *Advanced Business Communication*, 4th ed., Thomson South-Western, United States, 2001.

Raisel, Ethan M., *The McKinsey Way: Using the techniques of the world's top strategic consultants to help you and your business*, McGraw-Hill, Toronto, 1999.

Sparks, Suzanne D., *The Manager's Guide to Business Writing*, Tata McGraw-Hill, New Delhi, 2002.

Thill, J.V., C.L. Bovee, *Excellence in Business Communication*, 4th ed., Prentice-Hall Inc., Englewood Cliffs, New Jersey, 1999.

EXERCISES

Given below are some action words. You may keep adding to the list. Use them in your own sentences:

A Assent, applaud Advise, admit, Achieve, assert arrange, ascertain	**I** Invent, innovate Implement, imply Infer, inquire
B Believe, bail, beg, Benefit, bereave Begin,	**J** Jibe, judge, jail Join, jeer, juggle Jog
C construct, compose Complete, Consent, cheer	**K** Keep, know, knock Knead, knit, kill kick
D Do, deceive, debar Defend, defy, deprive	**L** Like, lessen, learn Last, lend, loan
E Endure, embrace encourage, express, Ensure, enthuse Expand, establish	**M** Manage, master Mediate, malign manipulate
F Forgive, found Formulate, forward Ferment, finance	**N** Negotiate, notice Number, nurture Nurse
G give, generate Garner, gamble Gauge,	**O** Organize, operate Observe, offend Omit, open, order
H Honour, head, Harass, have, hoard Hope	**P** Prepare, promise Persuade, plan participate
	Q Quote, quiz, quit Quiet, quip, quiver

R

Request, Regard
Record, receive
Reward, report

S

Succeed, share
Stimulate, serve
Support, schedule

T

Take, train,
transmit, target
Thank, titillate

U

Undertake, use
Undervalue,
utilize
underrate

V

vindicate, view
Verify, vouch,
vote
vulgarize

W

Write, wake, waive
Withhold, waffle
Waggle, work

X

x-ray

Y

Yawn, yelp, yeild

Z

Zoom, zone

Part 5

Communicating in a Multicultural World

CHAPTER 8

Communicating in a Multicultural World

Nothing is permanent except change.
— HERACLITUS (540–475 B.C.)

'Globalization', 'Global village', 'Multiculturalism', 'Cultural Diversity', 'Multicultural Communication', 'Multinational Organizations' and 'Global Competencies' are labels that are commonly used these days for businesses that transcend national and cultural borders. Never before have organizations joined forces to develop and deliver products on a worldwide basis like they have done during the last decades. It is as though a lightning has struck the business world. Companies from USA, Europe and East Asia have been expanding their markets by opening foreign subsidiaries in increasing numbers. General Motors Corp., Ford Motor Co., Toyota Motor Corp., General Electric Co., Royal Dutch/Shell Group, Hitachi Ltd., Siemens AG, Samsung, Pepsi, Sony, Coca-Cola, LG, Honda, Hyundai and many others are engaged in worldwide business expansions.

Indian companies such as the Tatas, the Aditya Birla Group, Reliance Industries, Asian Paints, Dr. Reddy's, Wipro, Infosys, Ranbaxy, BHEL, are all engaged in global operations. Multinational Corporations (MNCs) are dominating the world economy because business opportunities are aplenty in the new world and also the realization that talents which can sustain global businesses must come from the new multicultural world.

THE IDEA OF A GLOBAL WORLD

The new world is essentially a multicultural world that is inching towards an order that will have to embrace and absorb the cultural aspects of the diverse population from different religious, racial, linguistic, and ethnic backgrounds. The future business leaders will have to ensure that different cultural workforces are allowed to enjoy a free space to share their emotional reactions, aesthetic ideals, and religious beliefs within a broad framework of organizational culture and values.

The macro level, the society, from which the personnel is drawn, however, has to ensure that a free breathing space is given to people so that they grow with a sense of responsibility and dignity. Lawrence Harrison and Samuel Huntington in their book, *Culture Matters,* have succinctly captured this new ethos: "Imagine that in this world order various sanctioning mechanisms make it possible to enforce minimal rules of civility: exit visas are always available, and no aggression is permitted across territorial boundaries. Imagine that such a world system is set up to support decentralized control over cultural issues and hence to promote local cultural efflorescence ... this system would be two-tiered and operating at two levels—global and local—its personnel will belong to two castes."

According to the authors the cosmopolitan liberals will succeed in running global institutions because they are trained to appreciate cultural diversity. The non-liberals, on the other hand, separate themselves to form strong ethnic groups. Ultimately, the cosmopolitan liberals will form the global elite that will constitute the cosmopolitan culture of the new world system. In this new world system, the authors say, "your ancestry and skin colour will be far less important than your education, your values, and your travel plans."

The 21st century indeed has brought with it the challenges of a turbulent global market place where the key issue is to attract people, develop, retain and deploy them for sustained performance. Employees form the lifeblood of the truly global corporations of the future and today's managements must understand this sensitive point. The postmodernist world will have its chaos but the new cosmopolitan world will arise from this chaos to emerge as a single world that the Indian Vedas have already described as *Vasudhaiva Kutumbakam.*

How can communication help a world that is galloping its way to a well-connected and well-wired world? Can strategic use of human communication help address the cultural and linguistic perils of globalization?

THE COMMUNICATION DIMENSIONS OF MULTICULTURAL BUSINESS

Scholars, researchers and business consultants have been studying global developments of business from close quarters and many have expressed their views about the many ways globalization as a process has struck the world. The blitz of global changes in business patterns has taken its toll on the people who are serving or have served global organizations. Already we know about foreign companies that came to India but had to wind up their businesses because of absence of factors that were not conducive to global operations. A major part of delays in business decisions or failures is related to cultural and communication incompatibility or gaps or lack of training in understanding the nuances of a multicultural environment. Our values, beliefs, priorities, and style of functioning are shaped by the culture in which we grow up. Each culture is different from the other. If you have to do business successfully at a global level, as an expatriate manager or on short business trips, it is vital that you understand the local culture well enough to integrate with the people for a smooth business operation. This is not always very easy. Communicating in a global world is a challenging task!

The following incident happened to a very senior executive. The name of the executive and the names of the country and the foreign company have been withheld on request.

Example

Here is the experience of an Indian executive, who is the Marketing and Creative Director (fabrics and garments), from a well-known Indian organization, who went abroad on a small stint. He had a mission and that was to have an operational tie-up with an internationally famous fashion brand for export (of the brand) from India and also retailing the same within the country. He had a lot of task on his hands. Most importantly, he had to convince the people with whom he was expected to work why it would make sense to have an Indian operation in terms of business development, production and price competitiveness.

However, as days went by, things were far from being smooth and therefore didn't progress as expected. This very senior executive found it hard to put across his ideas to the marketing group in the company. He realized that mere product knowledge and functional skills were not enough for him to get into a fruitful discussion mode with the people he had to interact with. His ideas and specific proposals failed to elicit the required positive response. Every time he tried to explain his ideas in meetings, he experienced that he was in the 'discomfort zone.' He felt, he spoke to himself only with eyes that stared at him, faces that always looked like masks and a general feel of 'non-acceptance' that exuded from their body language.

It did not seem easy for him to break the ice. The executive realized that for business on foreign soil, one had to tune oneself more with the cultural intuitions and non-verbal cues of the people than merely loading oneself with hard knowledge of the product, supply chain, marketing, or retail management. He only wished that his company had oriented him to the culture of the country where he had to have continuous interactions with people of a different cultural background. Time was a crucial factor as with each passing day he was losing out on his business opportunities. He would have to do a lot of answering back in India!

What is it that you learn from this example? Shouldn't his company have realized that an expatriate executive/manager has a lot of alien issues to grapple with before he can show results?

IMPACT OF GLOBALIZATION ON ORGANIZATIONAL AND MULTICULTURAL COMMUNICATION

Globalization has brought in the challenges that a culturally complex world throws up. While it is accepted that information has to travel at the speed of thought, it is equally important to ensure that human communication travels not only fast but travels with accuracy and clarity. This challenge is experienced at both the levels of human communications in a multicultural business environment and within a growing organization.

Shuter and Wiseman argue that with the rapid pace of globalization, organizational communication has become more complex. Intercultural communication, interpersonal and small group factors in MNCs, including initial interaction, conflict communication, cultural issues, and non-verbal messages have emerged as key issues that need to be critically understood. Organizations are struggling to adapt their communication to global customers.

Companies that want to grow globally must build and maintain distinctive human resource in today's competitive, multi-cultural and technology-driven world. Unless organizations are able to combine vision and mission with the ability to inspire and lead people in a variety of organizational formations and cultures, they will cease to be a part of the globalization phenomenon.

For organizational communication to be effective, all MNCs must ensure the following:

1. All functional units are well coordinated ensuring that there is total interdependence.
2. All members actively communicate with one and all openly and clearly to ensure that breakdowns in communication do not occur.
3. A proper organization policy exists that will influence a healthy communication climate.
4. All members are trained to handle their organizational communication despite constraints or culture related problems.
5. All members are clear about clarity of tasks, organizational goals and expectations.

The model shows why it is essential for an organization to encourage, sustain, and promote a communication culture that will generate a healthy and cohesive pattern of organizational behaviour and understanding between its work-teams.

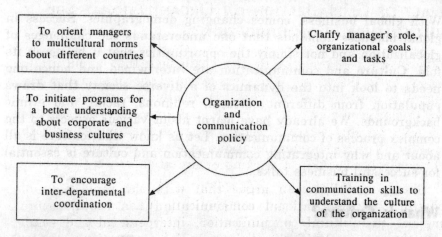

As business keeps growing, there is bound to be pressure or an organization. Complexities of globalization have triggered the realization that a more insightful knowledge is needed to understand the people dimension for both global business expansion and for a favourable working environment within an organization. Organizations, therefore, must be flexible and adaptable to the changing times.

Many researchers have expressed serious concern about the struggle of many firms with the concept of globalization, its interpretation, implementation, and impact on the everyday operations of companies and the lives of their managers. Most managers work in one industry, hone their skills to that industry, but have little time to look around for inspiration from others, or to rethink their own actions conceptually (Jean-Pierre Jeannet)

These are serious pointers that need to be addressed with a sense of concern. It is one thing to physically note that businesses are accelerating between developed and emerging economies and mega-mergers becoming a reality, but is an entirely different experience of the way the human process has to adapt and work. It has often been debated whether mergers and acquisitions actually merge people or it is only a physical process of merging companies on paper. Many have opined that mergers of two organizations are not necessarily the merger of two cultures. Globalization has a triggering effect on the need to create a harmonized environment so that the talents and the capabilities of people from different countries can be put to best use. It is, indeed, an overwhelming managerial challenge.

UNDERSTANDING CULTURE FOR GLOBAL COMMUNICATION

With global business, comes changing demographies. Success in global business demands that one understands the challenges of globalization and not simply the opportunities that it brings in its fold. Culture and communication are intertwined and hence one needs to look into the dynamics of a diverse society that draws population from different cultural, religious, racial, and ethnic backgrounds. We already have learnt about various aspects to the complex process of communication. Let us know what culture is all about and why integrating communication and culture is essential for successful business talks.

What is Culture?

Culture has been defined in many ways. The one commonly quoted is from anthropology:

Culture is a way of life of a group of people ... the stereotyped patterns of learning behaviour, which are passed on from one generation to the next through means of language and imitation (Barnouw*).

Culture has also been defined as *a set of values, beliefs, norms, customs, rules, and codes that influences people to identify and define themselves as a distinct group.* This process of identifying common habits and norms creates a strong sense of belonging in the minds of the members of the group. Cultural similarities attract people to one another. They create a bonding effect.

For your study on global communication, you need to understand the meanings of the three terms that are frequently used in the context of international business and communication.

1. **Intercultural communication.** It is defined as "the communication that takes place between people of different cultural backgrounds but living in the same country." In the course of regular interactions between these groups, patterns of behaviour and customs develop and take a concrete shape of culture and that, which comes to be associated with national communication and social behaviour.

2. **Multicultural communication.** When people from different cultural, ethnic, racial, and religious backgrounds, communicate with one another by making special adjustments to different cultural standards through tolerance and sensitivity, multicultural communication occurs.

3. **Cross-cultural communication.** In simple words, it can be defined as *miscommunication*. This happens when parties engaged in negotiations or any other form of communication are from different cultural backgrounds. More and more, people in organizations are facing the challenge of bridging cultural gaps in interpersonal relationships as cultural diversity in the workplace is increasing and as organizations are extending their global reach. The greater the difference between the cultures, greater is the risk of miscommunication. (Dalmer Fisher).

Business executives and students wishing to be dynamic and effective players in the global economy of the 21st century must acquaint themselves with the cultural parameters of different

---

*V. Barnouw, *Culture and Personality*, Chicago: Dorrsey Press, 1963, p. 4.

countries. Researchers have recorded their observations of cultural habits of people from different countries.

Sir John Banham, in his foreword to the book, *Globalization —The people dimension,* writes:

> The world is changing frighteningly fast. And, if we simply assume that the future is going to be like the past, we're going to be both surprised and disappointed. ... The organizations that are going to survive and prosper in this new world are those that understand better than anyone else—and better than their rivals—what's happening. They must also understand sooner than their rivals what's happening, and get ahead of the wave rather than getting buried by it.

AN EFFECTIVE COMMUNICATOR ALWAYS ADAPTS TO GLOBAL AUDIENCES

When you can present your own ideas clearly, specifically, visually, and most important, contextually—in the context of a deep understanding of another's paradigms and concerns— you significantly increase the credibility of your ideas ...

— STEPHEN R. COVEY

Knowledge about the cultures of the world becomes very handy in formal business communication as well as organizational communication, interpersonal communication and social communication, especially while entertaining business clients. Very often business decisions or deals are struck not in offices but over lunches and dinners. If you have some previous knowledge about the cultural traits of business clients, you may strike up conversations that can interest the client. People are sensitive about one's national culture. Integrating business with an understanding of culture gives executives a chance to place business situations in the right perspective.

The growth of multiculturalism is affecting the whole world, particularly the USA, UK, Canada, and now Australia. The immigrants from India, Hong Kong, Pakistan, Vietnam, China, and the Middle East and the Latin American countries have added to the diverse workforce. The more heterogeneous the workforce, more is the need to understand the cultural factors that can make a lot of difference to the working style of people in an organization. The challenges of cultural diversity at the workplace are exerting pressures on the workforce to understand the kind of behaviour that is accepted in an organization and the behaviour that is not welcome. An Indian is very different from his European counterpart or someone from a Far Eastern Asian country. Yet, when they are all working for the same organization, it is essential that they understand not only one another's cultural habits but also observe the cultural patterns or codes that an organization practices. Understanding cultural factors is a must for global communication.

In the context of global communication, the role of culture, however, must not be overgeneralized or evaluated as 'good' or 'bad'. People of different nationalities are bound to carry on themselves their cultural tags—good or bad. Cultural habits develop over a long period of time and may cause rigidity in the minds of people belonging to that culture. In global communication, one has to pay attention to the cultural factors of people with whom businesses are done.

Human beings express themselves through words and gestures and these can vary widely from country to country. Unless people are within one another's frame of reference for understanding a message, no communication can ever take place. Innumerable examples can be cited to illustrate how cultural habits get exposed subconsciously and cause either irritation to business clients from a different cultural background or substantial business loss. The following examples bring to the fore that cultural habits can become barriers in communicating a thought, for which one has to pay a price.

Caracas. An American manager is in a rush to close a deal for the products the Venezuelan government has already told his firm it wants. By refusing to take time to build good interpersonal rapport with a key minister, he loses what should have been a sure success. The price of his impatience: A sociable Swede gets the goods—$ 2 million in new business.

Tokyo. An American marketer enters a conference room expecting to begin superficial negotiations with the CEO. Instead, she faces a dozen department heads that want to know everything about her offer from A to Z. Unable to answer their minutely detailed questions, she loses face. The tab for being unprepared: A German with the facts on hand makes the $ 6 million sale.

Riyadh. An American exporter is trying to sell to a Saudi official. As the exporter sits back comfortably in his chair, he crosses his legs, exposing the sole of a shoe—an insult. He passes documents to the Arab with his left hand, which Muslims consider unclean. He refuses coffee, implying criticism of his host's hospitality. The cost of being a cultural klutz: A Korean, well versed in Arab culture, lands the $ 10 million contract (*The World Class Executive: Everything you need to know to do business around the world*, Neil Chesanow).

Mumbai. 1. An Indian IT firm is engaged in the long process of negotiation for selling its software to a Japanese firm. The Japanese firm insists that a full-length presentation be made, followed by extended talk before terms and conditions are mutually accepted. The young executive comes prepared for the presentation. He is enthusiastic about his presentation and dashes off a lot of data and information anticipating that his enthusiasm will be well received by the potential client and also be questioned on his data. At the end of the presentation, he is unable to understand whether his ideas have been appreciated or rejected. Obviously the gushing style of the Indian executive and the reticent style of the Japanese client were a mismatch.

2. A German garment-exporting firm on current business expansion plan in India is seriously considering the option of placing a final order with an Indian firm. The final stage of negotiation involved intense discussions over pricing, finish, colour, style, quantity and delivery date. Each time the German businessman indicated the specific requirements of his firm, the Indian businessman kept nodding his head from side to side giving an impression that he had understood everything and every detail that would be carried out and without any problem. At the end of the discussion when the German businessman sought reconfirmation of all the details, he discovered to his dismay that the 'nods' and the 'yes, yes' were no indication of what was actually understood by the Indian businessman. The German felt irritated at the end of the discussion. In a way, no discussion had actually taken place. It was a colossal waste of time.

The examples illustrate that, with increase in international trade and multinational corporations, the chances of interacting with people of different nationalities are not only on the rise but also make a demand that the cultural patterns of people with whom business interactions take place be respected and understood by parties involved in the whole process. Since the world population comprises people from widely social and cultural backgrounds, cross-cultural communication has emerged as a reality of a global communication. This is the greatest challenge that a global business faces. Verbal and non-verbal communication styles of people across the world are different.

ETIC AND EMIC APPROACHES TO CULTURE

An organization with a diverse workforce is a cultural mosaic of different patterns of behaviour. Scholars have observed that behaviour of people in organizations is influenced by their national culture. They have divided their study into two major areas: etic and emic approaches to organizations. The **etic approach** classifies culture on the basis of values and focuses on organizational behaviour. In contrast, the emic approach does not attempt to classify cultures on the basis of values; rather it draws conclusions about organizational dynamics by focusing on the communication styles of the people.

The **emic approach** has become increasingly popular in recent years because it offers insights into the cross-cultural aspects of organizational behaviour. If an organization has to be effective globally, it must develop effective internal and external communication. Multinational researchers must address issues that deal with ethnicity, national culture, corporate culture, organizational communication and how national culture influences the communication between organizations in different countries. (Shuter and Wiseman)

The emic approach helps us to understand that each person has his or her core beliefs that get expressed through *cultural display*. When we meet someone from another culture, we cannot be fully aware of his or her beliefs unless that person interacts. *Cultural display* helps us to get information in the sense that when we meet a person or persons in a meeting or social gathering, we can learn a lot about their national culture through our interaction over two or three minutes. We need to make certain observations: What are the topics that they are talking about? What are their business goals? How important is time to them? Do they talk to each other much? Do they greet each other? Do they shake hands, bow or touch each other? How much importance is attached to dress? Are they formal or informal? Do they show their feelings openly?" These are crucial observations for either a negotiation to take place or simply get into social business talks, points out Perkins. These non-verbal communication cues reveal a great deal of people's national and cultural habits.

In a multicultural working environment, the cultural displays make a great impact. We might either be pleased or be shocked by the cultural displays. For example, an American might be uncomfortable with an Indian, or a Japanese might find an American too aggressive, or an Englishman might think that Indians generally are loud speakers. It is a fact that Indians are habitual loud speakers and this has very often bewildered the westerners.

Here is an interesting observation in this context about British speakers and those from the Indian subcontinent living in London and communicating in English. Anthropological linguist John Gumperz and his colleagues found that their British conversational partners found the Asians to be angry in their talks when they weren't. The reason for this may be that their business-as-usual level of speaking is often louder than is typical for the British. The problem is exacerbated when an Indian speaker tries to get the floor. Whereas a typical British strategy for getting the floor is to repeat a sentence beginning until it is heard, the typical Asian way of getting the floor is to utter the sentence beginning in a louder voice. (Deborah Tannen—*That's not What I Meant*, p. 32).

HOW CAN WE OVERCOME CROSS-CULTURAL COMMUNICATION PROBLEMS?

People working in a multicultural environment must acquire new skills and knowledge about other cultures. The more sensitive a person becomes to the diverse cultural factors, more successful will the person be in getting into the right frame of reference for communicating ideas with people from the other culture.

The factors that generally cause cross-cultural communication problem, owing to lack of knowledge about the other culture, are:

- Social customs
- Values and beliefs
- Names and titles
- Sense of time
- Social conduct
- Language/speech for communication
- Non-verbal communication
- Exchanging business cards
- Raising a toast
- Being ethnocentric
- Believing in the stereotype

It is essential to know what intercultural researchers have said about contextuality as the main element for differentiating the communication behaviours of individuals of different cultures. Anthropologist Edward Hall identified two distinct ways in which people of different cultures express their messages.

- ◆ Low-context culture
- ◆ High-context culture

All countries that use language/words primarily to express thoughts, feelings, and ideas as logically as they can, belong to the *low-context cultural* group. To the people of these countries, the meaning of their message is in the words that they use. Verbal communication is of utmost importance to the people of these countries. A 'yes' is a yes, unlike it is in India where a mechanical head nod suggesting 'yes' can also mean 'no'. The countries that belong to the low-context cultures are mainly the countries from the western hemisphere. Mainstream communication pattern in the U.S., Great Britain and Canada, has more to do with words than with non-verbal cues as it is in the Asian countries.

The low-context culture

- Follows direct style of communication (don't beat around the bush).
- Relies heavily on straight talk and approach to a problem through plainly stated words (no use of ambiguous words).
- Uses explicit communication ('Yes' is respected).
- Is more aggressive/assertive in negotiations.
- Does not rely on the use of non-verbal methods of communication.
- Respects time (punctual).

Countries that belong to the *high-context culture* are all Middle East countries, Asian countries, including India, the Far Eastern countries, including Japan.

The high-context culture

- Follows indirect style of communication (beat around the bush).
- Relies heavily on subtle, indirect/contextual and non-verbal cues of a message.
- Avoids saying 'No' fearing that it might cause offence.
- Relies less on verbal/oral forms of communication.
- Interprets a verbal message in the total context of non-verbal delivery.
- Takes time lightly (not punctual).

NON-VERBAL COMMUNICATION

While we have the advantage of referring to the dictionary for checking the meaning of a word, we are unable to do so when we are confronted by non-verbal signals. In the context of multi-cultural communication, it becomes imperative that we train ourselves in decoding the non-verbal signs in a communication process.

Smiles, frowns, head nods, handshakes, keeping a visitor

waiting for long, who speaks to whom and from what distance—
are all cues that might indicate anger, frustration, irritation,
closeness and so on. In a multinational organization, the need to
know these cultural subtleties is felt all the more. An Indian
student may find it difficult to accept the racist attitude of a white
student. An American manager might think that our cultural
norms are too complex!

Refer to the chapter on non-verbal communication to understand how important it is to know the nuances and meanings of
eye contact, smiling, gestures, proxemics, chronemics and other
aspects of unspoken language.

Expatriate managers are now managing a large percentage of
global operations across the world. All such managers have to
make it possible to find a home by communicating within and
outside the organization with people all the time. It is a daily
reality for them. Think of Indian managers in the US and other
countries where competing with the language and cultural aspects
on a daily basis has become a necessary part of their job.

Pico Iyer in his travel book, *The Global Soul,* writes:

> For a global soul like me—for anyone born to several cultures—the
> challenge in the modern world is to find a city that speaks to as
> many of our homes as possible. The process of interacting with a
> place is little like the rite of a cocktail party, at which, upon being
> introduced to a stranger, we cast about to find a name, a place, a
> person we might have in common: a friend is someone who can
> bring as many of ourselves to the table as possible (p. 125).

As aspiring global managers, you need to make yourself
aware of the cultural determinants in different countries although
it must be remembered that one cannot achieve cultural
competence just by memorizing a list of characteristics about
different people from different countries. Multicultural competence
requires a positive attitude toward embracing cultural differences.
As Steven Covey says, "it is the amount of consideration we have
for the feelings of others."

How would you as a global manager fulfil your responsibilities
while communicating with people around? It is important to know
how to demonstrate your culture's positive characteristics without
practising ethnocentrism. A global soul has essentially to be one
who knows how to speak positively of the strengths of other
cultures. The global manager has to be one who has to have the
skills to bridge cultural gaps between people and thus become a
leader. The global manager must be one who knows how to
appreciate and accept differences.

OVERCOMING CULTURAL BARRIERS

The model depicted in Figure 8.1 demonstrates how a global manager can overcome cultural barriers and be an empathetic communicator:

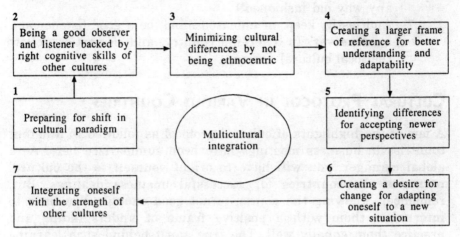

Figure 8.1 Model suggesting stages for multicultural integration.

To strike a sensitive chord with your business client from another culture, the following points should be kept in mind:

1. Know your own culture first—foreigners may ask you curious questions about social and cultural norms as followed in your country, e.g. they are eager to know why Indian women wear the red dot on their forehead and what is its cultural significance
2. Take interest in other cultures
3. Pay attention to the non-verbal cues of other cultures
4. Pay attention to how words are used in conversations, and the pitch, tone, and the grace with which you should utter your words. Use simple and common words. (Indians are generally perceived as racy speakers and Europeans find it very difficult to follow our speech)
5. At no cost must you make your business client feel that your country's culture is the best. Avoid being ethnocentric and judgmental. Every culture is as good as the other. Cultural habits develop over a period of time. Try to get into the frame of reference to understand another culture.
6. Practise flexibility in accepting a new way of looking at individuals—by doing this you will help yourself in not stereo-typing individuals. Try to look beyond cultural

stereotypes. Try to look beneath the surface for deeper knowledge. (An Indian woman executive may prefer the traditional sari to the western dress and yet be extremely efficient and knowledgeable in her work and business related matters. The traditional attire does not make her in any way old fashioned!)

7. And lastly, keep an unbiased mind, be a good listener and an observer. In a foreign country, and in parties, follow the local cultural norms.

CULTURAL PROTOCOL IN VARIOUS COUNTRIES

A few of the highlights of cultural protocol as followed in different countries in business meetings have been summarized here. As a global manager, you will have to orient yourself to the cultural norms of the countries for successful business dealings. But, remember, knowing the points, is not good enough. You have to internalize them with a positive frame of understanding and practice them equally well. The true spirit behind such learning should never be lost sight of.

When you are in **Japan**, make sure to:

1. Add the honorific 'san' to a person's last name as a sign of respect.
2. Use professional titles in place of actual names to acknowledge a person's status.
3. Never forget to bow in Japan. It is another important feature of the protocol. How low one should bow depends on the opposite person's rank and status.
4. Direct eye contact is not a part of Japanese business etiquette, although with modernization, things are changing.
5. Say 'hai' (yes) when listening to a speaker. It does not necessarily indicate agreement or confirmation of a deal. (The Japanese etiquette dictates that the listener should continually show that she/he is being attentive by saying 'hai', giving nods, or making affirmative sounds—very similar to what we do in India).
6. Avoid the American 'OK' sign as well as shrugging the shoulder or winking the eye. These are not welcome in Japan.
7. Apologize in order to show that you are ready to atone for not meeting the customer's expectations.
8. Use respectful language when speaking to a superior.

9. Learn to praise even if the work done is not up to the expected standard.
10. If you have to point out any faults in someone's work, use a third party to convey your point of view gently.
11. Observe silence to express your dissatisfaction.
12. Maintain close workplace proxemics.

When in **Australia**, it is to be remembered that Australians are very much like the British (culture and history) and many characteristics that we find in Britain are commonly observed in Australia as well. Yet, with its history of convict heritage and proud Aborigines, Australia has a spirit of its own that can be very infectious, because the Australians

1. Observe punctuality.
2. Use the direct style of communication like it is done in the Western countries.
3. Exchange business cards and greet people by shaking hands.
4. Remember to avoid sensitive issues like the status of the aboriginals, religion, and racism.
5. Respect their pioneering spirit.
6. Respect their healthy defiance of authority but also respect their hardy and friendly nature.
7. Respect their open mind to accepting other cultures.

In **Brazil**, one has to observe the following norms:

1. When meeting people for the first time, address them as Senhor/Senhora or Senhorita.
2. Make it a point to greet people by shaking hands in business meetings.
3. Although time tends to be a little flexible, punctuality is appreciated.
4. As in India, the presence of VIPs in meetings must be acknowledged by greeting the person. It is customary to do so.
5. All sensitive issues like religion, minorities and poverty must be avoided.
6. Using Brazilian Portuguese in conversations is appreciated.

It is important to remember a few details about business protocol when in **China**. Like the Japanese, the Chinese are also very sensitive about non-verbal communication in business relations. One should therefore remember the following:

1. Address people by their professional titles like Professor, Doctor, Advocate, Director, and not simply addressing them as Mr. or Mrs. or Miss.
2. Exchange business cards very carefully. It is appreciated if the cards are printed on both the sides in English and Chinese.
3. When you exchange cards, respect the local feelings by holding the card with both hands with the Chinese side up and show interest by reading the card. Not reading a business card and directly placing it in the card case or mechanically on the table or putting it in the back pocket can be interpreted as a breach of protocol.
4. The Chinese business protocol is hierarchical in nature. The senior person always leads the delegation. Ensure that when you lead a delegation, you are at the head of the group entering the conference room.
5. Do not speak fast. Use short, simple, sentences free of jargon and take pauses to make sure that people are able to understand you.
6. Do not use exaggerated claims.
7. Gifts may be given after the negotiation has taken place. Specify that the gift is from the company. Present it to the leader of the negotiating team.
8. Like in India, VIPs are an important part of a business gathering and hence need to be greeted first.

The **French** passion for individual liberty is well-known and hence learn a bit of French if you wish to enjoy the flavour of the country and its people, their endless babble of animated discussion on art, politics, fashion, gourmet food, music, and literature.

Remember to

1. Avoid loud or aggressive colours like red or yellow. The French like formal, sober colours for business meets.
2. Like in India, as we use titles like 'Sriman' and 'Srimati' for men and women, in France use the titles 'Monsieur' and 'Madame.'
3. Get your business cards translated into French on the reverse side. Ensure that your degrees and designation feature on the French side of the card
4. Learning a few basic French words will be appreciated but be very gracious with pronunciation as the French are very sensitive about their language.
5. The French take up the negotiation or business discussion

as an intellectual exercise, hence be prepared with the logic of business details.

6. Respect punctuality although people in the South of France are more lenient with time.
7. Gift giving is a good practice, but exercise discretion. French business etiquette dictates that you don't include your business card with a gift.
8. Greeting VIPs at the beginning of your speech is not customary.
9. Avoid sensitive topics like different ethnic groups, strikes, and do not criticise Napoleon.
10. Avoid giving opinion about anything and everything as Indians are generally in the habit of doing so. This kind of behaviour is strongly resented. Also avoid making personal enquiries in conversations. You must know how to handle your introduction!

The **Germans** are very hard working people and, hence, they have a lot of respect for time. Therefore, when you are in **Germany**, do the following:

1. Keep time. Every minute matters! Therefore do not underestimate the importance of punctuality. It is a vital part of German business culture. They respect time and work which must result into productivity. Indians must keep this in mind when doing business with the Germans.
2. Make your appointments well in advance. Casually changing the appointment time and place is not appreciated.
3. You must keep in mind the country's festivals and the German vacation periods.
4. Formal manners and direct communication style are appreciated.
5. Women are treated as equals.
6. Gift giving is a part of German business etiquette but ensure that it is not misinterpreted.
7. German business culture is equally hierarchical and you must therefore know the professional titles of people you expect to meet
8. Avoid topics like racism and the Third Reich, but topics like soccer, cycling, skiing, tennis and hiking are always welcome.

For most Indians, being in **England**, especially in London, is like being in India. However, excepting for the English language that Indians have inherited from them, the similarities end there.

The British/English are very reserved people and this needs to be kept in mind.

1. Respect formal behaviour as too much of informal body language is not appreciated.
2. Respect time.
3. The English are very formal people and hence observe all the formal protocol like exchange of business cards, shaking hands, addressing people with their formal names and so forth.
4. The dress code must be formal. Wear sober colours and be well-dressed.
5. Greeting VIPs is customary as it is in India.
6. Unlike the Americans who are very fond of using the superlatives, the British prefer to use understatements and sprinkle their talk with witty remarks. If you go to England, keep in stock, a repertoire of jokes and humorous stories and anecdotes. You will be considered an asset. But you must be natural in using them. Also pay attention to their understatements. They can use irony and sarcasm clothed on humour as a weapon in expressing disagreement.
7. Since they are by nature very reserved, they have a genuine dislike for people who blow their own trumpet.
8. Avoid sensitive issues like the monarchy, racism and the European Union.
9. When you make your business presentation, don't be surprised if you find the audience very quiet and almost non-responsive. This does not mean that the audience is not making its own observations. They will note the good points as well as the weak points but may prefer to remain silent.
10. Refrain from giving unsolicited praise, as it may not be welcome!
11. Gift giving is a part of the British business protocol.

Switzerland, the paradise on earth and arguably the cleanest country in the whole world, follows business protocols which are as immaculate as they can be. One should remember to follow the following customs:

1. Observe punctuality, for time is sacred as it is in Germany!
2. Greeting by shaking hands, dress code and addressing people by their formal names are customary

3. Like all Westerners, the Swiss also have a direct style of communication and are formal in their behaviour.
4. The Swiss, like the British, are very reserved people and hence do not like loud talk or behaviour.
5. Avoid topics like bank accounts or secrecy of accounts. The Swiss are very sensitive about this topic.

The **United States of America,** the only superpower in the world today, is perceived as an aggressive, dominating nation but also as a generous and tolerant one. People from all over the world—from all continents and of all races have gone to USA and many have become US citizens, thus exhibiting its capacity to accept people from different cultures, traditions and moves.

◆ Americans are very informal people, and hence Time can be as inflexible as business handshakes, and greetings can be very casual. The spirit of free expressions does not tie them down to the rigidity of business protocol.
◆ Do not be surprised if business cards are not exchanged sometimes as religiously as they are done in other cultures.
◆ However, the communication pattern is direct and assertive. Direct eye contact conveys that you are sincere.
◆ The concept of 'time is money' spurs them to get to the point immediately.
◆ Americans tend to be ethnocentric, and hence very often they appear ignorant about other cultures. Do not be surprised if they are not aware of the value systems prevailing in other cultures.
◆ Their presentations are very lively and they have a penchant for using multimedia techniques.

In his fascinating book *Understanding Global Culture: a cross-cultural journey*, Martin Gannon uses the metaphor approach to understand the cultural characteristics of some countries. All countries have strong cultural factors. We need to understand them so that we can integrate ourselves better with the cultural tradition. The cultural peepholes are a great help!

A study of the low context cultures in Western countries indicates that organizations attach greater importance to the idea of specialist workers and promotions or advancement in careers are given solely on the strength of accomplishments. Since they belong to the low-context culture, their communication style is direct and transparent even to the extent that grievances and disputes are addressed in meetings and not in chambers as it is in Japan.

As task oriented people, they are naturally aggressive; more individualized in workspaces, have immediate layoffs and hence are subjected to insecurity. They use a great deal of written/print communication. Their negotiation style is direct, assertive, argumentative, individualistic, short, quick, and can be confrontational.

What about India?

It will be interesting to cast a glance at how India, as a country that belongs to the high-context culture, comes across as a business partner in a global context. With mergers and acquisitions taking place for the past couple of years, and many global operations well poised, it will be motivating to know something about India's emerging global image.

The business environment in India is fast changing. One is witnessing swift changes in a number of family owned businesses that are in the process of transforming their overall organizational functioning style in the wider perspective of international business. The Aditya Birla Group, Infosys, Wipro, Reliance, the Tatas, Ranbaxy, Larsen & Toubro, Asian Paints are some of the leading Indian organizations that have undergone a metamorphosis in their organizations and have made their presence felt internationally. Then there are professionally managed organizations like Hindustan Lever Limited (HLL), Glaxo, Smithkline, Beecham Limited, ABN Amro, Citi bank, American Express, Standard Chartered Bank, HSBC, Deutsch Bank, Proctor & Gamble, amongst others that have become major players in a competitive business environment in an expanding India.

Any transitional change is always a time consuming and, very often, a painful process. For a country of India's size and complexities, it is understandable that the transitional process is taking a long time. Too many obstacles plague the changing process. A healthy business environment is a culmination of sound governance and integration of political economic, social, educational, and cultural factors. India is still grappling to adjust with these changes. Managing these changes by transcending beyond competition, reinventing and restructuring, synergizing resources and by bringing people together is a stiff challenge that tomorrow's managers will have to face.

However, here are three extracts that have been reproduced to give you some idea about the problems that come up with the process of change. The examples illustrate the tenuous nature of the process of globalization and more so when it concerns people skills. Unless the people dimensions of the complicated process are finely understood, losses in business are bound to take place.

1. **Signed, sealed and ... failed—Mergers and acquisitions—the cultural perspective:**

   *It does not come as a surprise that almost 50 per cent of mergers and acquisitions (M&A) in the past ten years have failed to deliver the expected results, because a major factor behind this is the failure to take into account the cultural incompatibility of the two organizations coming together. Research shows that between one-third to half of the M&A fiascoes can be attributed to employee problems arising out of cultural issues. Time, energy and crores of rupees are spent by top management, financial analysts as well as management gurus and consultants before these monumental decisions are taken. Yet scant attention is paid to the cultural ramifications of integrating separate companies. Often, an attempt to evaluate cultural compatibility is not feasible, due to the hostile, sudden and sometimes secretive nature of the process. (**Business India**, 1998, October 5–18.)*

2. **India's globalization scores worse than Pak, Bangla:**

   *India has slipped on a scale of globalization in the past year, says a latest report by A.T. Kearney and Foreign Policy magazine, ranking even below its neighbours— Pakistan and Bangladesh. The globalization index measures economic, social, political and technological integration in 62 countries, representing 85 per cent of the world's population and more than 95 per cent of world's economic output.... (**Business Standard**, January, 2003: Corporate Bureau.)*

3. In a passionate article **"Understanding the Global Customer," Azim H. Premji, Chairman, Wipro,** writes:

   *Globalisation is a new word in the Indian business lexicon. But it has unleashed a wave of unprecedented competition... to service a Global Customer we must become a global company. The paradox of being a global company is meeting world-class expectations. (**Times of India**, January 26, 2000.)*

In its annual issue **ET 500, 2001**, there is a special mention about how human resource is emerging as a vital factor in improving business performance. Business journals, special business columns, seminars and conferences have also been highlighting the need for India to change with the global time.

In his comprehensive book on global business leadership, Robert Rosen fondly writes:

> India's chaotic surface and underlying calm and its rapidly growing culture of entrepreneurs embracing ancient rituals are all reflections of its richly diverse, enigmatic culture. This melting pot of castes, languages, regions, and faiths is full to the brim and has created a culture of modest self-reliance and trusteeship...India is a grand tapestry of castes, languages, regions, and faiths, all coexisting—sometimes peacefully, as Gandhi hoped, and sometimes not so peacefully....

Yet when foreigners come to India, they are fascinated by our varied cultural practices. They are awed by the fact that while India has high technology and software, a major part of India is still living in the age of bullock carts and religious differences!

It is against the backdrop of this realization that the following exercise is taken up to ascertain how business people from other countries generally view our protocol.

1. *Social customs—Namaste* is the traditional style of greeting people (like the other high-context cultures, for example Japan/Arabia, the Far Eastern Countries like Thailand, Malaysia, Indian customs are deep rooted in the country's cultural habits).

   In the business culture, while men greet another by shaking hands, women generally greet by folding hands as "namaste" or also by shaking hands.

2. *Sense of time*—very flexible.
3. *Communication*—the oral form is preferred one to written communication as is the practice in most high-context cultures. Written communication needs to improve.
4. *Communication style*—it is a combination of both. It is direct at the senior level but indirect at the mid and junior levels.
5. *Nonverbal communication*—as accompaniments to oral communication, they form a very vital part. Smiles head nods are instant accompaniments and these sometimes can send very confusing signals to foreign clients. Indians tend to be obsequious, with foreigners and hence smiles that accompany such behaviour may often puzzle the clients.)
6. *Exchanging business cards*—they are exchanged upon meeting.

7. *Raising a toast*—Indians are uncomfortable with this, as it does not form a part of the national culture. Unlike in Western countries, where a short speech is made, as a part of raising a toast, in India it is good enough to say "cheers".

8. Being ethnocentric—in some business circles, ethnocentrism prevails over the need to have a global outlook. With modernization having set in, the outlook is changing.

A top executive from a German firm is greeted in a traditional Indian way with garlands and *tilak*.

An illustration of how cultural integration can be done.

Expatriate Managers' Experiences in India

A few expatriate managers from Scotland and USA were interviewed for the purpose of gathering their observations and experiences of doing business in India. They were very candid in giving their opinions about the style of functioning of Indians at the top, the middle, and lower levels of the management hierarchy. Some of their observations are reproduced here to give an idea about our strong and weak areas. These observations have a great feed back value and hence we do need to take them seriously to improve our organizational and communication skills.

Indians are generally viewed as both generalist and specialist types of workers. In fact, the specialist types, they say, are not only knowledgeable in their field but they can even surpass their western counterparts. At the junior level, workers are task oriented and rely heavily on seniors for guidance.

One area where the Indians need to pay attention, they say, is their organizational skills of communication. They are "disjointed" to be precise. While they are more personal in their approach to work and hence are warm and amicable in their interpersonal relations, their organizational skills are far less formalized and systematic. The lack of structured approach to their work makes them less focussed and a bit chaotic. If, however, they realize this and improve their organizational skills of communication, they will have a distinct advantage over "westerners on the day-to-day business level."

About oral communication the expatriate manager from Scotland has something very specific to say:

> At junior levels, like-minded people thrive on the oral interaction with their colleagues for re-assurance that they are on the right track. I believe an area that needs work on, is allowing the more junior individual to be open and honest in their opinion... Westerners are encouraged to use their initiative and be active in giving opinion and suggestions.

In a typically family run business and the less professionally managed organizations, business protocol as well as organizational skills and relations are more traditional. These organizations have more of vertical downward communication, with less of vertical upward. With lines of communication vaguely defined, informal style of communication takes over the formal channels, and in the process, causes hindrance to daily functioning. These are the organizations where one often hears the refrain "the boss is always right".

Many scholars are engaged in an exhaustive study on cross-cultural communication from a global perspective. Terence Jackson's book, *International HRM—a cross-cultural approach,* provides interesting data about cultural issues. Specifically writing about culture and Indian Managers, he offers the following information:

Culture and Indian Managers

England's (1975) study of the personal value systems of over 2,500 managers in Australia, Japan, Korea, India and the USA supported an assumption that despite the value differences among managers in the five countries and value diversity within each country, there is a common pattern of translation of values into behaviours across the countries. While pragmatists have an economic and organizational competence orientation, moralists exhibit a humanistic and bureaucratic orientation.

The study reports the **percentage** of pragmatists:

Japan	USA	Korea	Australia	India
67	57	53	40	34

The degree of moralistic orientation (in percentage):

Korea	Japan	USA	Australia	India
9	10	30	40	4

The study also highlights the values associated with Indian managers. These include:

◆ A high degree of moralistic orientation
◆ A valuing of stable organizations with minimum of or steady change
◆ A valuing of status orientation
◆ Valuing a blend of organizational compliance and organizational competence.

The implications of such values to the management of people in Indian organizations could be the following:

◆ Indian managers are more responsive to the human and bureaucratic consequences of their actions.
◆ They are more influenced by positions and approaches which utilize philosophical and moral justifications.
◆ They are more responsive to internal rewards and controls.
◆ Because India has a large proportion of managers considered moral, change in managers is likely to be slower and more difficult.

Another study that Terence Jackson has mentioned in his book is about cross-cultural differences between American and Indian managers. The study was undertaken in the 1970s (Smith and Thomas 1972), and it has identified the following differences in the area of authority and influence. The observations are reproduced here to enhance your understanding about how communication patterns and perceptions are influenced by cultural factors:

Indian Managers	American Managers
◆ Indian managers at both middle and senior levels in organizations profess a belief in group-based, participative decision making, but have little faith in the capacity of workers for taking initiative and responsibility.	◆ American managers, on the other hand, place a relatively higher faith in the capacity of individuals to take responsibility and less faith in group-oriented participative decision making.
◆ In contrast to American managers, Indian managers favour labour and government intervention in the affairs of the organization.	
◆ Middle-level managers in India have a greater belief in change and are less conservative than their American counterparts at this level.	

With India's increasing presence on the global business map, it would be interesting to know what some experts on cultural studies have to say about Indian management style.

According to Hofstede (1980) data, Indian culture is relatively high on power distance, medium in collectivism (on the same level as Spain and Japan), medium in masculinity, and low on uncertainty avoidance (p. 213). Another study presented by Jackson is by Smith et al. (1996). According to them, "India is midway on their conservatism-egalitarian dimension, and towards loyal involvement rather than utilitarian involvement. (p. 213)

However, with swift changes taking place in the Indian boardroom and organizational culture, various steps are being undertaken to move towards making business more *customer-centric*.

Indian Management Responses to Liberalization

According to study by Khanna (1996, pp. 213–14), cited by Jackson in his book, *The trends in Indian management since liberalization* have been as follows:

- ◆ CEOs are aiming their internal and external processes directly at customer satisfaction.
- ◆ People are becoming the principal instruments in delivering service to the customer, particularly as the service industry grows in importance.
- ◆ Corporations are discovering that their core capabilities lie not in particular products or product categories, but in unique expertise.
- ◆ Successful techniques are focusing directly on people instead of technologies or processes, based on the principle that devising systems for getting the best out of people will automatically maximize corporate performance.
- ◆ Although previously top management of the company thought that the resources of the company were its finances and other material assets, in the changed economic environment, a corporation's of resources are increasingly seen to be its people or the human resources, not all of this can be codified in rule-books and manuals.

Recent research on the human resource management approach as adopted in India reveals that the preferred term is **HRD** (Human Resource Development). "HRD addresses the need to arrest deteriorating values by building up organizational and cultural strengths, broadening the philosophy of tolerance and sacrifice and displaying deep concern for people" (Rohmetra, cited by Jackson, p. 214).

As a humanistic concept, HRD places a high degree of importance on the dignity and respect of people and is based on a belief in the limitless potential of human beings. It stresses that people should not be treated as mere cogs in the wheel of production, but with respect. It proposes that human beings should be valued as human beings, independent of their contribution to corporate productivity or profit. The various underlying attitudes symbolizing respect for people's dignity, trust in their basic integrity and belief in their potential, should lead to the creation of a climate in companies where individuals find fulfillment in work and seek newer horizons for themselves and the enterprise. (Rohmetra, 1998, cited by Jackson, p. 214).

It is strongly believed that HRD practices in Indian companies attempt to blend Western and Eastern ideas and systems of people management. This concept of HRD (from Pareek and Rao, 1992), says Jackson, attempts to be more comprehensive and meaningful than the utilitarian concepts evolved in the Anglo-Saxon countries. It has come to denote a planned way of developing and multiplying competences, and the creation of an organizational climate that promotes the utilization and development of new competences. Culture building is seen as a part of its agenda. (TJ, pp. 212–14).

SUMMARY

Use Communication as a Strategic Tool

In order to succeed as a global manager in any kind of challenging business role and situation, it is absolutely essential to pay attention to your communication skills for successful multicultural business dealings by adapting yourself to the situation on hand without being ethnocentric.

When we communicate, through speech and body language, we convey our values to people and in the process impact them in some way. Through our use of language, our adoption of rituals and norms, we create a cultural ripple and a common ground for acceptance of ideas and suggestions. We may feel comfortable with westerners like the French, Italians and Americans because they communicate their ideas swiftly. Other nationalities, such as people from Holland and Japan may take time to do so. The model on multicultural integration illustrates how by being an empathetic listener we can create better understanding.

You will not be able to change and build trust unless you communicate consistently and honestly. For an aspiring global manager it is essential to be socially and culturally literate. In the words of Robert Rosen "Beware. And be ready." For a borderless economy in a multicultural world, you will have to communicate deeply, sensitively and strategically.

TEST YOURSELF: ONLY ONE OPTION IS CORRECT. TICK IT. DO IT YOURSELF.

1. When we say, "The multi-cultural world is a global world," it essentially means:
   (a) The globe that holds all the cultures of the world.
   (b) People from different religious, racial, linguistic, and ethnic backgrounds can live together.
   (c) A frightening world that is layered by too many cultures.

2. **A truly global leader is one who is by nature**
   (a) cosmopolitan
   (b) ethnocentric
   (c) rigid

3. **The main barriers to multicultural functioning in an MNC are:**
   (a) too many employees from different cultural backgrounds
   (b) different values, beliefs, norms and perceptions of employees shaped by their individual cultures
   (c) too many people communicating in diverse ways

4. **The only way by which MNCs can effectively function is by**
   (a) forcing them to communicate in an expected manner
   (b) coordinating all functional units must for interdependence supported by a well framed organizational communication policy
   (c) expecting employees to perform anyway

5. **Match the following:**

   (a) Culture · People living in the same country make special adjustments to different cultural standards.

   (b) Inter-cultural communication · When tolerance and sensitivity mark the communication and relationship patterns of employees.

   (c) Multi-cultural communication · In simple words, it can be defined as miscommunication.

   (d) Cross-cultural communication · A set of values, beliefs, norms, customs, rules, and codes that influence people to identify and define themselves as a distinct group.

6. **Of the three quotations given, which one focuses on global communication adaptability and who expressed it? Tick the right answer.**
   (a) "The world is changing frighteningly fast. And, if we simply assume that the future is going to be like the past, we're going to be both surprised and disappointed..."
   (b) "When you can present your own ideas clearly, specifically, visually, and most important, contextually—in

the context of a deep under tanding of another's paradigms and concerns—you ignificantly increase the
credibility of your ideas..."

(c) "Most managers work in one industry, hone their skills to
that industry, but have little time to look around for
inspiration from others, or to rethink their own actions
conceptually."

7. **The concept of 'culture display' refers to**

(a) display of cultural artifacts

(b) handshakes, language spoken, greetings, and social
etiquette

(c) colourful ethnic clothes.

8. **Tick the factors that cause cross-cultural problems:**

(a) Greeting people with a smile and a nod

(b) Positive values and beliefs

(c) Unclear speech and wrong use of words

(d) Being rude and indifferent

(e) Being aggressive

(f) Being courteous

(g) Correct social manners

(h) Correct social greeting

(i) Polite tone

(j) Being ethnocentric

9. **People from low-context cultural countries are known
by their preference for**

(a) direct style of communication or straight talk and value
for verbal communication

(b) indirect style of communication or roundabout style of
talk

(c) mixed style of communication.

10. **People from high context cultural countries are known
for their preference for**

(a) indirect style of communication and less reliance on
verbal form of communication

(b) direct style of communication and reliance on words

(c) mixed style of communication.

11. **Tick the factors that will help managers to overcome
cultural barriers**

(a) Know your own culture first.

(b) Ignore others' culture.

(c) Be ethnocentric.

(d) Take interest in other cultures.

(e) Practice flexibility.

(f) Keep an unbiased mind.

FURTHER READING

Barnouw, V., *Culture and Personality*, Dorsey Press, Chicago, 1963.

Czinkota, M.R., I.A. Ronkainen, and M.H. Moffet, *International Business*, 6th ed., Harcourt College Publishers, Tokyo, 2002.

(For Association of Indian Universities Mysore, Karnataka, February 26–28, 2001).

Gannon, J.M. and Associates, *Understanding Culture: Metaphorical journeys through 17 countries*, Sage Publications, New Delhi, 1994.

Glenn Morgan, Peer Hull Kristensen, Richard Whitley, *The Multinational Firm: Organizing across institutional and national divides*, Oxford University Press, Oxford.

Harrison, A., E. Dalkiran, and E. Elsey, *International Business*, Oxford University Press, Oxford, 2000.

Harrison, L.E. and S.P. Huntington, *Culture Matters: How values shape human progress*, Basic Books, New York, 2000.

Jackson, Terence, International HRM: a cross-cultural approach, Sage Publications, New Delhi, 2004.

Jean-Pierre Jeannet, *Managing with a Global Mindset*, Prentice-Hall, Amsterdam, 2000.

Kreps, L. Gary, *Organizational Communication*, 2nd ed., Longman, London, 1990.

Locker, O. Kitty, *Business and Administrative Communication*, 5th ed., Irwin McGraw-Hill, Toronto, 2000.

Mendenhall, M., Punnett B.J., and David Ricks, *Global Management*, Blackwell, Massachusetts, 1995.

Richard L. Wiseman and Robert Shuter, *Communicating in Multinational Organizations*, Sage Publications, New Delhi, 1994.

Robert Rosen, *Global Literacies, Lessons on Business Leadership and National Cultures*, Simon & Schuster, Singapore, 2000.

Robins, P. Stephen, *Business Today: The new world of business*, Harcourt College Publishers, Tokyo, 2001.

Singh, P. and Asha Bhandarker, *Winning the Corporate Olympiad: The renaissance paradigm*, Vikas Publishing House, New Delhi, 2002.

Sohan Modgil, Gajendra K. Verma, Kanka Mallick, and Celia Modgil, *Multi Cultural Education: The interminable debate*, The Falmer Press, Philadelphia, 1986.

Terrance Brake, *The Global Leader: Critical factors for creating the world class organization*, Irwin Professional Publishing, Singapore, 1997.

Timm, R. Paul, *Managerial Communication: A finger on the pulse*, Prentice-Hall Inc, Englewood Cliffs, New Jersey, 1986.

CHAPTER 9

Keeping Pace with a
Changing World: The PR Way

*Public relations practitioners should demonstrate a
systematic approach leading to measurable results.*
— KIRSTEN BERTH AND GARON SJOBERG

We have seen in the previous chapter how a global manager today
has to be mentally and culturally groomed for various international business situations, since complexities always arise in
businesses that are related to social and cultural norms of the
multicultural diverse groups that one interacts with. Very often
cultural differences can be frustrating because they need to be
understood in the right perspective and one needs a lot of patience
to do that. Business people from Asia-Pacific region, the Middle-
East countries, the Indian sub-continent, (from high-context
cultures), with their 'relationship' style do find it difficult to
transact with the direct style of people from Europe and America
(from low-context cultures) and vice versa.

Mergers, acquisitions and global expansions have also brought
along with them the related problems of downsizing, cost cutting,
and restructuring within organizations. These are human problems
and they need to be addressed as sensitively as organizations can.
No organization can continue to move on its rails without taking
into account the feelings of its employees. Along with the 'global

face' of an organization, equally important is the 'people's face'. The human aspect cannot be ignored. Intense business competitions have also put pressures on organizations to take up developmental activities as a part of their corporate social responsibility at community levels.

In the wake of the catastrophic Gujarat earthquake in 2001, we have seen how many Indian organizations came to the rescue of the beleaguered people of Gujarat. Reliance Industries Limited, ever since, has undertaken the responsibility to rehabilitate the whole town of Anjar. Late Shri Dhirubhai Ambani pledged Rs. 15 crore to alleviate the sufferings of the victims. The Chairman of the Tata Group, Mr. Ratan Tata urged all individual Tata companies to provide relief supplies and funds. The Essar Group Chairman, Shashi Ruia said: "We have large investments in Gujarat and deem it our duty to provide as much relief as possible during this crucial period...."

The public relations person handles a large part of such type of social welfare activities. The function of public relations is to mediate in changing circumstances as well as keep the stakeholders informed about the company's policies and business plans. As businesses keep growing and changing and as organizations match those changes, text-books and subject courses also have to keep pace with a changing business environment. Perspective development in management education is an important area of learning.

Many of you might decide to specialize in PR or Corporate communications. Even if not so, some knowledge about the basic functioning of PR and media management will help you to function as a better manager and leader. As a manager, you will not only interact with people within an organization, but also with customers, vendors, distributors, competitors, investors, journalists, government, and community representatives, or send information to them. And this could include your views about your competitor's products and services, the shelf life of products in superstores, or crises like the Gujarat earthquake and what your company is doing about it or give an interview to the media as the spokesperson of your organization.

What is important to note here is that every time you express your views about various situations, you are sending some message through the media to the outside world, not as an individual but as someone who represents your organization. You will have to manage the organization's reputation with the media and the various groups. Hence, every manager has to play the role of a good PR person while communicating with the outside world.

WHY PR?

The aim of public relation is to acquaint the managers with the concept of public relations and make them aware about the need to be a good PR person. In this age of growing importance of human relationships, especially for the satisfaction of personal and professional needs at the workplace, it is urgent that we build a culture of trust and inter-dependence by understanding our mutual needs, which is the philosophy of public relations. With today's competitive environment that is besieged by such metaphors as 'the rat race' and 'dog-eat-dog' compounded by self-proclaimed and self-glorifying eulogies, it is all the more pressing why we need to address complex issues arising out of a competitive and stressful business environment. The chapter is designed to give an idea about how the PR functions, and most importantly, how one should handle the media if one has to write either a press release, address a press conference, or interact informally with the internal publics.

The concept of public relations has emerged as the discipline of anticipating and interpreting public opinion and issues that shape the destiny of an organization. The power of PR is rooted in the basic belief that any meaningful enterprise in modern society can prosper or perish only on the basis of public opinion. The proper role, therefore, for PR, is not to be the mouthpiece but to project the values of an organization. It is not always easy to manage this role. Bringing about insight and understanding is quite an uphill task. The principles of public relations therefore would help one to understand the spirit and the philosophy of a very responsible task such as dealing with the outside world, and perform better as a business manager.

DEFINITIONS OF PR

Many definitions exist on public relations. Some of them are quoted here.

1. The British Institute of Public Relations (IPR) has defined PR as

   planned and sustained effort to establish and maintain goodwill and mutual understanding between an organization and its publics.

2. The World Assembly of Public Relations Associations in Mexico City (1978) defined PR as

   the art and social science of analyzing trends, predicting their consequences, counselling organizations leaders, and implementing planned programmers of action which will serve both the organization's and the public interest.

3. H. Frazier Moore, and R. Bertrand Canfield have defined PR as a

> social philosophy of management expressed in policies and practices which, through sensitive interpretation of events upon two-way communication with its publics, strives to secure mutual understanding and goodwill.

4. Webster's New Collegiate Dictionary defines PR as

> the business of inducing the public to have understanding for and general goodwill towards a person, firm, or institution.

You will see that all these definitions emphasize that public relations is a deliberate and continuous activity. The key words "planned" and "sustained" suggest that public relations, as an activity, is not automatic or effortless. It has to be initiated and maintained for goodwill toward its publics—both internal and external.

MISCONCEPTIONS ABOUT PR

PR as a concept of essential management function developed with industrialization, urbanization, and modernization. The more complex a corporate grew with a large body of shareholders, dealers, suppliers and members of community, more was the need to reach a collective face of these disparate groups of people. Because most business managers have little or no training in PR, it is generally understood as a publicity function. Some organizations, in fact, tend to put undue emphasis on the 'cosmetic communication' aspect of PR (being nice and sweet to people) in the belief that it would enhance their corporate communication. This is far from the truth of PR philosophy. PR is serious business. It must be clearly understood that PR is not

- ◆ propaganda and lobbying
- ◆ a mouthpiece of an organization
- ◆ a glamorous vocation.

For obvious reasons, PR became a pejorative word since it shifted away from the core objective of communicating truthfully to the larger audience.

THE REALITIES OF PUBLIC RELATIONS

Managers who have an embracing attitude to understand the

needs of the publics are the Renaissance people—in love with enlightening ideas that benefit the entire organization and the stakeholders. Such a manager does not project an image, rather builds an image that can withstand the test of time. Labelled as 'in-house activists', managers with PR principles make it their business to understand the environment of an organization so that they can practise what is secularly good. The power of PR is not in its ability to create only better images, but create a better organization itself. The PR manager is trained in the principles of truthful dissemination of information and this gives an opportunity to the receiver of the information to either enjoy it or reject it. But it is the bounden duty of the PR manager not to indulge in half-truths.

Newsom, Turk, and Kruckeberg in their book, *This is PR: The realities of public relations* have listed basic principles that managers can follow. As earlier said, as a manager you have certainly to face situations where a press release or a speech or a promotional matter has to be sent to the press for information to be passed on to the stakeholders. This is a responsible work because the perceptions by the publics must not be different from the real behaviour of the organization. Some of the principles are reproduced here.

1. PR deals with reality, not false fronts. (It deals with facts, not fiction).
2. PR is a service-oriented profession in which public interest, and not personal reward, should be the primary consideration.
3. PR practitioners must have the guts to say 'no' to a client or refuse a deceptive program.
4. Because the public relations practitioner reaches many publics through mass media, which are the public channels of communication, the integrity of these channels must be preserved. (PR practitioners should never lie to the news media, either outright or by implication.)
5. Because PR practitioners are in the middle between an organization and its publics, they must be effective communicators—conveying information back and forth until understanding is reached.
6. To expedite two-way communication and to be responsible communicators, public relations practitioners must use scientific public opinion research extensively. (PR cannot afford to be a guessing game).
7. To understand what their publics are saying and to reach them effectively, public relations practitioners must employ

the social sciences—psychology, sociology, social psychology, public opinion, communications study and semantics. (Intuition is not enough).

8. The PR field requires multidisciplinary applications.
9. Public relations practitioners are obligated to explain problems to the public before these problems become crises. (PR practitioners should alert and advise, so people won't be taken by surprise.)
10. A public relations practitioner should be measured by only one standard: ethical performance. (A PR practitioner is only as good as the reputation he or she deserves.)

Public relations, as a concept of effective management, has to be understood as a discipline that is concerned with the reputation of an organization and building understanding with all stakeholders. It is the result of what you do, what you say and what others say about you! It is a management function, an interactive process, about relationships with publics—both internal and external. A manager, during the course of his or her business dealings with customers and clients, will not be in a position to refrain from following the PR principles or sideline the demands that PR will make. It is imperative for a manager to be

- a people's person
- a good communicator
- socially sensitive
- experienced in using managerial skills
- conscious about the environment (inside and outside the organization)
- ethically strong
- possessing writing skills and the knowledge of media

These qualities will get reflected in his/her relations answers and responses to the media.

USE OF COMMUNICATION SKILLS FOR MEDIA AND PUBLIC RELATIONS

As a manager, you may be required to interact either with business groups or social groups for various purposes. Your knowledge about the process of communication with the vital factors involved—stimulus, motivation, frame of reference, encoding and decoding, the importance of message, the importance of choice of language, noises in the environment, feedback and how to overcome the noises—all will motivate you to fine-tune your communication skills for your day-to-day activities. However, while, a two-way process of communication happens to be transactional/interpersonal in nature, PR communication focuses on the end receiver, the 'mass' that may seem invisible but is not. PR communication is not a verbal exchange of thoughts between individuals who are visible. You have to make them visible by establishing the right kind of frame of reference through accurate and truthful communication.

Figure 9.1 illustrates how the target groups receive messages and how they send their feedback to the organization.

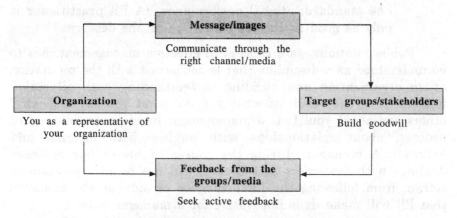

Figure 9.1   Corporate communication strategy model.

For someone who would like to specialize in PR, it would be essential to know all about:

- ◆   Corporate image and how to build it
- ◆   Qualities of a good PR plan
- ◆   Research in PR
- ◆   Target segmentation and message designing
- ◆   Media mix
- ◆   Budgeting

and also have prerequisite knowledge of media, and how to manage information through newsletter, bulletin boards, house journal, annual reports, and promotional kit for the internal publics.

The details of these requirements are not discussed here because the chapter only aims at the millennium manager who must know how to handle the media, feel comfortable while doing so, handle press conferences, write press releases and send relevant information to the media about the kind of work that the company has been doing, and the objectives of social development programs.

Most managers think that press relations/public relations are handled entirely by the company's PR department. Not all organizations have a PR department. In such a case, the manager has to learn how to deal with demands that the media make on them. Actually, most senior executives spend a great deal of time on communications and a significant component of that time is devoted to press and public relations. All managers need to be sensitive about the way the press has to be handled for public relations. The media today have become far more pervasive than what they used to be. Information explosion and the power of technology have given that extra edge to the media. Any manager would feel the need to spread a good word about his or her organization, its policies, products and developments to the stakeholders. The PR department can always give you words of advice about how to deal with media.

Hence today's managers must know:

◆ How the press and media function
◆ What the press and media need
◆ The jargon used by the press
◆ How to write a well-constructed press release for informing the external publics.

The details of clear and simple writing have already been discussed in chapters two and seven. However, it is essential to understand what makes public relations writing different from other forms of business writing.

The purpose of a press hand-out is to keep the general public informed about important events, seminars, conferences, visit of a V.I.P., launching of a new product, reaching the earthquake victims, as earlier stated, any social welfare activity, sponsoring an event, or any occasion that the organization thinks is of importance to the public.

EXHIBIT

Sample of a press release/hand-out:

ABC COMPANY
Lal Bahadur Shastri Marg
Mumbai 400 001

For Immediate Release: **Contact Gracie Singhal**
January 27, 2001

PRESS RELEASE

New Age Technology for Earthquake Victims in Gujarat

The Managing Director, Ms. Kalyani Gupta, at an urgent meeting called today, said that in the wake of the terrible earthquake in Gujarat, it was necessary to take special steps to deal with the enormous human tragedy. She said that while it was absolutely urgent to donate money, blood, medicines and relief materials of all kinds, the company had to have a more strategic plan for rehabilitating the victims of Gujarat.

Speaking to the top management on this issue she said, "The company has decided to adopt the border villages for rehabilitation of the earthquake victims." She said that the company also plans to take up a project that would educate the people about the materials to be used for building houses in their region. The special project aims at helping the villagers to understand that losses, in terms of human lives and property in earthquakes, can be minimized if the building materials used are human-friendly. The conventional methods of using old-fashioned housing materials will not be useful anymore. It is necessary to have earthquake-resistant materials that will be cost-effective and also not cause extensive damage.

She further said that engineers from Japan had agreed to build safe houses by using PVC material so that the use of cement concrete, bricks and mortar would be minimum and thus less liable to cause damages. It was also necessary for villagers to know about this new technology so that it could be used in future. Already a team of officials had left for Anjar, Bhuj, and Ahmedabad, to find out how best the rehabilitation work could be carried out in phases.

The company realizes that the quake-ravaged Gujarat and Kutch will take time for a complete human recovery. It is not easy to deal with the trauma of people. It, therefore, plans to outsource the services of counsellors and social workers who can study the human problems and help the victims to come out of their trauma.

A sum of Rs. 1 crore has been initially earmarked for the rehabilitation program. The managing director, however, hopes that the efforts put in by ABC Company would attract other companies to come forward and be partners in the cause of welfare that would transform the lives of thousands of people in Gujarat.

WHAT IS A PRESS RELEASE?

You will see that writing a press release is like telling an interesting story to the press about the work that your organization is doing in several areas such as, launching of new products and services, financial results, special projects, or any other important 'happenings'—almost anything that would make sense to the target audience. A story is vital to any press release.

In essence, a press release is a short message from the organization to the press and is written in the hope that it will get coverage in the newspaper.

How to Write a Good Release?

It is essential that managers should have functional knowledge of writing a release that does not end up in the waste-paper bin. Editors are aware that most press releases are written to please the bosses/management, and hence may not contain factual truths. In such cases, the editors reject such releases because they do not fulfill the requirements of the media. The language of puffery and platitudes does not please the editors and hence they view the PR releases with a question mark. Building and managing the corporate reputation of the organization is not only the function of the PR but of every manager. And hence before the press release is dispatched to the press, every detail has to be checked.

Rules to follow in a Press Release

1. Present complete news—The golden rule is to answer the five W's—**Who, Where, When, What, Why** while writing the release. The basic information will help you to present your release in greater depth. Editors like to receive sufficient information. You can do so by answering all these questions either in the first sentence or in the first paragraph of the release. Each answer can be elaborated in the following paragraphs in order of importance.

    The first paragraph in the example above answers the five W's:
    Who: The Managing Director
    What: Special steps taken
    When: Today
    Where: Company premise
    Why: To alleviate the sufferings of the victims of Gujarat earthquake

2. The release must contain information that is real and not claim simple promises. Concrete data, and factual details make a release interesting.

3. The release must have local interest to the reader (for instance, Gujarat earthquake)

4. A simple, conversational style that encourages a two-way communication and makes reading interesting.

Style for the Press Release

As in business communication, the style for writing a good press release also has to be clear and concise. The release should be easy to read. The following tips will be useful:

1. Avoid floweriness or effusion—stick to facts
2. Avoid long words
3. Use words appropriately—(for instance the words 'alleviate', 'rehabilitate' used in the example)
4. Avoid adjectives and adverbs (editors generally like understatements, and not advertisements)
5. Use strong verbs
6. Break up long sentences and keep paragraphs short
7. Avoid a casual/chatty style (occasionally may be used)
8. Avoid buzz words, acronyms, and jargon
9. Justify statements
10. Make the release brief
11. Eliminate all extraneous facts
12. Be specific

HOW TO HANDLE A PRESS CONFERENCE?

A press conference is as important a tool of communication as a press release to a manager. Once you learn the technique of writing a good release, you are likely to succeed in handling a press conference. The difference, however, is in the nature of the communication medium. In the case of the release, you may revise and edit your release several times before you send it to the press like you will do with business letters. The press conference, on the contrary, will demand a lot of 'thinking on feet' skills from you for answering all the questions from the media people. Therefore, your ability to express yourself through effective oral communication skills will be tested.

To handle a press conference well, you need to be clear about:

1. The purpose (why the press conference has been called).

2. Details about what you are going to say (facts).
3. News value of the details, i.e. information about the five W's since media personnel have little time for frivolous stories. You may run the risk of earning a negative impression if you are not prepared with your facts.
4. The location and time—choose the right location and time for the conference.
5. Create a conducive environment for discussion, questions and answers to take place.
6. The people to be invited—prepare a list of all who are to be invited.
7. The information to be given—ensure proper briefing of the media with press hand-outs/releases, photos, facts and figures related to the matter that you are going to talk about.

Media Interviews

During the course of handling business operations for your organization, you will face situations when giving interviews to the media will also have to be handled. A business presentation of the company's launch of new products or services cannot be done without inviting the media people for obvious reasons of publicity. This means that you need to anticipate questions that may arise from your presentation and the answers that you might give to questions asked.

Media people do not have much time. Their questions need to have appropriate answers that should be short, crisp and related to the topic.

The interviews of business and corporate executives on channels like CNBC, Star News, Zee News, Aaj Tak, BBC, and other channels will acquaint you with the way the media personnel ask questions and the kind of answers that are expected. The mass audience that is listening to the interview must be able to understand clearly the text of the message.

Very often, media people conduct telephonic interviews about projects that your organization may have announced or an advertisement that has triggered interest in them or a corporate social project that the organization may have undertaken. When the media people, whether from the print medium or the electronic medium, meet you face-to-face or speak to you on telephone about your organization's work, they not only come prepared with a list of questions but they also expect well-structured and meaningful answers to be given.

Hence a few tips will be useful to you to prepare for such interviews:

1. Anticipate the questions that you may be asked
2. Gather background information on the topic in case some answers need more elaboration
3. Be sure to remember the sources of your information in case the interviewer desires to know
4. Organize your thoughts well so that you are able to answer in a structured manner
5. Speak clearly, confidently, and authoritatively
6. Listen to the question well for a suitable answer (there is every possibility of a tricky question being asked)
7. Avoid jargon
8. Show enthusiasm in your answers and at the same time appear to be sincere
9. Be prepared for complex and spontaneous questions
10. Let your body language match your words
11. Try and ignore the camera and be natural
12. Use positive words
13. Avoid the "Yes"/"No" answers
14. Avoid the "No Comment" type of responses
15. If you do not know the answer, please say so.

According to a reporter from a financial newspaper, the manner in which business executives often handle questions from the media is unfriendly and mistrustful.

The general approach is one of 'hyperbole.' It is always the success story that executives are excited about sharing with the media. If asked about what 'roadblocks' or 'hurdles' the company had to face in order to overcome them to make the project a success, very often the request is turned down, or circumvented, possibly because they do not want to speak about the difficulties faced. From media point of view, the reporter said that the aim in asking such questions was not to delve into the details (the organization might possibly fear that the details might give a chance to the media to sensationalize the story) for any other purpose but to put the facts before the readers. It is this element of mistrust that often mars a good story. "Executives", he said, "do not know how journalism functions."

Other than writing a press release for the external publics, as a manager you should also be able to deal with the needs of your internal employees. Besides, functional communication, which is a part of the formal process, informal contacts with employees, forms a vital requirement for sustaining the spirit of togetherness in an organization. If the organization has a PR department, it will look into the prospects of bringing out

♦ house journals,
♦ video journals,
♦ electronic newspaper,
♦ bulletins, and
♦ brochures.

These are important tools of PR communication for the internal public. Managing employee interest is an important function of PR.

As a manager, you will have to be a part of such internal PR programs because such communications are directly connected with the mood, the morale, and the communication climate of an organization. When you interact with employees in informal functions such as picnic, social functions, events, sports, or give an interview for the house journal, the communication climate becomes positive and transparent. Employees regard such communication as interesting and encouraging. You not only become a part of their world, but by doing so, you gather bits of information that give you an idea about the employees' interest in the organization, their participation in organizational activities, their non-verbal cues, their smiles, and general conduct. Participation in internal PR activities has real time value in terms of enriching employee relations and sustaining genuine interest in them.

CONCLUSION

A healthy internal and external PR and media policy is a reflection of the organization's corporate culture. Every manager needs to contribute to the growth of such a corporate culture. The organization's values, human interactions, traditions, ideals and vision of growth give a place its identity. Like human beings, organizations too have their distincitive image and this rests in the hands of responsible managers. By learning the new skills of PR and media, you as a global manager, will be able to handle situations with confidence and knowledge. These new skills, meant for handling corporate situations, complement your basic knowledge of effective communication skills.

SUMMARY

The chapter gives important inputs on why it is necessary for today's smart managers to understand the relevance of effective communication skills for work that transcends the boundary of their organizations. Interacting with the world outside, as an organizational person, is both an interesting and a challenging task. Today's managers must perfect their communication skills for handling welfare activities as well as the media.

The first part of the chapter gives the philosophy of public relations to enable the reader comprehend and appreciate the human face of business. Corporate social responsibility figures as a major factor in a business growth model for a responsible business organization. To understand the spirit of such work, one needs to imbibe the spirit of a 'Renaissance' person who is in love with ideas that enlighten the human soul. A socially sensitized manager will be able to place a business situation in a better perspective.

The second part of the chapter illustrates why and how a manager can meaningfully communicate to the outside world about the organization's social and business activities by writing a good press release. The section provides tips on writing a good press release. A manager's knowledge of correct language and communication adaptability are reflected in a press release.

A manager also has to learn the skills of handling a press conference and a media interview. The tips offered will help you prepare well for successful handling of questions from the media, which is not a simple task. One needs to have not only the background information about the topic, but also the ability to handle the questions on the spot. 'Thinking on feet' skill (responding to the questions in an appropriate manner) is an important managerial ability. It helps you to be proactive while handling the questions and send out positive image to the media.

The tips will help you to conduct yourself in a cool, confident, and convincing manner regardless of the questions asked and the style of the interviewer.

TEST YOURSELF: ONLY ONE OPTION IS CORRECT. TICK IT. DO IT YOURSELF.

1. PR has been defined as:
   (a) Corporate social service to people
   (b) Planned and sustained effort to establish and maintain goodwill between an organization and its publics
   (c) Rendering charitable service
2. One of the misconceptions of PR is that it
   (a) is a glamorous profession

    (b) involves hard work/client servicing

    (c) is an uninteresting profession

3. **The reality of PR as a profession is measured by**

    (a) glamorous performance

    (b) networking performance

    (c) ethical performance

4. **The end receiver of PR communication is**

    (a) you

    (b) the public

    (c) the World

5. **Today's managers must know PR as a function of**

    (a) responsible corporate communication for external as well as internal public

    (b) responsible promotional communication for both external and internal public

    (c) responsible provisional communication for external as well as internal public

6. **One golden rule to follow for writing a good press release is to follow the**

    (a) ten W's

    (b) seven W's

    (c) five W's

7. **Draft a release for newspapers about your company's launch of a new product/scheme. Ensure that it is not more than 500 words and that it has a correct format.**

8. **The left column has errors in the sentences. The correct options are given in the right column. They are jumbled up. Choose the correct option for the relevant sentence.**

    (a) Our love and respect are common.   · Complement

    (b) The colour of this curtain will compliment the décor of the conference room.   · May

    (c) "Can I come in please?"   · Mutual

9. **"Financial statements of ABC consulting firm indicate that the company's financial situation was negatively impacted during the preceding twelve months."**

    Only one option is correct. Tick it. Do it yourself.

    (a) ABC consulting firm lost money last year.

    (b) ABC consulting firm negatively impacted the market

    (c) ABC consulting firm mismanaged financial matters last year.

10. As a manager handling a press conference, you will succeed only if you carry out

(a) background research, know the purpose and create a conducive environment for addressing questions

(b) background research and mix well with the audience

(c) background research and answer all questions.

FURTHER READING

Argenti, Paul A., *Corporate Communication*, Irwin McGraw-Hill, Boston, 1998.

Ghosh, G. Subir: *Public Relations Today in the Indian Context*, Abhinava Printers, Calcutta, 2001.

Jefkins, Frank, *Public Relations*, The M&E Handbook Series, London, 1994.

Lesley, Philip: *Handbook of Public Relations and Communications*, Jaico Publishing House, New Delhi, 1992.

Macnamara, Jim, *Public Relations Handbook for Managers*, Prentice-Hall Australia, 1996.

Moore, H. Frazier and R. Canfield Bernard, *Public Relations—Principles, cases and problems*, Richard D. Irwin, Ontario, 1977.

Newsom Doug and Bob Carrell, *Public Relations Writing: Form and Style*, 5th ed., Wadsworth Publishing Co., Washington, 1998.

Newsom, Turk, Kruckeberg, *This is PR: The realities of public relations*, 7th ed., United States, 2000.

Penrose, Rasberry and Myers, *Advanced Business Communication*, 4th ed., Thomson South Western, United States, 2001.

Saffir, Leonard with Tarrant, John, *Power Public Relations*, NTC Business Books, Illinois, 1992.

Theaker, Alison, *The Public Relations Handbook*, Routeledge, London, 2001.

Urech, Elizabeth, *Speaking Globally*, Kogan Page, London, 2000.

Answers to Test Questions

CHAPTER 1 COMMUNICATION AS THE MOST IMPORTANT MANAGEMENT TOOL

1. When I think of communicating with someone, I generally
   (a) focus on the correctness of speech
   (b) focus on the content
   ✓ (c) focus on the 'how' and the 'what' of the presentation

2. The ability to communicate effectively is
   ✓ (a) a learned behaviour
   (b) an acquired behaviour
   (c) a casual behaviour

3. Gestures, voice, pitch, facial contact, are
   (a) powerful verbal signals
   (b) not important to oral communication
   ✓ (c) natural accompaniments of oral communication

4. Common frame of reference between the sender and the receiver of a message means
   (a) the sender and the receiver are still caught up in their "message noises."
   ✓ (b) both the sender and the receiver have common understanding of the message
   (c) the mirror reflection of the message has not been established

5. Grapevine is active in an organization when
   ✓ (a) formal network of communication is weak
   (b) too many people meet at the same time to talk
   (c) there is problem at workplace

6. **The biggest barrier to downward communication is when**

   (a) the organization is small
   ✓ (b) there is a long line of communication from the top level to the lower levels
   (c) upward communication is considered more important than downward communication

7. **The other name for horizontal communication is:**

   ✓ (a) Lateral communication
   (b) Collateral communication
   (c) Collaborative communication

8. **Jack Welch's "walk the talk" mantra illustrates**

   ✓ (a) Open door policy
   (b) Check on employees' policy
   (c) Encourage grapevine policy

9. **Today's organizational communication climate by and large is**

   (a) more formal and less informal
   (b) more informal and less formal
   ✓ (c) more professional and less casual

10. **Transformational communication is at the very basis of**

   ✓ (a) corporate social responsibility
   (b) corporate stakeholders responsibility
   (c) corporate financial responsibility

CHAPTER 2   LISTENING SKILLS

1. **Listening to me is not as important as**

   (a) speaking to explain ideas because I am better at it
   (b) writing to get response because I believe in accurate information
   ✓ (c) equally important as all other communication skills

2. **Listening is not the same thing as hearing because it**

   ✓ (a) is a psychological process and hence far more demanding
   (b) a physiological activity where the ears play an important role
   (c) the same thing as hearing the words and responding to them

3. **Listening as a process involves**

   (a) only two main stages—sensing and memory stages
   ✓ (b) five stages—sensing, interpreting, evaluating, responding, and memorizing stages
   (c) catching the strong stimulus and converting it into a message is the only important stage

4. **There are many barriers to listening. Tick the ones which you think are the most applicable to you.**

   (a) Close mindedness
   (b) Hasty evaluation
   (c) Egocentrism
   (d) Anger/jealousy
   (e) Different cultural background
   (f) Wandering mind
   (g) Hearing impairment

5. **Which type of a listener are you? Tick the one that applies to you.**

   (a) I am able to separate my negative emotions from facts when I listen to people and hence I am an active listener
   (b) Long speeches and poor speaking skills force me to skip listening for the real matter and hence I am an evaluative listener
   (c) I have a wandering mind and cannot stop day dreaming when listening to people and hence I am a marginal listener

6. **Which bad listening habit do you suffer from? Tick the one that applies to you.**

   (a) Uninteresting subject
   (b) Poor content of the speech
   (c) Poor speaking style
   (d) The urge to spar

7. **Write down the full meaning of the acronym CARESS.**

8. **The body language of an active listener is reflected in**

   (a) shifting body posture
   ✓ (b) attentive facial expressions
   (c) covering of mouth and talking to the person sitting by the side

9. **Active listening is**

   (a) nodding head as an attempt to appreciate the point
   ✓ (b) trying to see the point as the speaker sees it
   (c) ignoring the speaker's point and framing one's own

10. **There are many misconceptions about listening. Tick the one that you agree with the most**

   (a) Listening is the same thing as breathing.
   (b) All listeners receive the same message.
   (c) Listening is the same thing as hearing.

CHAPTER 3   BASIC SKILL-SETS OF A MANAGER

1. A manager's effectiveness depends on the style of functioning. Which style should be adopted by a manager?
   - (a) Closed style
   - (b) Blind style
   - (c) Hidden style
   - ✓ (d) Open style

2. Indicate which of the four styles refers to the following statement:
   "Do not lecture me please! I know exactly what I am doing."
   - (a) Open style
   - (b) Closed style
   - ✓ (c) Blind style
   - (d) Hidden style

3. Managers with poor interpersonal skills have
   - (a) a blind style functioning
   - ✓ (b) a closed style of functioning
   - (c) an open style of functioning
   - (d) a hidden style of functioning

4. The term 'disclosure' means the person
   - ✓ (a) voluntarily discloses information about self to others
   - (b) keeps information about self hidden in the closet
   - (c) does not bother to share information with others

5. The term 'feedback' means
   - (a) seeking only positive response
   - ✓ (b) seeking response from others and not waiting for it
   - (c) selecting only the positive response and rejecting the negative one

6. Handling criticisms effectively means
   - (a) criticizing immediately
   - ✓ (b) keeping the 'you view point' in mind
   - (c) being judgmental while dealing with the person

7. A manager is said to have a closed style of functioning when he
   - ✓ (a) does not seek feedback and does not share information
   - (b) blocks information and does not allow it to be passed on to others
   - (c) wants more information but does not share the information

8. A manager is said to have a blind style of functioning when the manager is
   - (a) high on feedback and disclosure
   - (b) neither high nor low on feedback and disclosure
   - ✓ (c) low on feedback but high on disclosure

9. **A manager is said to have a hidden style of functioning when he**

    (a) keeps ears and eyes open to collect feedback

✓ (b) is low on disclosure but high on feedback

    (c) is neither interested in gathering feedback nor in disclosing information

10. **A manager is said to have an open style of functioning when he/she**

✓ (a) Gathers feedback and discloses sensibly

    (b) Is biased in giving feedback and disclosures

    (c) Is indifferent to both feedback and disclosures

11. **Assertive communication style refers to**

✓ (a) Empathetic communication

    (b) Sympathetic communication

    (c) Apathetic communication

CHAPTER 4 **USE OF WORDS AND SENTENCES**

1. **We used to get on well ...**

    (a) and we still keep in touch

    (b) but now we have made it up

✓ (c) but now we have lost touch

2. **Tick the correct expression**

    (a) He and me volunteered to go.

✓ (b) He and I volunteered to go.

    (c) Me and him volunteered to go.

3. **Use the correct form of verb**

    Rice and dal ... his staple meal

✓ (a) is

    (b) are

    (c) have been

4. **Which of the three sentences is a polite expression? Tick it.**

    (a) Sign here...please!

✓ (b) Would you please sign here?

    (c) You must know that you have to sign here.

5. **Which of the three sentences has greater clarity? Tick it.**

    (a) Admission to you has not been granted because of non-submission of relevant documents.

✓ (b) We could not admit you because you did not submit the original mark sheet at the time you deposited your form with us.

    (c) Non-submission of original mark sheet is a serious violation of our admission rules and hence admission has not been granted to you.

6. **Which of the three sentences has better conciseness? Tick it.**

    (a) Last year the conference was entirely organized by the management trainees who spent late hours working on the details and who went out of their way to spend on the eatables and the decoration so that the event would turn out to be a major success.

    (b) Last year the management trainees worked hard to organize the conference and did not mind spending time and money for its success.

    ✓ (c) Last year the management trainees organized the conference by spending time and resources for its success.

7. **What is wrong with the following sentence? Tick the correct option.**

    'We would deem it a favour if you inform us at the earliest.'

    (a) It is a correct expression.

    (b) The sentence lacks courtesy.

    ✓ (c) The sentence is wordy and lacks conciseness.

8. **Use correct preposition**

    There is no exception...this rule

    (a) by

    (b) in

    ✓ (c) to

9. **Only one word is correctly spelt. Tick the word.**

    ✓ (a) Hierarchy

    (b) Heirerchy

    (c) Hieararchy

10. **The phrase 'ad valorem' in the sentence All imported goods are subject to ad valorem duty' means:**

    ✓ (a) According to value

    (b) According to quantity

    (c) According to import rules

CHAPTER 5 **PRESENTATION SKILLS**

1. **The popular understanding of the word 'presentation' is that it**

    ✓ (a) has to be a power-point presentation

    (b) must have colourful slides

    (c) must have many slides

2. **The term 'speech presentation' refers to**

    (a) a long speech

    ✓ (b) instant oral presentation

    (c) a power-point speech

3. **What makes a power-point presentation memorable are**

   (a) well-made power-point slides

   (b) sincerity with which the presentation is delivered and how well punctuation is

   ✓ (c) a combination of oral communication skills and well-designed power-point slides

4. **The acronym WIIFM means**

   (a) 'What's in it for managers?'

   (b) 'What's in it for most?'

   ✓ (c) 'What's in it for me?'

5. **The presentation style that applies to corporate executives is**

   ✓ (a) cool zone

   (b) hot zone

   (c) dull zone

6. **Choice of a presentation format (narrative, descriptive, deductive) depends on the**

   (a) presentation matter

   ✓ (b) kind of audience attending the presentation

   (c) venue where the presentation is to take place

7. **A power-point slide is perceived as a 'poor slide' when it has**

   (a) too much of textual matter

   (b) loud colours and ornamental fonts

   ✓ (c) a combination of the two

8. **The body language of a presenter should be**

   (a) closed

   ✓ (b) open

   (c) diffident

9. **Which of the qualities of a presenter, according to you, are important during presentation? Tick them.**

   (a) Enthusiasm

   (b) Involvement

   (c) Audience-focus

   (d) Self-control

   (e) Monotone

   (f) Addressing only a select section of the audience

   (g) Flinging arms

   (h) Keeping arms across the chest

10. **'Thinking on Feet' skill in handling Q&A means**

    (a) standing on feet

    (b) standing and thinking simultaneously

    ✓ (c) answering the questions calmly and confidently

CHAPTER 6 NON-VERBAL COMMUNICATION

1. **Non-verbal Communication means**
   - (a) the absence of verbs in our communication
   - (b) the presence of action in our communication
   - ✓ (c) communicating through our body movements

2. **The adage 'Actions speak louder than words' means**
   - (a) Actions are more important than words.
   - (b) Actions are like words we speak.
   - ✓ (c) Body language has a greater impact than words.

3. **Match the pairs:**

   (1) Kinesics • Science of the movement or our eyes (2)
   (2) Occulesics • Science of space (4)
   (3) Paralinguistics • Concept of time (6)
   (4) Proxemics • Language of Touch (7)
   (5) Artifactics • Pitch, tone, modulation (3)
   (6) Chronemics • Postures, gestures, head nods etc. (1)
   (7) Tactilics • Appearance, clothing, personal objects (5)

4. **The expression 'gesture clusters' means**
   - (a) a universe of people
   - ✓ (b) a combination of different body gestures
   - (c) gestures that are clustered

5. **Match the pairs**

   1. Open palms • Indicate defensiveness (2)
   2. Crossed arms • Indicate superiority (5)
   3. Mouth guards • Indicate evaluation (4)
   4. Tilted head, hand under chin • Indicate suspicion (3)
   5. Steepled fingers, feet up on the desk • Indicate openness (1)
   6. Tapping fingers, shifting body weight • Indicate nervousness (6)
   7. Broad smile, wide eyes • Indicate enthusiasm (7)

6. **Which of the following dimensions refer to the human body and its appearance? Tick them.**
   - ✓ (a) Posture
   - ✓ (e) Dress
   - (i) Seating Arrangement
   - (b) Volume
   - (f) Interior décor
   - (j) Tone
   - (c) Space
   - ✓ (g) Gestures
   - (k) Rate
   - ✓ (d) Height
   - (h) Touch
   - (l) Pitch

7. Which of the following dimensions refer to the human voice? Tick them.
    - ✓ (a) Modulation   ✓ (e) Pitch
    - ✓ (b) Intonation   (f) Time
    - (c) Handshake   ✓ (g) Volume
    - (d) Posture   ✓ (h) Articulation

8. NLP stands for:
    - (a) Neural-language Processing
    - ✓ (b) *Neuro-Linguistic Programming*
    - (c) Non-Linear Programming

9. Establish the relationship between the matter on the left-hand column with the matter on the right-hand column:
    1. Matching   To act of observing the behaviour of the person on the other side and match the same (1)
    2. Mirroring   The complete integration of matching, mirroring, and pacing (4)
    3. Pacing   The act of watching the non-verbal gestures of the other person (2)
    4. Calibrating   The manner in which you match and mirror (3)

10. State true or false
    - (a) A speaker whose voice has tremors and may gulp and perspire could be a liar. (T)
    - (b) Hands interlocked at the crotch level indicate confident body language. (F)
    - (c) "Pointing index finger at someone is a negative behaviour and should be avoided. (T)
    - (d) A person who shuffles feet, lick lips, and drum fingers could be a liar. (T)

Chapter 7 WRITTEN COMMUNICATION

1. Clarity in written communication is achieved by using
    - ✓ (a) exact words
    - (b) complicated words
    - (c) jargon and clichés

2. The expression 'Kindly favour us with a reply' should be redrafted as:
    - ✓ (a) 'Please reply...'
    - (b) 'I want you to reply...'
    - (c) 'You must reply...'

3. The expressions "man hours," "policeman" "fireman" are
    - ✓ (a) gender specific
    - (b) gender neutral
    - (c) non-gender

4. Use of active voice makes sentences

    (a) slow and stretched

✓ (b) dynamic and forceful

    (c) ambiguous and complicated

5. "I communicated the message to him" is in

✓ (a) active voice

    (b) passive voice

    (c) neutral voice

6. In business, we must

    (a) speak at the customer

✓ (b) speak to the customer

    (c) speak over the customer

7. The sentence "We will be pleased to deliver your order by the end of this week" is poorly drafted because the

    (a) customer is not so important to the writer

✓ (b) writer is more important than the customer

    (c) writer respects the customer

8. The tone of the sentence "Items desired should be checked on the enclosed form" is

✓ (a) rude

    (b) polite

    (c) threatening

9. All email messages must be

✓ (a) short because they save bandwidth and cause less strain on the reader's eyes

    (b) long because sometimes situations demand long e-mails

    (c) both short and long

10. Tick the characteristics of effective business writing:

✓ (a) Clear writing

    (b) Impossible to read quickly

✓ (c) Familiar words

    (d) Colourful tone

    (e) Ambiguity

✓ (f) Courteous and complete

✓ (g) Simple and plain language

✓ (h) Short, clear sentences

✓ (i) Concrete expressions

    (j) Jargon and big words

CHAPTER 8 COMMUNICATING IN A MULTICULTURAL WORLD

1. The sentence 'The multi-cultural world is a global world' essentially means:

    (a) The globe that holds all the cultures of the world

✓ (b) People from different religions, racial, linguistic, and ethnic backgrounds can live together

    (c) A frightening world that is layered by too many cultures

2. **A truly global leader is one who is**
   ✓ (a) cosmopolitan by nature
   (b) ethnocentric by nature
   (c) rigid by nature

3. **The main barriers to multi-cultural functioning in an MNC are**
   (a) Too many employees from different cultural backgrounds
   ✓ (b) Values, beliefs, norms and perceptions of employees shaped by their individual cultures are different
   (c) Too many people communicating in diverse ways

4. **The only way by which MNCs can effectively function is by**
   (a) forcing them to communicate in an expected manner
   ✓ (b) a well-framed organizational communication policy based on the principle that all functional units must be coordinated for inter-dependence
   (c) Expecting employees to perform anyway

5. **Match the pairs**

   (a) Culture
   • People living in the same country make special adjustments to different cultural standards (b)

   (b) Inter-cultural communication
   • When tolerance and sensitivity mark the communication and relationship patterns of employees (c)

   (c) Multi-cultural communication
   • In simple words it can be defined as miscommunication (d)

   (d) Cross-cultural communication
   • A set of values, beliefs, norms, customs, rules, and codes that influences people to identify and define themselves as a distinct group. (a)

6. **Of the three quotations given, which one focuses on global communication adaptability and who expressed it? Tick it.**
   (a) "The world is changing frighteningly fast. And, if we simply assume that the future is going to be like the past, we're going to be both surprised and disappointed..."
   ✓ (b) "When you can present your own ideas clearly, specifically, visually, and most important, contextually—in the

context of a deep understanding of another's paradigms and concerns—you significantly increase the credibility of your ideas..." (Stephen Covey)

(c) "Most managers work in one industry, hone their skills to that industry, but have little time to look around for inspiration from others, or to rethink their own actions conceptually."

7. **The concept of 'culture display' refers to:**

   (a) display of cultural artifacts
   ✓ (b) handshakes, language spoken, greetings, and social etiquette
   (c) colourful ethnic clothes

8. **Tick the factors that cause cross-cultural problems:**

   (a) Greeting people with a smile and a nod
   (b) Positive values and beliefs
   ✓ (c) Unclear speech and wrong use of words
   ✓ (d) Being rude and indifferent
   ✓ (e) Being aggressive
   (f) Being courteous
   (g) Correct social manners
   (h) Correct social greeting
   (i) Polite tone
   ✓ (j) Being ethnocentric

9. **People from low context cultural countries are known by their preference for**

   ✓ (a) direct style of communication or straight talk and value for verbal communication
   (b) indirect style of communication or roundabout style of talk
   (c) mixed style of communication

10. **People from high context cultural countries are known for their preference for**

    ✓ (a) indirect style of communication and less reliance on verbal form of communication
    (b) direct style of communication and reliance on words
    (c) mixed style of communication

11. **Tick the factors that will help managers overcome cultural barriers:**

    ✓ (a) Know your own culture first.
    (b) Ignore others' culture.
    (c) Be ethnocentric.
    ✓ (d) Take interest in other cultures.
    ✓ (e) Practice flexibility.
    ✓ (f) Keep an unbiased mind.

CHAPTER 9 KEEPING PACE WITH A CHANGING WORLD: THE PR WAY

1. **PR has been defined as:**
    (a) Corporate social service to people
    ✓ (b) Planned and sustained effort to establish and maintain goodwill between an organization and its customers
    (c) Rendering charitable service

2. **One of the misconceptions of PR is that it**
    ✓ (a) is a glamorous profession
    (b) involves hard work/client servicing
    (c) is an uninteresting profession

3. **The reality of PR as a profession is measured by**
    (a) glamorous performance
    (b) networking performance
    ✓ (c) ethical performance

4. **The end receiver of PR communication is**
    (a) you
    ✓ (b) the Public
    (c) the world

5. **Today's managers must know PR as a function of**
    ✓ (a) responsible corporate communication for the external as well as the internal public
    (b) responsible promotional communication for the external as well as the internal public
    (c) responsible provisional communication for the external as well as the internal public

6. **One golden rule to follow for writing a good press release is to follow the**
    (a) ten W's
    (b) seven W's
    ✓ (c) five W's

7. To be done by students. Draft a release for all newspapers about your company's launch of a new product/ scheme. Ensure that it is not more than five hundred words and that it has a correct format.

8. The left column has errors in the sentences. The correct options are given in the right column. They are jumbled up. Choose the correct option for the relevant sentence.

    (a) Our love and respect are common · Complement (b)
    (b) The colour of this curtain will compliment the décor of the conference room. · May (c)
    (c) "Can I come in please?" · Mutual (a)

9. "Financial statements of ABC consulting firm indicate that the company's financial situation was negatively impacted during the preceding twelve months."

   Only one option is correct. Tick it. Do it yourself.

   ✓ (a) ABC consulting firm lost money last year.

   (b) ABC consulting firm negatively impacted the market

   (c) ABC consulting firm mismanaged financial matters last year.

10. **As a manager handling a press conference, you will succeed only if you**

    ✓ (a) carry out background research, know the purpose and create a conducive environment for addressing questions

    (b) carry out background research and mix well with the audience

    (c) carry out background research and answer all questions

Officialdom
Exude
ubiquitous

Index